IN THE SHADOWS OF THE KREMLIN AND THE WHITE HOUSE

*Africa's Media Image
From Communism to Post-Communism*

Charles Quist-Adade

University Press of America,® Inc.
Lanham · New York · Oxford

Copyright © 2001 by
University Press of America,® Inc.
4720 Boston Way
Lanham, Maryland 20706

12 Hid's Copse Rd.
Cumnor Hill, Oxford OX2 9JJ

Library of Congress Cataloging-in-Publication Data

Quist-Adade, Charles.
In the shadows of the Kremlin and the White House : Africa's media
image from communism to post-communism / Charles Quist-Adade.
p.   cm
Includes bibliographical references (p.) and index.
1. Africa—In mass media. 2. Mass media—Soviet Union.
3. Mass media—Russia (Federation) 4. Mass media—United States.
5. Africans—Russia—History. 6. Racism—Russia—History. I. Title.
P96.A372 R876   2000   00-048899 CIP

ISBN 0-7618-1913-4 (cloth : alk. paper)

TM
⊖ The paper used in this publication meets the minimum
requirements of American National Standard for Information
Sciences—Permanence of Paper for Printed Library Materials,
ANSI Z39.48—1984

To three people who matter to me:
Yayo (Mother), Dada, and Maayaa.

TABLE OF CONTENTS

Epigraph

This was the image laid
upon the dark skin of
the black people by
those who had the
power to do it.

Philip Haile, 1982

I see our brothers and
sisters, mothers and
fathers, captured and
forced into images they
did not devise, doing
hard time for all of us.

Alice Walker, 1982.

Preface

Contemporary Russia is riddled with ethnic, racial, linguistic and territorial conflicts. While we know much about ethnic and territorial cleavages, our knowledge of racial attitudes—especially in relationship to Black peoples—is extremely limited. This book traces two factors critical to expanding our understanding of these attitudes. First, it investigates the Russian historical and cultural background of racial attitudes and prejudices concerning Africa; then the book analyzes the role of the press in shaping, reinforcing, or perpetuating these attitudes and prejudices.

It provides empirical study of Soviet/Russian attitudes towards Black Africans. It provides the first comparative study of the Soviet/Russian and western press coverage of Africa. It analyzes Africa's image in the ex-Soviet and Western press by comparing news coverage of Africa in general under the two press systems. In comparing the ex-Soviet and Western press coverage of Africa, the study demonstrates how the ideologies underlying the two press systems influenced the portrayal of distinct images of the African during the periods under review.

This study explores the extent to which the Cold War and its subsequent death affected the ideological premises assumed by the Soviet Union press that covered events on the African continent. I argue that, as in the West, the reigning powers in the Soviet Union used the press to promote and protect their interests first and foremost. All other considerations were held hostage, as it were, to these interests.

Although, content analysis of the Soviet/Russian press coverage of Africa covered the period up to 1991, more recent data on Russian press coverage of the continent have been included in the general discussion and analysis.

This book results from nearly eight years of research, which includes my M.A. thesis and Ph.D. dissertation at Leningrad [St. Petersburg] State University.[1] Although, I wrote and defended both works during the era of glasnost and relative academic freedom, I met considerable opposition from those who matter at the faculties [of

Journalism and Sociology], as my conclusions did not appear acceptable to them. They compelled me to present a watered-down version of my M.A. thesis, [which I defended in 1988], since my supervisor flatly rejected the conclusion that PRAVDA was racist and elitist in its coverage of Africa—although I had given more than adequate proof. While my supervisor chided my M.A. thesis for not quoting enough of Lenin and for using too many "bourgeois" sources, my Ph.D. supervisor complained that I had quoted Marx and Lenin too liberally. By 1991, Lenin and Marx were no longer fashionable in Russia, and I could not convince him that even Western anti-Marxist social scientists regard Marx as an authority on large social groups and social institutions.

The behavior of my supervisors is symptomatic of constraints and dilemma, both students and their professors had to face, in the academia in the former Soviet Union. It required considerable courage to dissent from the general Marxist-Leninist doctrine in the pre-glasnost years; it became equally difficult to steer the Marxist-Leninist course when Mikhail Gorbachev launched his reforms in the mid 1980s. Not that academia in the West is totally free of constraints and pressures. While the pressures to toe the 'capitalist line' in the West are subtle, students and scholars faced overt 'hand-twisting' to conform to the Communist Party ideology in the pre-glasnost years.

This book has taken a number of years to write and many people have helped me along the way. I am indebted to several people for the help and encouragement they gave me to complete this book. First I thank Dr. Marlene Cuthbert of the Department of Communication Studies, Dr. Kwasi Ansu-Kyeremeh of the School of Communications, University of Ghana, Legon, Dr. Tanya Basok of the Department of Sociology and Anthropology, and Dr. L. D. Majhanovich of the Department of Classical and Modern Languages, all of the University of Windsor. They all read the original manuscript, making corrections and useful suggestions. I am equally thankful to my dissertation supervisor, Professor Alexander O. Boronoev of the Department of Sociology, St. Petersburg State University, who encouraged me to make a transition from journalism to sociology. His interest in my study spurred me on to the end in spite of all the dangers and difficulties I faced in collecting data for my study.

I am also thankful to Wayne State University for giving me a grant under its Women and Minority Research Program to update this book. The Department of Communication Studies of the University of Windsor in Canada also deserves my sincere gratitude for granting me the opportunity to convert my dissertation into this book during my postdoctoral stint at the university. However, all errors, factual and typographical, are solely mine.

Introduction

When the doors of the Victor Vorster prison eventually opened for Nelson Mandela to walk to freedom in February 1990, the media in the Western and Developing worlds virtually exploded with the news. Television and radio gave the story top billing and the print media ran full-page spreads on the man who had not been seen outside the prison walls for nearly three decades.

In what was then Gorbachev's Soviet Union, the picture was quite different. Central Television allotted less than 30 seconds at the tail end of its main evening news program, Vremya. The media producers obviously considered the day's sports news more newsworthy. The following day, PRAVDA, the main mouthpiece of the now disbanded Communist Party, buried the story on page five—a short, unremarkable biographical sketch of Nelson Mandela, under a commentary on Soviet-US relations on page five. IZVESTIYA, the Soviet parliament's newspaper, carried nothing at all on Mandela's release. Instead, it published a report by its Southern African correspondent on threats by white South African nationalists to kill Mandela if he were freed.

What explains the poor coverage given to Mandela's release? Was it a slip of journalistic memory? Was it an isolated case? Or was it the trend in glasnost-style and post-Cold war era journalism in the former Soviet Union, now the Commonwealth of Independent States? Long before the invention of yellow and market journalism, Africans and their continent captured the headlines of the Western mass media with largely adverse coverage, which deliberately or unconsciously capitalized on its real and imagined weaknesses. During the colonial period, Rider Haggard's[1] type of romantic popular tales, coupled with yellow journalism and pseudo-scientific reportage, had painted the image of a dark continent inhabited by rude savages and godless heathens. The colonial remedy to this myth was the civilizing and proselytizing mission of the Christian West.[1]

Even a cursory glance at the contemporary Western news media shows that that coverage has not shifted far away from this colonial tradition of deforming the image of Africa as a place where anything but drought, disease, pestilence and a host of other tragedies occur. The media now project Africa, as writers did in the colonial era, as a *tabula rasa,* making no meaningful contribution to the human race. Much of the Western media today sees Africa as a continent of paralysis and chaos, terminally blighted by the so-called coup-famine syndrome.

Not as well known, however, is how the media in Communist and post-Communist Russia has covered Africa. Supposedly, these media developed from the Marxist-Leninist principles of "proletarian internationalism" and the much-vaunted "solidarity with peoples fighting for their spiritual, political and economic liberation."[2] The extinction of Communism in Russia and Eastern Europe has led to the appearance of extreme right-wing ideologies, nationalistic, anti-Semitic, and even Fascist ideas hitherto suppressed by the authoritarian system. Their influence in both society and the press is growing. In the former Soviet Union (FSU), national chauvinists and Fascists have expressed their ideas in the mass media and in parliament. Mainly, they fault the FSU's policies in the Third World generally, in Africa specifically.

In several mainstream press articles, politicians and journalists on the left-right political and ideological spectrum, have found a scapegoat in the Kremlin's Africa policy. For example, a member of the Russian Parliament complained in the newspaper LITERATOR that the former communist leadership "wasted precious Soviet resources on peoples who have only begun to call themselves a people, who have just descended from the palm trees, and have only managed to pronounce the word 'socialism'.[3] Of course, the FSU's economic crisis could easily explain away the current mood; but certainly currents run below the surface of economic distress and the resultant scapegoating. We may have to dig deeper to find the real factors.

For instance, what explains the Soviet/Russian media's Cold War propensity to depict Africans as *bednie rodstvinki,* "poor cousins," exploited and subjugated by the imperialist and neo-colonialist West, whom the USSR must salvage—in line with the Marxist-Leninist principle of proletarian internationalism? What lies behind the Soviet/Russian version of the "White man's burden"? The media's portrayal of Africa as [Russian] Communist man's burden, as I shall argue, expressed more of ethnocentric, paternalistic, and even racist urges, than of a Marxist-Leninist ideological inclination.

The questions I attempt to answer include:

1. In what different way[s] did the press in the FSU shape, project, and reinforce the existing image of Africans?

2. To what extent did the Marxist-Leninist ideology and socio-cultural praxis that set the past agenda continue to dominate the news coverage of Africa after Communism's collapse and the Soviet Union's disintegration? In other words, do the principles and practice of Soviet/Russian journalism continue to influence press coverage of Africa in post-communist Russia?

3. Was the Marxist-Leninist ideology as altruistic as its purveyors claimed?

4. When ethnocentric instincts and values clash with ideological inclinations and concerns, which of the two takes the upper hand? In short, is ethnocentric "blood" thicker than ideological "water"?

5. How far has the current infatuation with Western ways and wholesale repudiation of Communism affected Russian media coverage of Africa?

6. How different was Soviet media coverage from that of the West?

7. Finally, how do the interaction of Kremlin politics and press [journalistic] practice affect the coverage of Africa?

After independence in the sixties, many African leaders came to see the Soviet system as a more humane alternative to Western capitalism. They had hoped for a more realistic and balanced coverage of their continent, especially when—in the 1960s and 1970s—the "Soviet-East" pitched camp with the non-aligned nations, demanding "a new and more just, balanced and democratic" international information and communication system. However, they hardly suspected that media coverage of international news in the first Socialist country followed not only the logic of Cold War politics, but also the "basic instincts" of ethnocentrism.

The Cold War ended with the close of the 1980s. "New Thinking" and glasnost, the fruits of Mikhail Gorbachev's perestroika[4] revolution, united the two former superpowers and bitter rivals, the FSU and the United States. A new world order of "common human interests" and cooperation began to take shape. Old stereotypes and prejudices began to disappear. In Africa the main peace dividend from the fledgling new order has been the end of proxy wars by the superpowers in Angola, Ethiopia, and Mozambique as the United States and Russia[5] agreed to end arms supplies to their minions in these countries.

Up to the end of the Cold War, North-South relations depended largely on the East-West conflict. Under the banner of anti-imperialism, the Soviet Union pursued its own imperialist ambitions in Africa and other parts of the developing world, and the U.S tended to misinterpret anti-Communism as a supposed synonym for freedom. The previous fixation on the East-West conflict by the loyal press of the two power blocks distracted attention, serious problems and relevant issues in the so-called Third World.   In the best expression of loyalty to the opposing power blocks, the ex-Soviet and Western press amplified the ideological and psychological warfare to such a deafening extent that they drowned out the distant voices of desperation in the developing world. It is no overstatement to say that the Cold War was fought more on the battlefield of the press than anywhere else.

The end of the Cold War meant less ideologizing of Third World issues, less patronage, less coerced or bought loyalty, and less internationalizing of regional conflicts. This lessening was bound to have a rub-on effect on the international mass communication media. The prospect was that the international media would stop looking at Third World issues merely through the prism of the East-West confrontation and within the narrow framework of superpower stereotypes.

This prospect created room for optimism among many writers and commentators in Africa, other parts of the Third World, and elsewhere during the early years of "New Thinking." At long last, they thought, the international mass communication media would begin to look at issues concerning the developing world on their own intrinsic merits and not as an extension of East-West ideological and psychological warfare. The international system was becoming polycentric. It would be easier now to identify numerous problems in the developing world, which the East-West conflict had previously pushed behind world focus.   But the unfolding of world events before and after the demise of Communism and the fall of the Soviet empire following the unsuccessful putsch in August 1991 have more than eroded such optimism. An African proverb says when two elephants fight it is the grass that suffers, and when they make love the grass suffers too. Precisely that wisdom seems to lie behind the logic of post-Cold War world politics, now controlled incontestably by the U.S.

For Africa and much of the Third World the new world order is another cause for concern. Apart from increasing marginalization, the end of the Cold War brought with it an unprecedented upsurge of racism in Europe and a condescending, dismissive attitude toward immigrants from Africa and other parts of the developing world. New stereotypes and prejudices are being created where old ones have disappeared or began to disappear. To a large extent we may blame the spread of these new stereotypes on the media. I argue that the media do not necessarily create these stereotypes, but they play no small part in shaping, reinforcing, and entrenching them. This role underscores their importance in the creation of images in this study.

The scientific-technological revolution has led to an information boom, turning our planet into Marshall McLuhan's global village. In a single day, a hurricane of events literally assails us. In a single country, the number of events are so overwhelming that its citizens are hard-pressed to keep track of them. The problem is complicated in the international arena, where the simultaneous and successive flow of happenings in all parts of the globe makes it humanly impossible to follow every single event.

We are handicapped by time, distance and other factors. So we must depend on the mass media for much of our information about the rest of the world. But ethnic stereotypes and racial prejudices become new stumbling blocks to complete comprehension of the information we receive, as we have no time for personal inquiry and verification. Moreover, we mustn't forget that media people are themselves constrained by their own stereotypes and prejudices.

In this light, then, the responsibility of the international communication media in shaping social attitudes and feelings assumes enormous importance. Their role in molding, educating, and organizing people for good or bad ends remains unchallenged. The social responsibility of the mass media in molding the average person's feelings and perceptions about international affairs becomes even greater, considering the diverse cultural norms, beliefs and practices of peoples in different parts of the world.

The aim of this book is to explore the extent to which the Cold War and its subsequent death affected the ideological premises on which the FSU press covered events in Africa. It argues that, as in the West, the press in the former Soviet Union is used by the powers-that-be to promote and protect their interests first and foremost. All other considerations are held hostage, as it were, to these interests. The argument is based on the following two premises:

1. The ideology of dominant ruling classes as exemplified by corporate [in the West] and nomenkulatura [in Russia] interests set the agenda for the press during and after the Cold War.
2. The press, just as in politics, hankers after permanent interests, not permanent friends.[6]

It is my view that the ethnocentric "blood" is thicker than the ideological "water," and precisely because of that I contend that ethnocentric interests informed the ideological stances of the press systems of the two former superpowers. Also, it is my view that the more racist a publication, the more it will marginalize Africa. But the main thrust of the book is to determine how the Soviet communist press shaped the projection and reinforcement of existing images of the African. In other words, I intend to investigate what factors lie behind the formation of specific images of or stereotypes and prejudices about the African and Africa and how these images are amplified and communicated in the mass media. I also aim to explore the ways press coverage of Africa by the Russian media influenced, and if they did, how the perception of Africans was formed in the minds of the average Russian. For this purpose, sociological, social psychological, and mass communication theories were applied to determine the basis of stereotyping, prejudice-formation, ethnocentrism, and how the ethnocentrism of the Soviet press or society influence the perception of Africans by the audiences of the two press systems.

In addition, I intend to determine if, and to what extent, the Marxist-Leninist ideology and socio-cultural praxis that set the agenda in the past continue to hold sway in the news coverage of Africa after the collapse of communism and the disintegration of the Soviet Union. By way of comparison, I aim to discern if there have been any changes in the Western press coverage of Africa during the glasnost/"new thinking" or "neo-detente" years and since the end of the Cold War and subsequent collapse of the Soviet Union. I proceed from two main hypotheses:

1. Press or mass media systems are influenced by and influence or reinforce socio-cultural, psychological and ideological systems of any given society. The more

ethnocentric and racist a press system is the more likely it is to perpetuate both the "Tarzan" image of Africa and the so-called "coup-famine syndrome" as the dominant African reality.   This, in effect, will influence or reinforce audiences' views or opinions of Africa and Africans.

2.   The Western media, loyal to the capitalist tradition and propensity to maximize profits, look for sensationalism in Africa, in order to sell it at the expense of balanced information. The Russian media, on the other hand, did not hanker after profits, and until 1990 considered it an affront to Marxist-Leninist ethics to carry advertisements. As an alternative to the Western capitalist, profit-oriented press, the ex-Soviet media should cover African issues much more comprehensively, and from a more dispassionate angle.

To explain why the media in Russia portray Africa as they do, I explore the socio-cultural, ideological, and psychological factors underlying the formation of specific images and stereotypes about Africans and their continent in the FSU press. I draw analogies to the West, and analyzed the image of Africans as perceived and projected in the ex-Soviet press. Part of this analysis considers the Kremlin's Africa policy, specifically the influence of its dynamics and metamorphosis on this stereotypical perception and projection.

This book compares news coverage of Africa in general under the two [Russian and Western] press systems. As a sociological study it employs sociological methods and analysis. In addition, I have used a large body of Soviet and Western literature on communication theory. Various studies and theories in sociology and mass communication on the many factors involved in the formation of stereotypes, their dissemination, and/or reinforcement, led me to a sweeping conclusion. Namely: rabid ethnocentrism in the international mass communication media—straight-jacket evaluation of all phenomena based on value systems in the media gatekeepers' own ethnic origins—has much to do with the abiding negative stereotyping of Africans in the media and in the minds of people in the FSU and the West.

Hence, the tendency to evaluate African issues from a purely Eurocentric viewpoint, and to measure African lives and developmental activities from solely European standards, norms, and expectations has led to rash conclusions about the African personality and the perpetuation of unhealthy stereotypes by the international mass media. I advocate a realistic, cultural-relativist approach[7] in media coverage of

African issues, through which practitioners can evaluate African events from the perspective of African values.

I know there is nothing like "instinctive objectivity;" but I believe the conscientious efforts of media people to appreciate and respect other cultures' norms and practices can lead to at least "scientific" objectivity in media reports about other peoples and races. Such efforts will mark the first step toward reducing the cultural arrogance and ignorance that blights Northern hemispheric media coverage of much of the Third World today. While not calling on the dominant world media to act as public relations agencies extolling the virtues of African life, I insist that in the midst of apparent despondency and helplessness, Africans are not mere spectators of their own mishaps; that they are struggling under very harsh conditions to overcome these problems, many of which are not of their own creation; and I make a case for the international media to cover creative efforts of these people to overcome their problems.

Journalists can achieve this aim when they and their master gatekeepers (editors) learn to see the cultural and historical relevance of the African reality. In comparing the Soviet and Western press coverage of Africa, I aim to define the relationships to Africa of the media systems of the former ideological adversaries. These relationships I view through their images of Africans, the spread and reinforcement of these images, and the influence of these images on their various audiences. My study also shows how the ideologies underlying the two press systems influenced the portrayal of distinct images of Africans in the Cold War and post-Cold War periods. Finally, I argue that the international mass media's comprehensive, balanced and accurate coverage of African issues benefits not only Africans in their quest to play their role on a multi-cultural, multi-faceted world stage, but also our entire global village. For the world will have no peace until peace prevails in all its constituent parts, including Africa.

Chapter One discusses the history of the Kremlin's Africa policy since Khrushchev's thaw years [1956-64] through Brezhnev's neo-Stalinist period [particularly 1969-82] up to the Gorbachev perestroika-glasnost-"New Thinking" years [1985-91] and Yeltsin's post Communist era [August 1991 and afterward].

Chapter Two attempts a conceptual analysis of the media's role in inter-ethnic and inter-racial image formation. It also looks at the historical, social, cultural-psychological and ideological factors underlying the formation of inter-ethnic and inter-racial relationships. I also analyze the dynamics of the image of Africans in the ex-Soviet (C.I.S.) press, with parallels drawn from the western press. I briefly analyze the following:

- The role of the media in the formation of ethnic and racial images (stereotypes);
- The media and attitudinal formation and change;
- The significance of images and stereotypes, by means of which societies, with the help of the mass communication media, influence their inhabitants;
- Cultural and socio-psychological differences as factors in inter-ethnic and inter-racial image formation.

Using ethnographic methodology — in-depth video interviews — I sought to assess the African images in the minds of Russians and how African students, diplomats and African-Russians perceive these images.

Chapter Three presents a comparative analysis of Russian and Western press coverage of Africa. In Chapter Four I test my hypotheses against a body of empirical data—an opinion survey of Russian students and their professors, plus Western exchange students and visiting scholars at various St. Petersburg institutions of higher learning. The survey inquires about their images of Africans, and seeks to determine what influence the press has in forming these images. In Chapter Five, I summarize the findings of my research.

1.   I make a detailed analysis of the coverage, which reflects the broad socio-cultural and ideological spectrum that the book seeks to cover. Both cross-sectional and longitudinal approaches are applied. Opinion polls (of students and lecturers at Leningrad [St Petersburg] educational establishments) were the cross-sectional means, and content analysis of Russian and Western publications (NOVOE VREMYA and NEWSWEEK) after a five year interval (1985-1990) and *Novoe Vremya* (THE NEW YORK TIMES for 1985-1990-1991) was the longitudinal study.

2.   For comparison, the book analyses three Western and three ex-Soviet publications for frequency and value-loaded coverage of African issues for November and December 1987, and 1985 and 1990.[8] These publications are: THE NEW YORK TIMES, THE DAILY TELEGRAPH, and NEWSWEEK; and IZVESTIYA, PRAVDA, and NOVOE VREMYA. I chose these

publications for their reputation as the major news sources for Soviet and Western readers, not as random samples. All coverage of Africa is coded according to the following categories: frequency, approximate number of words, and article subject. I used frequency and approximate number of words to determine the degree of marginalization of Africa, while I used article subject to measure the extent of value-loaded treatment (stereotyping) of African issues by these publications.

Periodization of Research:

i.   The Khrushchev and Brezhnev eras [which coincided with the independence and post-independence periods in Africa] i.e. 1956-1982;

ii. Early glasnost/perestroika period (October-December (1985)

iii. Glasnost-perestroika or the Gorbachev years (October-December 1987; February-May 1989; and January-December 1990)

iv. The post-Gorbachev (Communist) period (September-December 1991, January-June 1992 and March 1993).

3.   Opinion Survey: To determine the press's influence or lack of it on the Western and Russian audience concerning the formation and dissemination of specific images of Africans, I polled ex-Soviet students and lecturers and short-term course Western (U.S. British and Canadian) students in various St Petersburg educational institutions.

4.   I also conducted in-depth video interviews of a cross-section of Soviet citizens, African Russians-products of mixed marriages and relationships between Soviet women and black students.

As with other kinds of communication channels, the intelligibility of press coverage depends on language or codes shared by communicators and recipients of the message transmitted. In the press, these codes include not only verbal language (in this case, Russian and English), but also many other codes (still photographs, editing styles or techniques, news-hole-advertisement juxtaposition, placement of articles, etc.). Communication, always political, occurs in texts that readers understand in relation to the codes organizing them. This study's principal focus is the discovery, reading, and decoding of these coded signs (images) referring to Africa.

This present study does have its limitations. Empirical data collected to test the propositions of the study are limited to the immediate pre-glasnost and immediate post-glasnost periods, although the general discussion extends much further beyond this time frame. The scope of the study therefore compelled me to concentrate on a portion of the media and selected statements as indicative of Soviet/Russian perceptions of Africa and Africans. The selection raises a host of methodological questions, most critical of which is the role of other media, for example, television in the transmission of images and text about Africans and their continent. It is equally difficult to ascertain the role of other agents of socialization, such as the family and the educational system.

Although the findings of the study cannot be used to provide generalized explanations of the motivations of Soviet/Russian press coverage of Africa and the perceptions of people of the FSU of Africans, they nevertheless, one will hope, will serve as useful snapshots and preliminary basis for further studies. It is hoped that this book will give future researchers a firm enough pedestal from where to see what Russian images of Africans were during the past century and how they will unfold in the new millennium.

I acquired great insight as a participant/observer of the Russian scene, particularly due to almost a decade's stay in the FSU. It is a well-known fact that the touchstone of the scientific method is the objectivity of its practitioners. Researchers must stand above the fray, as it were, or state their views as boldly as they can, no matter whose ox is gored. However, we all are human beings, susceptible to bias and value judgments. In matters of race and ethnic relations particularly, it is hardly possible to divorce one's values from one's research or writing. By the very nature of my subject, the approaches taken in this book are not value-free or value-neutral; they are influenced by my socio-cultural baggage, personal experiences, and points of view. However, I have attempted to state things as succinctly as I see them. If I felt a contest was warranted, I tried not to let traditional or commonly accepted viewpoints or long-standing ideological premises go uncontested. But at the same time, I do not want to give the impression of simply having an axe to grind. I do have biases, and some are bound to show.

Scholars of various hues have tended to see the differences in the worldviews of the FSU and the West as ideological: Communism versus Capitalism. This book demonstrates that we are more than ideology makes us. Above all, human beings can rise above their ideological selves. We may trace many of the world's ills to unmitigated ethnocentrism, not ideology. While ethnocentrism is a balm that soothes our feelings of inferiority and fear of isolation, it can also be a bane, pitting us against others, sometimes unnecessarily. It blinds us to what the sages of the past always stressed: that humankind belongs to the same species, in spite of differences in skin and hair color, and language. And as a species we are obviously capable of maintaining our sense of unity and homogeneity.[9]

The most important lesson, as Dr. Wilbur Schramm has emphasized, is respect for the members of another culture, race and nationality. An African, a Japanese, a Russian, a Chinese and a German are first of all human beings, with many common qualities and desires. In our modern setting this idea has given birth to the concept of a global village, which sees our planet as a mosaic of cultures, where respect and understanding rule.[10] We must also remember that ideologies will emerge, flourish, change, go out of vogue, and even die; but human essence and worth remains unchanged through the centuries. People may use ideologies to rationalize racism under various guises, but it is impossible to break the bonds uniting the human species. Most human evils spring from ethnocentrism, from limited awareness, and lack of sympathetic feeling with others and with the world outside us.

Like the Biblical mote in the eye, these evils are easy to see in others. However, it is much more difficult to find them in ourselves. For example, it was easy for politicians and media personnel in the FSU to blame Western racism, but difficult for them to see the same problem in their own backyard. The greatest challenge is: how do we respond to the evil in others without becoming infected by the same disease?

Charles Quist-Adade
August, 2000
Windsor,Ontario

Chapter One
Prologue: Africa In The Shadows Of The Kremlin And The White House

Between the breakdown of the grand alliance of World War II in the late 1940s and the razing of the Berlin Wall in 1989, the conflict between the United States (USA) and the former Soviet Union (FSU) dominated international affairs. The rivalry between the superpowers not only shaped the pattern of events in post-war Europe, but also had a stifling impact on political and economic developments in the developing world, particularly in Africa. The climate of suspicion and hostility created by the Cold War paralyzed wider developments in international relations. Many emerging leaders from the developing world were sacrificed in the East-West ideological and psychological crossfire.[1]

Many sound ideas about nation building, self-governance, and world peace emanating from the so-called Third World were drowned in the clatter of ideological and psychological warfare between the "Soviet-East and "American-West."[2] During the Cold War, it was fashionable to interpret the tensions between the superpowers as resulting from the clash of ideological differences or principles.[3] Most often people saw little beyond the East-West divide but the incompatibility of Capitalism and Communism. This was a flawed approach. The tensions were, more than anything else, vectored onto geo-strategic considerations bordering on national and narrow ethnocentric interests, which belonged to the ruling elites in both the USA and the FSU. The geopolitical considerations of the superpowers led to a frenzied quest for spheres of influence, securing firmer footholds, and the militarizing of Africa and much of the Third World.

Until the end of the Cold War, the major form of foreign "aid" to Africa was the supply of arms. In 1980, Washington provided military aid to 43 countries, about half of which were in Africa. By 1991, 102 countries, including Botswana, received US military aid.[4] Similarly, the Soviet Union exported 32 per cent of its arms to 56 Third World countries in 1989. Throughout the 1980s the Soviet Union supplied Third World countries with 7,925 tanks and self-propelled gun mounts, 20,470 artillery pieces, 17 submarines, 2,620 supersonic aircraft, 1,705 helicopters and 32,210 SA class missiles. These weapons went to the "hottest" flashpoints in Africa, notably, Angola, Ethiopia, Mozambique, and to Asia, the Middle East, and Latin America.[5]

Moreover, while its arms deliveries were worth more than $5.9 billion, the USSR provided $2.1 billion in economic aid to sub-Saharan Africa between 1980 and 1984. For North Africa the comparable figures were even more dramatic: $7.9bn in arms transfers and only $650 million in economic aid. In 1985-89 the Soviet Union exported $66,209 million worth of arms to various Third World countries, more than half of which were in Africa."[6] Even in 1991, when the Cold War seemed to be winding down, nearly 89 per cent of the total Soviet "disinterested" assistance to Africa was in the form of military supplies.[7]

Notwithstanding much rhetoric, the FSU like, its arch-rival the US, was a status quo power. Like the Americans, the Soviets did not have much sympathy for the demands associated with the New International Economic Order (NIEO) and its adjunct New International Information and Communication Order (NIICO) put forward by the non-aligned countries in the 1970s.[8] Through various international institutions such as the International Monetary Fund (IMF), the World Bank, United Nations Educational, Scientific and Cultural Organization (UNESCO), the "American-West" managed to preserve the status quo. Up to the time Soviet President Mikhail Gorbachev took the reins of power, and until the demise of Soviet-style Communism, the FSU also became an ardent champion of the status quo.

This is hardly surprising. Nations, as Hans Morgenthau asserted, act to preserve the status quo, and in the case of the superpowers, to advance imperialist aims and to gain prestige. Thus FSU not only did not seek to overthrow the existing distribution of power, it actively negotiated adjustment within the general framework of the existing status quo.[9]

If in the past Soviet leaders advised Third World nations to make a fundamental break with the capitalist-dominated world economy, then in the mid-1970s they began to recommend a more moderate course of action. The Soviet leaders became much more reluctant to guarantee economic support to Third World countries that sought to escape the grip of Western domination.[10]A vivid example was the case of Ghana. In 1982 Flight Lieutenant John Jerry Rawlings seized power for the second time in two years. With his coup d'etat he proclaimed he was launching an Ethiopian-type revolution. He then sent a delegation to Moscow, seeking economic support. But the Soviets advised the revolutionary Ghanaian government to go to the IMF instead.

According to Frank Furedi, a striking convergence existed between the views of Soviet and Western experts on Third World development matters during the last decade or so before perestroika and glasnost in the FSU. Both groups of experts were increasingly united in opposition to radical economic critiques of imperialist domination.[11] Valkiner cites a collection of essays by the Soviet [now Russian] Institute of Africa, published just before Gorbachev came into power, which challenged Samir Amin's[12] recommendations that Third World countries raise the prices of their raw materials.[13] Soviet scholars took issue with writers of the dependency school, accusing them of "exaggerating" the harmful impact of the world economy on the Third World.

Soviet contributors to the debate about the NIEO became increasingly conciliatory towards the existing order. At the 1979 summit of the fifth United Nations Council for Trade and Development (UNCTAD), Soviet delegates insisted it was possible to "democratize" the prevailing world economic system. The Soviet International Affairs monthly wrote in the same year, "In today's interdependent world, the USSR has no choice but to integrate into world economic relations, for participation in the division of labor has become a necessity facing every big or small nation."[14] The conservatism of the Soviet approach was apparent in the recommendations issued from Moscow to Third World regimes.

B. Zaslavsky commented on the pro-western drift of Soviet perspectives: "Soviet authors now advise Third World countries to remain attached to the capitalist world market to attract western capital for the development of the natural economy, to make maximum use of their own resources instead of relying on foreign aid."[15] The last version of the Communist Party of the Soviet Union (CPSU) program of 1986 endorsed the status quo orientation of Soviet foreign policy. The program dropped previous references to the Soviet Union's "internationalist duty to assist the peoples" of the Third World in fighting for their independence from the capitalist world order.[16]

The Information War

In the same vein, the Soviet position vis-a-vis the (NWICO) meant a dramatic shift toward the status quo before the demise of Communism. Yuli Magari best sums up the "Soviet-East" position during the early years of the debate: "For the Soviet Union, the entire Socialist community and the world communist movement and working-class movement, the efforts to set up a new information and communication order are inseparable from the struggle for complete elimination of exploitation, inequality and discrimination in relations among states, for peaceful coexistence and cooperation of countries with different social systems."[17]

Since the 1917 Bolshevik revolution, the West, jealous of its unswerving world dominance, never tired of finding ways and means of "consigning Communism to the ash heap of history." Treating the Communist revolution as "a mistake in history," the whole Western propaganda machine was let loose on the "evil empire." With its longer reach—by means of superior technology and expertise and centuries of its unchallenged sway—Western propaganda sought to isolate the Soviet Union and later its satellite states in Eastern Europe by creating a fog of fear and hopelessness around Soviet-style socialism. In this respect, the media played a leading role.

For example, a THE NEW YORK TIMES editorial from June 1970 says: "Our greatest adversary is now, and will be the Soviet Union. We shall be engaged against the Communist world in one way or another all our lives."[18] In their desire to create a *cordon sanitaire* around the world of Communism, Western mass media resorted to anything from "unbalanced objectivity, active opposition to outright lies," interpreting much the Soviets did as "international Communist conspiracy."[19] Hence the fear of isolation by the powerful, all-pervasive Western propaganda machine, more than anything else, prompted the "Soviet-East" to join forces with the developing countries in the call for a NWICO.

In other words, the position of the "Soviet-East" once again reflected its strategy of taking advantage of conflict between the "American-West" and developing countries. Since the West had practically monopolized the sphere of communication, information about the communist countries had insufficient access to Africa, Asia, and Latin America, let alone the Capitalist world. Hence, the essence of the "Soviet-East" position was to counter Western "imperialist expansion" in information dissemination by widening and strengthening its own information network and media infrastructure base. According to Yuri Kashlev, by the early 1980s the Soviet news agencies, Telegraphic Agency of the Soviet Union (TASS) and Novosti Press Agency (APN) were "among the largest in the world," and the Soviet press, literature and films circulated widely abroad. Soviet information, he continued, "is enjoying growing popularity on all continents. Radio Moscow broadcasts in more than 70 foreign languages."[20] Radio Moscow beamed 273 hours of broadcasting in 10 languages in Africa each week, compared with 219 hours for the British Broadcasting Corporation (BBC) and 135 hours for the Voice of America.[21] In addition, the FSU circulated numerous press reports aimed at the continent, and sponsored the publication of journalistic and academic articles with the African audience in mind.

Almost all party documents on the press stressed "an urgent need for an offensive in countering bourgeois ideological diversion, and in the truthful information about the real achievements of Socialism and the Socialist way of life."[22] Thus, as we have seen, the instinct of self-preservation, rather than altruistic solidarity with the developing world, was the underlying motive behind the Soviet Union's stand in the NWICO debate. Even when it realized the debate had reached a stalemate, and probably was unwinnable, the USSR gradually began to shift its initial stance in support of the status quo. By 1989, it wholeheartedly embraced the position of the "American-West."

By 1985, Soviet experts had begun to adopt a conciliatory position. Tatayana Lebedeva of Moscow State University wrote, "The policy of confrontation for which both sides—both the advocates and opponents of a new international information order—opted made it impossible to use the opportunities for dialogue and cooperation."[23] Lebedeva did not stop there. She moved on to deliver what can only be interpreted as a stab in the back to the non-aligned countries, until then described by the Soviet Union as its "natural allies." "It is time to abandon the interpretation of a new international information order (NIIO)[24] as a 'threat of information imperialism' or an attempt to impose total government control."[25]

Meanwhile, Nikolai Yermoshkin wrote that the international information exchange aspect of the new Soviet foreign policy is its search to promote "broad, concrete and constructive cultural cooperation for the sake of mankind, and for the benefit of general progress and peace all over the world."[26] And Soviet Foreign Affairs Minister Eduard Shevardnadze said at the 43rd session of the UN General Assembly, "the leadership of the Soviet Union has tried to elaborate a deeper perception of the original idea of Marxism about the interconnection between the interests of various classes and those of humanity as a whole, giving priority to the interests that are common to all nations."[27]

Craftily using verbal gymnastics, the USSR was not only trying to tow a middle line, it was also moving towards agreement with the West in maintaining the status quo. The convergence of the Soviet Union's interests in the Third World with those of the USA in maintaining the existing world economic order is understandable, not only because of geo-strategic considerations. There was very little difference in the ideological orientation of the ruling elite in the Soviet Union and that in the USA. This is not surprising, since socialist construction in the FSU not only followed the laws of capitalism [accumulation and competition]; the Soviet system was also part of the Capitalist system.[28] In Russia, as in the West, everything is subordinated to accumulation. Accumulation, in turn, results from the competitive relationship between the Russian ruling class and its rivals. They transform the output of Russian[29] industry into production dominated by the essentially Capitalist criterion of exchange value.[30]

Acting as the agent for the accumulation of capital, the Russian party and government bureaucracy, the apparatchiks, emerged as the collective capitalist—at the same pace as the economy itself took on the same features of the giant corporations in the nations of the West, against which Russia was competing.[31] Soviet experts themselves, admitting the "interdependence of the global economy," concluded, "it is not only the Third World that depends on the USSR and other socialist countries, but the socialist countries themselves have in a way become "hostages" to the crisis-ridden and dead-end modernization models on the former periphery of the world capitalist economy."[32]

A body of literature in the West and the Developing World demonstrates that the Soviet Union was indeed an imperialist power. Its economy functioned according to the laws of capital and where a bourgeois ruling class held power.[33] For example, Patrick Clawson of Seton Hall University and Santosh K. Mehrotra, who studied at India's Jawaharlal University, have graphically shown that the pattern of the "Soviet-East"-South trade and aid relations was very similar to the pattern of "America-West"-South trade and aid relations. The USSR profited from its aid and trades just as much as any imperialist power did.[34] The Soviet theory of 'non-capitalist development' fashioned in the 1950s, justified Soviet capital exports. Clawson and Mehrotra rightly contend that Soviet aid led to the development of capitalism—in fact, to the development of dependent capitalism.[35]

Several criticisms from the Chinese Maoists, although tainted by their bickering with the FSU following their ideological split, point to the status quo ambitions of the Soviet leadership. The Maoist leadership characterized the conduct of FSU in international politics as "obscene" Soviet "capitulation" to and "collusion" with American "imperialism."[36] The FSU's policy of peaceful-coexistence with the United States was a demonstration of Moscow's attempt to protect and service the status quo in international relations.

Given the same geo-strategic reasons and narrow interests of the Soviet Union's ruling elite, it is hardly surprising that during the 31st Session of the UN's General Assembly (1976-77), the USSR and the Western countries voted together on such vital resolutions as: (1) The Debt Problems of the Developing Countries [Resolution No. A/31/14]; (2) Industrial Redeployment in Favor of developing Countries; and (3) Ways and Means of Accelerating Transfer of Real Resources to Developing Countries on a Predictable, Assured and Continuous Basis.

Strategic-military competition, which dominated the process of capital formation in the USSR, became the cornerstone of its relationship with the West; it also served as the pivot around which Soviet policy in Africa and the rest of the Third World revolved. This geo-strategic competition served as the basis for the ideology behind the new "scramble for Africa" and the whole Third World by the "American-West" and the "Soviet-East" during the Cold War era. But the real linchpin of the East-West ideological warfare was the fears and anxieties of both ruling elites about losing their hold on power and wealth. These fears found expression in and determined the logic and dynamic of Cold War politics and the superpowers' confrontation.

To assess the extent and the dynamics of this confrontation, it suffices to focus on the horn of Africa, where the Russians and Americans exploited domestic and regional tensions, carving out spheres of influence and controlling important arteries to valued sources of raw materials. But first we must understand the background of their rivalry by noting these facts:

*   The horn straddles that region containing the world's most extensive oil reserves. Somalia, Sudan, and Ethiopia themselves now have or are likely to have significant reserves.

*   The West depends upon Middle-Eastern supplies;
      Soviet dependence upon Persian and North African
      oil increased substantially before the implosion of
      the Communist regime.

*   Largely, via the silver water of the Red Sea and
      Suez canal, Atlantic and Mediterranean trade links
      to that of the Indian Ocean, the Pacific, and the US
      West Coast,. Fully three-quarters of Western
      Europe's raw materials travel via Bab El Mandeb
      and the Suez.

*   Similarly, if less crucially, the Indian Ocean is one
      of three means of linking the east of the Soviet
      Union with its west. The northern sea route is
      passable in only three months of the year; the
      trans-Siberian route is immensely long (the USSR,
      about 5,000 miles wide, is subject to the vagaries
      of singularly harsh winters, and would be acutely
      vulnerable to external (Chinese) attack in case of
      war).

*   The USA has nuclearized the Indian Ocean, and
      thus threatened the Soviet Union in a weak spot.[37]

Against the backdrop of these facts the "American-West" and the
"Soviet-East" vied to court and cultivate, with varying degrees of
success, Egypt, Sudan, Ethiopia, Somalia, Uganda and Kenya.[38] The
concern of the "American-West," as then Secretary of Defense Casper
Weinberger told the US Congress in 1983, was to prevent the spread of
Soviet influence and the consequent loss of freedom and influence
which it entailed; to protect Western access to the energy resources of
the area; and to maintain the security of the key sea lanes of this region.
As Preston King rightly notes, the above statement could equally well
(suitably amended) be a declaration of the Soviet Union's policy in the
horn.

King provides a vivid account of the "physics" of the East-West
conflict in the horn: "British emplacement at the straits of Bab El
Mandels was challenged by Nasser, supported by the Soviets, and these
pressures culminated in Britain's withdrawal from Aden. Insufficient
Anglo-American support for Somalia's irredentism claims invited

Soviet entry after independence (1960). Soviet influence reached its apogee in 1976, being reversed by the 'switchover' of 1977. Soviet influence was expunged from Somalia by virtue of the critical military assistance the USSR gave Ethiopia (under attack from Somalia). US influence in Ethiopia, by virtue of the refusal of military assistance, was equally expunged. The USA, by virtue of the physics of superpower relations, was suctioned, in its turn, into Somalia."[39]

In the struggle to cut their slices in the Indian Ocean and the Red Sea regions, the "American-West" managed to pull into its orbit Egypt, Sudan, Somalia and Kenya. The "Soviet-East" got allies in Ethiopia and across the water in Aden.[40] Thus the confrontation in the horn between the "Soviet-East" and the "American-West" emerge summarily from King's words: "The American-West attempts to maintain its dominance, the Soviet-East to break that dominance.[41]

The consequences of this confrontation brought misery to the horn's people. Thus, to paraphrase the popular African proverb, when the superpower elephants fought, the African grass suffered. The region's people suffered and indeed continue to suffer, even after the Cold War, because of their own deep-seated animosities. And they suffer because "the great powers found it politic to exacerbate these animosities, to nurse and to arm them." Drought struck recurrently, "but the limited energies of the Ethiopians, Somalis and Sudanese are harnessed to the machine of war."[42] It became evident that the superpowers did not want to fight each other. An unwritten agreement between them seemed to exist.   Wherever the Americans bombed Libya, the Soviets stayed away.   Wherever the "Soviet-East" deployed its forces in Ethiopia, Angola, and Afghanistan, the Americans steered away.

Superpower rivalry in Africa, as we shall see, did not stop at the quest of military supremacy. It also extended to the media "battlefront," influencing the flow and content of news originating from Africa in the international media. Regardless of the ideological premise informing media coverage of African events, the specter of the superpower rivalry cast its ominous shadow over the news media in both camps. For instance, both Soviet and Western media often used ideological stereotypes like "freedom fighters," "bandits," "terrorists," "insurgents," and "puppets" to describe the same group of Africans fighting either to liberate themselves or to end counter-revolutionary activities.[43]

Both systems' media misinformed the public, and omitted and distorted facts about the developing world to suit their ideological biases and preferences. When the media in the USSR media talked about East-West issues they were East-biased; in the same fashion,

Western media were West-biased. They all saw Third World issues mainly through the prism of East-West ideological confrontation.

Africa And The Kremlin: From Revolutionary Messianism To Platonic Friendship

Communist Romance - Courtship And Honeymoon

The Soviet Union's direct involvement in Africa, unlike the "American-West's," was relatively recent. Under Nikita Khrushchev in the mid-1950s, the Soviets first began to adopt an active orientation towards Africa and the whole Third World.[44] The shift was influenced by several considerations. China was fast emerging as a competitor of radical allegiance in Africa and the rest of the developing world. The instability following the departure of Britain and France from their former colonies in Africa and Southeast Asia created openings for extending Soviet influence.[45] Probably the Kremlin's most pressing preoccupation was to checkmate the USA from turning Africa and other parts of the Third World into anti-Soviet bases and launch pads for surprise western attacks.

Several African nationalists and post-independence leaders were impelled to embrace Marxism-Leninism, due to the widespread negative response to colonialism that Africans associated with capitalism—or, more broadly speaking, with the Western forms of economic, social and political organization, democratic institutions and spiritual values. In the early 1960s the view prevailed in Africa and other parts of the developing world that socialism, with its planned economy and political stability, would ensure incomparably higher rates of production than capitalism. Many African leaders also proceeded from purely pragmatic considerations. They believed that by recognizing Marxism and Leninism as the state ideology, and declaring loyalty to socialism, the USSR and other countries of the socialist community would start providing them with massive aid.[46]

The Kremlin's ideological and propaganda planners artfully prompted that they "viewed the example of the USSR, where the peoples of the erstwhile fringes of the tsarist empire, who at the beginning of the 20th century had stood at approximately the same level as the newly-free African countries, had within an exceptionally brief span of time, indeed in the lifespan of just one generation, overcome their age-old backwardness thanks to the socialist choice."[47]

Thus the Kremlin, self-styling itself as godfather of left-wing radicalism, sponsored the national liberation movements that had sprung up in Africa, Asia, and Latin America after the end of WWII, particularly in the fifties and early sixties. Having realized the appeal of radical thought and Marxism in the developing world during this period, Moscow sought to spread the "Red Empire" to the "Dark Continent," to further its strategic empire-building aim.[48] George Padmore was much more forthright. Writing as a Soviet Communist Party renegade in the fifties, he observed that, "Africans and peoples of African descent are courted primarily to tag on to the white proletariat; and thus to swell the 'revolutionary ranks' against the imperialist enemies of the 'Soviet Fatherland.'"[49]

The Kremlin leadership needed radical African and other Third World leaders as pawns in their political and ideological confrontation with the West. It cultivated and wooed radical regimes to steer the "Marxist-Leninist course," hence serving as sources of tangible or potential military bases, valuable raw materials, and as a means of accomplishing "world Communism's basic objective of securing global triumph for the teachings of Marx, Engels and Lenin."[50] The opportunistic and cynical behavior of the Soviet communists dates to the early years of the Bolshevik revolution.

Padmore, who was forced to break ranks with the Soviet communists when he discovered that the Soviet Communists looked upon Africans as political pawns to be maneuvered in Russian interests alone, noted as far back as the mid fifties, that, "the oppressed Negro workers and peasants are regarded by the Communists as 'revolutionary expendables' in the global struggle of Communism against Western Capitalism."[51]

At the outset, Khrushchev's diplomacy was directed at the Middle East. As Fukuyama noted, in this region the "American-West's" presence constituted the greatest military threat to the USSR: "Moscow's chief concern was to undermine the series of US-sponsored pacts being erected around its borders, the most important of which was the Baghdad Pact with the SAC bases in the Northern tier."[52]

To counter the USA, Moscow cultivated friendship with Egypt under Gamal Nasser in the 1950s and 1960s. The evolution of the links between the Soviet Union and Egypt set the pattern, which was repeated again and again in relations with Africa over the next 30 years.[53] Egypt had been rebuffed by the American-led-West. Washington's refusal to help finance the construction of the Aswan dam, a major prestige project for the Nasser government, annoyed the

Egyptian leader. He reacted by moving closer to Moscow and he "hit decisively" at the West by nationalizing the Suez Canal. After the invasion of Egypt by a joint western task force, Nasser became entirely dependent on Soviet arms.[54]

Triumph in Egypt combined with modest gains in other parts of Africa. Two sorts of situations favored Moscow's penetration into Africa. First, the USSR could step in where demands for economic or military assistance had been denied or ignored by the USA. Somalia followed the Egyptian example of the mid-1950s in the early 1970s. Secondly, the Soviet Union could make important gains by establishing relations with radical regimes, which were at loggerheads with the "American-West." For example, the "Soviet-East" forged strong links with new radical leaders such as Ben Bella in Algeria, Modibo Keita of Mali and Kwame Nkrumah in Ghana during the 1960s.

Perhaps the most cogent statement of the Soviet Union's objectives in Africa was the "Statement on African Policy," released on June 23, 1978. Among other things, the statement said the Soviet government sought to strengthen and expand its "peaceful relations" with all legitimately ruling African governments; to aid national liberation movements throughout Africa in their struggles against outside domination; to oppose colonialism, neo-colonialism, and racism; and to support progressive programs adopted by African governments that embarked on the non-capitalist path of development."[55]

This statement, originally released as an apparent reaction to American charges of "Soviet expansionism" in Africa, became the blueprint of post-Kruschev Soviet African policy, which successive Soviet leaders and the media repeated throughout the Brezhnev-Andropov-Chernenko era (1964-85). Soviet accusations of Western interference and warnings of the "insidiousness of American imperialism" in Africa appeared in the Soviet media regularly throughout the 1970s and the early 1980s.[56]

Behind the Soviet media accusation of the "American-West" striving to maintain its neo-colonial sway and to establish hegemony in Africa lurked a geo-political consideration: protecting the USSR's interests.[57] This central objective was supplemented by a stratagem of opportunistically taking advantage of the difficulties encountered by the USA in Africa.

However, generally the FSU lacked the economic weight to compete effectively with the USA, although in specific situations, such as in Egypt, Soviet economic assistance played an important role. The fundamental lack of dynamism in the Soviet system accounted for its satellite states' ability to pull out of its orbit easily. As former Soviet experts Zevelev and Kara-Murza have recently explained, the Soviet Union ensured the military-political survival of the radical regimes, but could not become a full-fledged guarantor of their advance towards a new social mode of production, due to its own economic and technological drawbacks and serious deformations in its social system.[58]

Moreover, A. Izyumov and A. Kortunov lamented that, "even the most consistent of the USSR's allies such as Angola, Ethiopia, Mozambique and others began an active search for political and economic contact with the West."[59] And they grieved that, "it transpires that the US shifts the main burden of sustaining political stability" in these countries to the Soviet Union, while deriving economic benefits from this stability itself. "Sometimes the situation is ridiculous: for instance, in Angola Cuban troops often defend installations of American oil corporations from attacks by UNITA gangs financed by the West itself."[60]

Thus, although the most important resource available for boosting their influence in Africa was military hardware, and Soviet supplies of arms were key to diplomatic success in Algeria, Egypt, Angola, Mozambique, the Soviets discovered that their role as super arms dealer did not guarantee lasting influence in Africa.[61] In fact, the Soviets were more adept at establishing a foothold in Africa than they were at retaining it.

The ruling elites in Africa were happy to accept military assistance from the "Soviet-East," but they treated it as a temporary expedient before moving on to forge links with the "American-West." Striking examples are Egypt, Angola and Mozambique. Other examples are Angola and Ethiopia, both of which relied on the Soviet Union for political and military support.

According to Zeebroek, in 1986 only 9.8 per cent of all Angola's imports came from the FSU, while 56.6 per cent came from Western Europe, and a further 11 per cent from South Africa.[62] Ethiopia was critical of the Soviet assistance it had received in the form of famine aid between 1984 and 1986.[63]

Although Soviet propaganda maintained that trade and economic aid were instruments for "strengthening national and economic independence" and were therefore "useful weapons" against imperialism, the FSU did not use either in its policy objectives in Africa.[64] Its share of overall trade in Africa declined throughout the 1970s to a meager 2-3 per cent in 1985.

By the close of the 1980s, the FSU's total imports from Africa were a mere $1.227 billion. Its exports to Africa (minus South Africa) amounted to $5.3 billion.[65] Years of nearly hysterical striving to achieve (nuclear) military parity with the US had sapped and undermined Soviet potential to offer any meaningful economic assistance to prop up client states in Africa. Many of the pro-Soviet African regimes sooner or later succumbed to Western pressures.[66] The overthrow of such Soviet allies as Ben Bella in Algeria, Patrice Lumumba in the Democratic Republic of Congo (the former Zaire) and Kwame Nkrumah in Ghana underlined the insecurity of the Soviet presence in Africa. It also marked the end of the era of "revolutionary messianism" in Soviet-African policy.

These setbacks provided the background to the most crushing defeat for Soviet African diplomacy: the Soviet Union's expulsion from Egypt. Moreover, instead of creating a flexible, pro-active and comprehensive aid program, the Soviet became bogged down by the argument that the socialist world could not "genetically bear responsibility for the backwardness of the former colonies",[67] thereby unnecessarily ideologizing and limiting its economic assistance in Africa. Brenda Wolf writes: "...However, the level of assistance must correspond to the possibilities for deepening relations and the level of intensity with which the anti-imperialist struggle is fought" by a given African country.[68] This means that "Soviet-East" assistance was greater when an African government embarked "on the road of anti-imperialist, non-capitalist development."[69]

Soviet aid became restricted to the countries of the so-called socialist orientation, Angola, Benin, Congo, Ethiopia, Mozambique, etc. Thus huge, showy projects meant exclusively for the state sector were built mostly in countries where "anti-imperialist forces," pro-Soviet leaders were "in full control of political power."[70] While these projects were supposedly built for the "benefit of the broad masses," they become conduit pipes for the bureaucratic-political elite to amass wealth.[71]

While this principle did not undergo any discernible changes before the Gorbachev era, disappointments suffered by the Russians particularly in Egypt, Ghana, Mali, and Somalia injected a note of caution in the modeling of Soviet African policy through the late 1970s and early 1980s. Less mention was made of "disinterested" aid. Instead, "mutually-profitable" credits became the new buzzword of Soviet assistance to Africa. By the same token, African countries adopted a rather cautious stance to Soviet activities and overtures on the continent. Even in countries where Soviet activities or policies came under a shadow of suspicion or cynicism, due to ideological shifts in these countries, the general attitude towards the Russians was uneasy tolerance, not open hostility or total rejection.

Except for Doe's Liberia, Sadat's Egypt, Somalia, and of course, apartheid South Africa, which showed varying degrees of anti-Sovietism at one time or another, the Soviets were generally in the good books of most African governments. Attempts by hawkish politicians in the US to spread the anti-Communist scarecrow of Russia's imperialist grand design to import Communism to Africa had little impact on most African leaders. In short, the relationship between the USSR and most African countries in this period could be described as platonic.

The Gorbachev Era And The End Of A Platonic Relationship

New Thinking and Old Vision

Novoe politicheskoe myshlenie ("New Political Thinking"), which served as the motor in the Gorbachev reforms, became the driving force of a new era in world affairs during the second half of the 1980s. Although "new thinking" was not an entirely new idea—it has been echoed since Albert Einstein's[72] times – it was popularized and translated into concrete action by Gorbachev soon after he became General Secretary of the Communist Party of the Soviet Union (CPSU) in the spring of 1985. The beginnings of Gorbachev's new thinking go back to the CPSU Central Committee Plenum of April 1985, when he called for "civilized relations between states based on true adherence to the norms of international law."[73] After that historic plenum, through his state visit to France in October 1985, and until his first meeting with President Reagan on November 21, 1985, he expressed his philosophy of new thinking in various terms.

In the French Parliament he referred to the ever-growing "interdependence between continents and countries" and the need to ensure that mankind and civilization survive at any cost."[74] He praised Europe as "a cradle of spiritual values."[75] But the most comprehensive and systematic elaboration of new thinking appeared for the first time in Gorbachev's 1987 book PERESTROIKA AND NEW THINKING FOR OUR COUNTRY AND THE REST OF THE WORLD[76] and an article in PRAVDA[77] on September 17, 1987.

To protect perestroika and make it acceptable to the West through foreign policy, Gorbachev, citing Lenin, tried to establish the

precedence of common human interests over class interests. He also
tried to give his reforms a stamp of "Europeanism," a European image,
by stressing the European character of the Soviet Union. Often he
spoke of Europe as "our common home," or "house," or "space."

In a speech on November 4-5, 1987, Gorbachev claimed that because
of the changed East-West configuration of world politics, one could
"no longer regard development of the world from the standpoint of the
struggle between two opposing systems."[78] It is important he went on,
"to take the realities into account and be aware of the fact that we are
all sitting in one boat, and must behave in such a way that it does not
capsize." He stressed the significance of seeing "peaceful co-existence"
"in a new light," i.e. primarily as competition and cooperation.[79]

Addressing the United Nations Assembly in December, 1988,
Gorbachev again summed up the basic principles of new political
thinking, saying human development had entered a "new era" in which
progress would be determined by the priority of values common to all
mankind."[80] The solution to global problems, he said, is only possible
through a new dimension and a new quality of cooperation between
countries, plus societal and political currents "irrespective of
ideological or other differences."[81] He declared that, "violence and the
threat of violence cannot and may not be instruments of foreign policy
any more."[82]

New Thinking was also meant to extend to the international
exchange of information. In his book, PERESTROIKA AND NEW
THINKING IN OUR COUNTRY AND THE REST OF THE
WORLD, Gorbachev proposed a universal information exchange
program and a new international communication system under the
auspices of the United Nations Organization (UN), to give peoples the
opportunity to understand one another, to know the truth of their lives,
and not the interpretations of western propagandists. This program, he
said, must eradicate from the flow of information the stereotype of the
enemy, bias, prejudice, absurd lies, the deliberate distortion of facts,
and their dishonest manipulation.[83]

Furthermore, Gorbachev assigned the mass media a new role in the
post-Cold War world. "To humanize international relations, there have
to be appropriate actions in the humanitarian field, too, notably as
regards information exchange, human contacts, etc. That will help
create moral guarantees for peace and hence contribute toward working
out the material safeguards."[84] The cultural arrogance expressed in the
"information aggression" and journalistic color-sensitivity practiced by
the Western media not only "leads to mental degradation" and spiritual

poverty, but also "hampers cultural mutual [inter-] enrichment.[85] It also breeds ill feeling and alienation between peoples. On the other hand, you must agree that a people that knows and values the culture and art of other peoples can have no ill-feeling toward them."[86]

Explaining the information exchange in the new thinking, T. Lebedeva wrote: "Conscious of the existing realities and imperatives in the field of information, we are also fully aware of the need for a change not only in the structure, but also in the content of international information exchange. The first task is, above all, to discard deep-seated stereotypes, which tune us in to a certain wavelength of expectations and assessments, and so far made it impossible for us to use the opportunities for dialogue and cooperation."[87] Lebedeva, calling for adjustments to the concept of the New World Information and Communication Order (NWICO), advocated new thinking in world information policies. She claimed communication policy should be determined by the priorities of universal human values.[88]

New Thinking And Africa: The Peace Dividends

In the immediate post-Cold War period (1986-1990), or what some have called the "neo-detente" era, glasnost (openness), perestroika (restructuring), and the New Thinking in the Soviet foreign policy became key elements in world politics generally, which specifically affected the tenor of regional conflicts in developing countries.[89] The combined effects of the Soviet New Thinking and the resultant US-Soviet neo-detente set in motion a process of conflict resolution in Africa and many parts of the Third World. This period saw the gradual transformation of the antagonistic relationship into "adversarial cooperation" between the superpowers, which characterized the bipolar Cold War relationship as positive collaboration.[90]

The Reagan-Gorbachev summit meetings in 1987 and 1988 set the tone for increasing Soviet-US cooperation. The two superpowers embarked on parallel efforts that positively affected long-standing conflicts and disagreements over Third World issues. In Africa, the era of constructive collaboration began with the Angolan/Namibian peace process in 1988. For the first time in the post World War II period, US and Soviet officials cooperated in an open and cordial manner to end a bitter political conflict.[91]

By June 1988, the two powers had agreed to support a target date of September 29 for reaching a peaceful settlement that also included independence for Namibia. Shortly afterward, Cuba, South Africa, and

Angola agreed on the withdrawal of Cuban troops from Angola. On December 13 they reached a final agreement, resulting in the formal tripartite treaty signed on December 22 at the UN. South Africa, Angola and Cuba agreed to the phased withdrawal of Cuba's troops over a 27-month period and the independence of Namibia by November 1989.

Thanks to New Thinking, the civil war in Mozambique saw considerable progress towards peaceful settlement with a ceasefire agreement already signed. The combined effects of the Soviet, Cuban, and former East German withdrawals showed quick results in the outcome of the Ethiopian civil war, leading to the overthrow of the Mengistu regime and the end of four decades of civil war. The de-ideologization of international relations, one of the premises of New Thinking, diminished the specter of the Communist bogeyman, which South Africa's apartheid regime had hitherto used to justify its oppression of the black majority and also to ensure Western support. Little wonder that, South Africa's leader, F.W. de Klerk, took steps toward dismantling the inhuman apartheid system. He even went to the extent of un-banning the South African Communist Party.

In all the conflict settlements discussed above, the Soviets had used their leverage over their former clientele to ensure success. But they did not act out of sheer altruism. Besides the Kremlin's objective to scale down its costly commitments, it also believed that successful cooperation with the US in the African conflicts would probably contribute to progress in other areas of US-Soviet interaction.

From New Thinking And Passive Disengagement To Post-Communist Active Disengagement

Before setting out on his historic nine-day African visit in March 1991, former Soviet Foreign Affairs Minister Eduard Shevardnadze gave, what observers saw, as the bare outline of the FSU's African policy in the era of glasnost and perestroika.[92] He pointed to a shift from traditional methods and outlook to "new criteria in Soviet policy in Africa and broadening of external political horizons."[93] He described the shift as qualitative, a process that became manifest after Gorbachev inaugurated his perestroika/glasnost revolution in the spring of 1985. Here was a shift from what Soviet scholars termed past "ideological fantasies," "political wishful thinking," "paternalism," and "economic gigantomania" toward ideological "soberness'" and economic pragmatism based on cost effectiveness and rationalism.[94]

This meant that in the new era, economic consideration had to outweigh ideological cooperation. It also meant that Soviet economic assistance would now spread much more broadly throughout the continent, not being restricted to "special allies" or "traditional friends," as in the past. Thus, while formerly Soviet Africa policy strategists were preoccupied with winning more ideological friends on the continent, they now seemed to adopt a new formula vectored onto Lenin's injunction: "More economics, less political trivialities" and "politics is the concentrated expression of economics."[95]

Spelling out the new parameters of the Kremlin's new African policy, former Deputy Foreign Minister Anatoly Adamishin stated: "We seek to be down-to-earth and realistic and avoid wishful-thinking, to do business thriftily."[96] He said Soviet policy in Africa should be made more "active, realistic and closely bound up with the interests of our national economy."[97]

What the USSR wanted now, said Adamishin, "is maximum efficiency with economic, scientific, technical and other forms of cooperation being of immediate benefit to all sides. From now on, local conditions, instead of Soviet yardsticks, are to be applied when embarking on projects in Africa."[98] Gorbachev's foreign affairs spokesman, Gennady Gerasimov, said on the eve of Namibia's independence and Shevarnadze's maiden African visit, that "new thinking has signaled the end of the platonic and ideological relationship between African countries and the USSR."[99]

For the first time in Moscow, people said, that in the past the USSR undertook too many ventures around the world, becoming bogged down in Africa on several issues not linked with the country's immediate interests. If in the immediate pre-perestroika era Soviet ideologists and propagandists presented Soviet-built large scale projects in, for example, Angola, Benin, Egypt or Ethiopia as "selfless socialist internationalist assistance" to help these countries "ward off imperialist blackmail," now they said most of these projects had become white elephants and a running sore in the Soviet economy, as large sums of rubles were spent yearly to keep them functioning.[100]

Soviet assistance, propagandists asserted, brought only "fleeting results in the period of struggle for power and in the first years of existence of a progressive government."[101] "Not infrequently," wrote A. Izyumov and Andrei Kortunov, "together with aid, Moscow also exported the worst principles of the [Soviet] administrative economic system: red tape, a dominance of 'gross output,' an expense-based approach. As a result most recipients of Soviet aid were never to overcome the stagnation of their economy, and in some of them production is generally dwindling."[102] "It is no secret," Kortunov continued, "that many Third World recipients of Soviet aid are notorious for their authoritarian or dictatorial methods of rule, the cults of their leaders, a ruthless suppression of the opposition, and for corruption."[103]

Concluding, he writes: "At a definite stage of history, Soviet [military] aid assisted in strengthening newly-emergent states' independence. But in many cases it also added to the deformation of their political development, the excessive influence of the military, and the militarization of the whole social life. Sometimes the aid encouraged bellicosity in relation to neighbors. Soviet military aid has been used by repressive regimes to suppress domestic opposition and religious movements."[104]

Thus the new arguments, much to the consternation of Moscow's pre-glasnost supporters in Africa, made outright nonsense of previous talk of the virtues of socialist aid to the developing world. For example, both Kremlin leaders and their admirers in Africa had loudly proclaimed that Soviet aid to the newly independent states was more effective and advantageous than that offered by the West. Soviet economic assistance, they said, "helps create the economic basis for independent development of African countries to consolidate their position *vis-a-vis* imperialist capital and to be more independent in their economic links with the capitalist world."[105] Giant projects were also considered beneficial because "they help resolve the problem of unemployment" in African countries.[106]

In 1990, Soviet economist G. Polyakov, expressed the new mood in Moscow concerning Soviet-African relations. "Socialism," he stated "cannot and should not be a guarantor of regimes, which do not enjoy widespread social support and are unable to defend themselves." Further he stated: "Aid programs should henceforth be made commensurate with the means available for Africa," and there should be fewer large-scale projects.[107] Instead, he advocated more trade in such things as washtubs and kitchen utensils. He even suggested the dumping of junk, "un-purchased Soviet-made goods" on African markets, arguing that, "if the Americans do not feel ashamed to do so why should Russians?"[108]

Polyakov continued, "Those who advocate continued cooperation with African countries do so because they argue that it is the only way to recoup debts owed to the FSU. They argue that the continent is the "cheapest source for raw materials, consumer goods cheaper than anywhere in the world," and a market for made-in-Russia goods which "do not yet attain Western standards."[109] Africa, he contends, could also become a hunting ground for unemployed or underemployed Russian specialists.

Almost all the perestroika-style commentators on the Kremlin's Africa policy fault "Stalinist barrack socialism" and its latter-day manifestations, Brezhnevism or neo-Stalinism, for the neglect of Africa or blunders in official policy and a one-dimensional presentation of Africans in the mass media.

However, side by side with the self-criticism, the glasnost media and politicians began a new marginalization, stereotyping and trivializing of African countries and events. For example, when Foreign Minister Shevardnadze made his historic visit to Africa in March 1990 –the first ever by a Soviet foreign minister—press and television coverage was officious and scanty. Reports by the state-controlled Central Television did not include shots of the minister's visit. In place of pictures, Soviet viewers saw a blank map of Africa, as though to confirm their long-held prejudice that Africa is without modern apartments, roads, railways, just a continent of sunshine and crocodiles.

In a TV panel discussion dedicated to African liberation day a month later, a Soviet journalist taking part in the discussion kept repeating that famine persists in large parts of the continent. Finally, his American colleague reminded him that famine is not Africa's main problem. The problem is food storage and distribution, as it is in the Soviet Union. As the media and the apparatchiks continued to attack Soviet policy in Africa, ordinary citizens also began repeating a question the Deputy Director of the Moscow-based Africa Institute, Alexei Vasilyev, had posed in an IZVESTIYA article: "Why Do We Need Africa?"[110]

Many Russians, upset and threatened by their country's apparent economic dislocation, began to scapegoat Kremlin's African policy. The primary grievance carried by mainstream media with either left or right political trappings, as well as the neo-Communist press, was that scarce Soviet resources were "generously" thrown away in Africa and other parts of the developing world in the frenzied chase for ideological fraternity and spheres of influence during the Cold War era. One critic said: "We gave to Africa without receiving anything in return." To him, Africa had nothing to offer Russia, so continued relations were unprofitable: "We have nothing to lose by cutting our ties with these backward countries but our chains of implacable aid."[111]

In another IZVESTIYA article, "Africans Want to Work With Us But We Do Not Need the Dark Continent", the author sums up these sentiments thus: "Enough is enough. After all, we saved them from starvation, we healed them, we educated their military officers, bureaucrats, doctors, engineers and agronomists."[112] Vasilyev's attempted to answer the glasnost-era critics, and ostensibly to diffuse the current anti-African mood of the country. "We have something to give to Africa, and Africans have something to give us in return," he argued. In a passionate appeal for Russia's continued cooperation with African countries, Vasilyev enumerated several achievements by Africans in science, culture and economics. Without such information, he contended, it is not surprising that Soviet citizens should regard Africans as having nothing at all to offer their country. "It is ridiculous to underrate the contribution of Africa to human civilization," he stressed, and offered this advice to his fellow countrymen and women: "Many of our compatriots must overcome the psychological barrier in their relations with Africans, whether from the north or south of the continent, banish from our minds the racist and confusing official slogans we learned in childhood."[113]

Several articles akin to Vasilyev's by Soviet journalists and Africanists appeared frequently in the mainstream press and specialized publications on Africa and the Third World during the early years of the Gorbachev reforms. The most notable among them came from former Soviet Africanist-diplomat, Boris Asoyan, in the Soviet Writers' Union mouthpiece, LITERATURNAYA GAZETA, "Africa—So Far Away: How We Looked at it Yesterday and How We See it Today,"(October 7, 1987) In KOMSOMOLSKAYA PRAVDA he published "About the Black Colour Without Exaggeration" (August 19, 1989). These two articles came to serve as the pivot around which post-Communist Russia discussed Soviet-African relations.

Exit Gorbachev, Enter Yeltsin

The Gorbachev era was buried under the rubble of the failed communist revanchist coup in August 1991. With it also died what remained of the "platonic friendship" existing between Africa and the FSU. Boris Yeltsin of the Russian Republic and his team of Western-style democrats, the new masters of the Kremlin and heirs to the disbanded Soviet Union, had yet to emerge with a clear-cut policy on Africa. Meanwhile, however, they were busily selecting their friends in Africa. Certainly, their African friends were bound to be radically different from those of their predecessor Communist rulers.

But although they said economic considerations determined the selection, the new rulers' official statements and diplomatic maneuvers indicated other considerations also.[114] If the first African tour at the end of 1991 by Russian Federation Foreign Affairs head Andrei Kozyrev was indicative, it seemed that Russia's new rulers seemed to have these three priorities in Africa:

* To maintain and even strengthen economic ties with countries of the Magreb. This was mainly due to the Middle East factor. Having become the legal heir to the disintegrated Soviet Union, Russia wanted to be considered a great power and a force to be reckoned with in the region for strategic and politico-religious reasons. In the words of Kozeryev, "Russia wants to continue and enrich its participation in the affairs of Africa as a normal, great power."[115]

* In Sub-Saharan Africa, old debts owed to the USSR had to be repaid with Russia's lessening involvement (progressive disengagement), although military cooperation could continue to earn money for the hard cash-starved Russian economy. The motive here is that most countries in this region were poor and economically backward. There were few or no economic benefits to gain. Further credits, even if this were possible, risked not being returned, as most of these countries were more or less insolvent.[116]

* Relations with South Africa had to improve fast and broaden.[117] The white minority-ruled country appeared like a new El Dorado, a haven for thousands of Russian emigrants. Thus in Angola, the first port of call by Kozyrev, the youthful foreign minister demanded the payment of debts (mainly military) owed to the USSR by the Angolan government. Although, the mammoth Soviet military base in Angola was to be closed, military cooperation, Kozyrev told reporters, should continue.

This meant that Russia was ready to sell more kalashnikov machine guns to the Luanda government when it needed most was economic cooperation to rebuild its war-ravaged economy. The minister made that statement, bearing in mind President Yeltsin's new decree to step up the sale of military hardware by Russia's industrial-military complex, to obtain much-needed hard currency to revamp the ailing economy. The decree gave directors of ammunition-making factories the freedom to export arms without resorting to Kremlin sanctions, as was the past practice. Although economic cooperation was part of a new agreement with the government in Luanda, the cardinal aim was to have debts swapped on a compensatory basis.

In South Africa, diplomatic relations severed in 1956 were restored, and economic and trade links established. A protocol agreement between the Russian Foreign Affairs boss and his South African opposite number, Rulof 'Pik' Botha, paved the way for the opening of embassies, consular sections, and commercial centers in various cities of the two countries. The May, 1992 visit by South African President F.W. de Klerk sealed relations between the two countries, which had been developing at breakneck speed since Gorbachev had promulgated perestroika and glasnost seven years earlier.

The new orientation of the Russian Federation's fledgling foreign policy rooted in Gorbachev's "new thinking" and perestroika-cum-glasnost ideology. Yeltsin made a major change to Gorbachev's "New Thinking" in substituting Gorbachev's "reasonable sufficiency" with "minimal sufficiency," and abandoned what remained of Gorbachev's messianic Marxist commitments. But still the mainstay of the new Kremlin's foreign policy remained Gorbachev's triple concept of "Perestroika-cum-Glasnost-cum-New Thinking."

Gorbachev's team set out to fashion a brand-new foreign policy, which became increasingly Western-oriented and pragmatic. These new planners of Russian policy in Africa announced that they were shedding the ideological ballast of their old stance. Soviet-African relations, like those with other parts of the developing world, were now to rest on Lenin's injunction: "More economics, less political/ideological trivialities" (emphasis mine). During the six-year Gorbachev rule, this injunction was followed to the letter as the Kremlin gradually cut aid and support for its allies. Gorbachev stated that the Soviet Union got bogged down in useless ventures in Africa, always gave but received nothing in return for its ideological investments. Politicians and the media, both right wing and left-wing, have made capital of "generous" and "disinterested" aid given to African and other Third World countries ever since Gorbachev raised the issue in a speech in Minsk, the Byelorussian capital, during the early years of his reforms.

Post-Communist Glasnost And Africa

However, the tone of the argument surrounding the issue became a crescendo after the botched August 1991 coup, when the so-called democrats led by Yeltsin took the reins of power.[118] Events in the wake of Communism's demise have proven that if the Communists and their media were friendly but patronizing, even solicitous in their approach to Africa, the "democrats" and the new press now appeared largely disinterested, condescending and even racist. Communists had prided themselves on offering "free," and "generous" aid to Africa, never tiring of drumming home to the Soviet citizenry how the USSR was performing its "Marxist" internationalist duty by assisting poor African countries in their "just struggle against western blackmail and exploitation."

The democrats, on the other hand, chose a less pompous yet infamous role. They lost no time, after taking over from the Communists, in giving full rein to their suppressed racist sentiments. They used the mass media to air not only their loss of interest in Africa, but also their anger and disdain toward Africans in the fullest expression of glasnost. Before and after the failed coup in August 1991, Yeltsin went on record as saying socialism should have been experimented with in a small African country, not in the huge Soviet Union.[119] This statement implied that Africans are nothing but guinea pigs, suitable only for experiments. Going as far as Africa to find a subject for this analogy—when there were as many small countries in Europe or in his own Russian Federation, composed of over 80 tiny tribal and ethnic groups—indicated not only his condescending, dismissive attitude towards Africans, but also the blind chauvinism and racial bigotry of Russia's new leaders.

For Russia's new political bureaucracy and the media, using Africa as a metaphor for poverty, backwardness, and hopelessness has become a fad. Lambasting the former communist leadership for "wasting" Soviet resources in Africa became a popular for catching applause and votes at political gatherings and in parliament. In 1991, Vladimir Zhirinovsky, founder of the Liberal Democratic Party of Russia, returned from a visit to the USA, told Russians he was appalled by the huge presence of blacks and Asians in New York. According to him, America's current problems rooted in the large concentration of colored people in that country.

Fascists have also obtained access to state media, in what seems like the new leaders' calculated attempt to use the media to scapegoat

Africa. In April, 1992 a talk show program on the state-owned Central Television had Fascists openly expressing their resentment against Africans and blacks in general.[120] This is hardly surprising, considering that Russia's so-called new democrats differ very little in their attitude towards blacks from the motley national-chauvinistic and Fascist groupings that have mushroomed all over Russia. Most of them were yesterday's Soviet-style Communists, who, despite their public pontification about the brotherhood of man and racial harmony under Communism, nurtured and spread racism, anti-Semitism, and ethnic hatred among the Soviet citizenry.[121]

Much more recently, the unholy trinity between the communists, democrats and nationalists was demonstrated most dramatically when Yeltsin, Communist Party leader Genady Zuganov and ultranationalist Zhirinovsky all attended an openly anti-black, anti-Jewish, and anti-foreigner art exhibition put up by the overtly racist painter, Illya Glazunov in Moscow. That the art show, which featured paintings of bulbous-lipped black men carting off naked white women and heavily bearded Hasidic Jews raising to their lips crystal goblets of Russian blood, was attend by these prominent politicians goes to further demonstrate the fact that when it comes "Great Russian nationalism" the three main political orientations in post-communist Russia are united.[122]

Excluded from this attitude was apartheid South Africa. During the immediate post-Communist period, which coincided with the last days of the apartheid regime in South Africa, Russians referred to it as a land of eternal spring, "a corner in Heaven,"[123] "Heaven for Whites."[124] It was reported on liberally and described in glowing terms. The press traced Russia's historical links with the racist regime to the Anglo-Boer War, when Russian soldiers supposedly fought on the Boer side against the English.[125] The ANC was called the "world's richest" liberation movement; the state media, including IZVESTIYA, called for cutting aid to it.[126] The injustice of apartheid, the pet topic of Soviet journalists during the Cold War era, was hardly mentioned in reports.

From all indications, the new Kremlin leadership seemed less interested in the ANC than in the white minority regime in Pretoria. It also did not appear concerned about the future prospects of majority rule under an ANC government. An IZVESTIYA article warned Russia's new democrats, most of them yesterday's Communists and staunch ANC supporters, not to throw out the baby with the bath water. "The ANC will play an influential role in post-apartheid South Africa, issuing export and import licenses. Soon the South African Foreign

Ministry is likely to be headed by a black, and that country's future ambassador to Russia may be black too, possibly an ANC man."[127] But to many Russians, pragmatic considerations about where today's bread and butter come from outweighed all else; only business with the white minority would bring much-needed assistance. Tomorrow will take care of itself. A Moscow entrepreneur summarized it all in telling an IZVESTIYA: "Good white guys came from South Africa with excellent and lucrative proposals. Later they offered goods. Should I refuse them because the ANC or the U.N. is against apartheid?"[128]

If under Communism the media and politicians singled out the white minority for castigation, for perpetrating atrocities against the innocent black majority, now the blame shifted to the black majority, for unleashing "black" terror against whites and "senseless" black-on-black violence. If in the past the media expressed compassion for the miserable living conditions of the black majority, now that sympathy transferred to the white minority. An IZVESTIYA article caught this shift clearly. "In the past 20 years, the wages of black miners went up by 67 per cent, while those of their white counterparts fell by 24 per cent. For black education, the South African government earmarked 3.3 billion Rands, and in 1992, 4.5 billion Rands. Each day eleven classrooms are built. Education for black children will be free, while that for white kids will be paid for by their parents."[129] ZNAMYA YUNOSTI also portrayed the white minority as victims of the transition process: "Life is becoming increasingly difficult for the whites, as more and more blacks take on jobs which were reserved exclusively for [the whites]."[130] Clearly the configurations of the Kremlin's relationship with the ANC needed detailed consideration.

How De Klerk Beat Mandela In The Race To The Kremlin

During his historic visit to Moscow in May 1992, de Klerk reportedly asked ANC Leader Nelson Mandela to visit Russia, to see the consequences of socialism for himself. This statement not only reflected the euphoria and triumph of the white minority leader over the demise of Communism in the FSU; it also revealed de Klerk's own feeling of personal victory in winning the Kremlin leaders' invitation to visit before Mandela. For a long time speculation had been rife about which leader would win the race to the Kremlin: which one would first have the honor and privilege of seeing the white marble walls of the Kremlin, walking the cobbled grounds of Red Square, and seeing the mortal remains of Soviet-style Communism's father, Lenin, in his mausoleum.

It is a reflection of post-Cold War realities and irony of the times that the apartheid leader, who had used the Communist scarecrow to justify persecuting members of the pro-Communist ANC, was the first to visit the Communist shrine. Mandela had to languish in prison for nearly three decades because the regime considered him a Communist agent and collaborator with the Kremlin. This event also confirmed one of the hard-to-beat truths of politics: there are no permanent friends, as Lord Palmerston reputedly said, there are only permanent interests. Yeltsin brought this message home powerfully to Mandela and his followers. And so de Klerk won. He would have done so, even if Communism had not suddenly collapsed the previous August.   Originally, the Russians wanted the ANC leader to visit Moscow before de Klerk. But this was not to be. Relations between the ANC and the Kremlin had been going through a bad patch that had begun soon after Gorbachev began his perestroika and glasnost reforms.

As perestroika progressed and the Russian leadership began to shed most of the old Communist paradigms, Moscow tried to improve relations with the South African regime without harming relations with the ANC. The ANC grudgingly accepted the new development, but the crunch came when high-ranking Russian officials gradually began paying regular visits to Pretoria without their traditional consultation with comrades in the ANC.   The ANC protested, but without much bite, for it still depended on Kremlin assistance and support. All too soon, another golden rule was broken. Taking advantage of glasnost, the media began criticizing the ANC. Adverse newspaper articles about it, with Moscow's tacit approval, called for an end to Soviet help. The cooling of relations between the ANC and the Kremlin showed in the surprisingly poor media coverage of Mandela's release from jail in February 1990.

While the Western and Third World media virtually exploded with the news, Moscow's Central Television allotted a mere 30 seconds to the man who had not been seen outside prison walls for 27 years. IZVESTIYA did not carry information about the freeing of this long-standing ally and comrade of the Soviet Union when it appeared the next morning. PRAVDA did so, but only in an unremarkable, dry, non-committal four-paragraph biographical sketch buried under an article on Russian-US relations. Still, when Mandela was freed, ANC insiders in Moscow said, Russia was the first country on his visiting list "because that country, more than any other outside Africa, supported the cause of the suffering black majority in South Africa."[131]

Seven years passed before Mandela could visit Russia on April 30, 1999. An IZVESTIYA article, "N. Mandela Cannot Come to Us. He is now in the USA," accused him of deliberately making the visit impossible. It claimed that instead of visiting Moscow, Mandela had decided to prolong his visit to the USA because "he has made new friends there, who would shower dollars on him."[132] However, the ANC rejected this allegation as baseless and irresponsible. Its mission in Moscow said the Kremlin had precluded Mandela's visit. It said Mandela had twice entered in his diary a visit to Moscow, as part of his foreign thanksgiving tours; but that "either no confirmation was received or confirmation came too late."[133]

Moscow had invited the ANC leader to visit Russia in a statement issued by TASS soon after his release.[134] But the Kremlin did not really find Mandela's visit very pressing, as the Cold War's end meant a Mandela visit would score no ideological point. This position explains the poor coverage given his release. Had Mandela been released even three years earlier, Moscow would have spared no effort to highlight yet another victory of Communism over Capitalism. Furthermore, the Kremlin was playing a Western card. Both Gorbachev and Yeltsin were unwilling to receive Mandela before the Group of Seven (G-7) summits in London in 1991 and in Munich in 1992, where the two had gone begging for much-needed Western financial assistance.

A Mandela visit before the summits was likely to get the Western interpretation of continuing Kremlin support for the ANC, which could block Western aid flow to a beleaguered Russia. In Moscow, African diplomatic circles speculated that the West's hidden agenda was to weaken the ANC, paving the way for a two-party post-apartheid South Africa. Then the only viable parties would be de Klerk's Nationalist Party and Chief Buthelezi's Nkatha Freedom Party. Margaret Thatcher supposedly brought that message to Gorbachev when she stopped in Moscow in May, 1991 enroute to South Africa, where she received an award for her support of the white minority regime.

The growing anti-ANC mood in the C.I.S, Commonwealth of Independent States, might also have given the Moscow leaders cause for caution. The possibility of Russian Fascists organizing anti-ANC demonstrations during Mandela's visit could not be ruled out, although this possibility seemed remote. According to the ANC's Moscow mission, its flag was torn down three times during the first two years of the glasnost/perestroika "revolution." Its Russian secretary and driver were threatened, and the mission received hate letters. One posted in St. Petersburg asked the "ANC of Kaffirs" to "go away to Africa."[135] The threats began after Russian press articles had attacked the ANC, questioning the wisdom of a bankrupt Russia continuing to support what was variously described as a "terrorist" organization and the "richest" liberation movement in the world.[136]

While the press campaign continued against Russian aid to the ANC, it encouraged Russians to migrate to South Africa. The early 1990s saw a stream of ex-Soviet journalists visiting South Africa for the first time and returning with a new apartheid story. In place of what one St. Petersburg journalist described as "stale tales" of white policemen and their dogs chasing and shooting "stone-throwing black protesters," they filed stories about "the land of eternal spring", "disappearing apartheid," "the African superpower."[137] Although more recent articles tended to reduce the color in this rosy picture with warnings of South Africa's internal problems of unemployment and recession, the current wave of emigration that Russians and other ex-Soviet nationals showed they were ready to take such risks.

These people saw the continuing violence in the black townships as a black problem that had nothing to do with white people. There was a rush for South African visas as far back as 1989-90; by the end of 1991, the first and largest group of 2,500, the first batch of 10,000 visa applicants, reportedly too left for the country tagged by the ex-Communist press as a "racist inferno." According to the Giperion Company, the South African-Hungarian joint venture that recruited skilled workers in the former Communist countries of Eastern Europe and the C.I.S. for South African firms, up to one million Russians and nearly half-a-million other citizens of the C.I.S. planned to settle in South Africa.[138]

St. Petersburg State University, which now teaches Afrikaans, the official language of the minority white regime in South Africa, became a hunting ground for labor contractors. Advertisements for job opportunities replaced students' murals on the evils of the apartheid system. Even before Communism's collapse in 1991, district and city party soviets (committees) had begun to set up South Africa sections to foster economic links with the white minority-ruled country. And while various Soviet-African friendship and solidarity societies were closing or becoming redundant, Soviet-South African Friendship associations and clubs mushroomed across the country.

When Pik Botha first toured the new Russia in November, 1991, leaders of ethnic Russians in Estonia called on him to open his country's doors to their people, who, they claimed, suffered discrimination by native residents. Botha was supposedly receptive. His white minority government had always sought to increase the white population, and his diplomatic maneuvers in the former Communist countries seemed like nothing but part of that recruiting exercise. The collapse of the Soviet empire brought the best chance of all; its 280 million-plus population offered a fertile recruiting ground for thousands, perhaps millions of white people—Russians, Ukrainians, Byelorussians, and Latvians, who were already itching to flee their crises-riddled countries.

Already several thousand Lithuanians and Hungarians, who fled their countries at various times, are permanent residents of South Africa.[139] African diplomats expressed fear that South Africa might take advantage of the situation to recruit Russian nuclear experts, although South Africa's later revelation that it already had the bomb render such worries anachronistic. Diplomatic ties between Moscow and Pretoria were severed in 1956, to protest the regime's apartheid policy. But the Kremlin collaborated secretly with the South Africans in marketing gold and diamonds through the monopoly Central Selling Organization controlled by South Africa's Oppenheimer interests.[140]

Chapter Two

The Russian Soul Comprehending And Communicating The African Spirit: The Mass Media, Attitudes, Prejudice And Stereotypes

In the preceding chapter, I traced the evolution of the Kremlin's Africa policy against the background of the East-West confrontation and through the New Thinking and neo-detente years. I argued that the Kremlin's policy in Africa was determined by geopolitical and ethnocentric factors rather than the classical East-West ideological fission. The FSU was a super- and status quo power, which, while using attractive Marxist rhetoric to express support and sympathy for African charges against Western neo-colonialism, also sought to establish a foothold on the continent.

Self-serving motives rather than ideological altruism were the basis of the Kremlin's African venture. The demise of Communism and the implosion of the USSR decisively tore the veil from the faces from the Kremlin and its media. This chapter discusses the role of the press in shaping a specific image of Africans in Russia and the various factors that influenced the FSU's press coverage of Africa.[1] But first it is worthwhile to give a brief historical account of the presence of Africans and people of African descent in Russia.

The African Diaspora In Russia: A Short Historical Excursus

Ancient Russia

Accounts of the first Africans in pre-Revolutionary Russia are very sketchy and contradictory. In fact, Russian historians after the October 1917 Communist revolution tended to write about the history of

Africa's links with Russia as an extension of Europe, following the fashion of their western counterparts. Thus it was fashionable to write about the history of Russian and African interactions in accounts by Russian explorers and travelers to the continent.[2] Among these explorers were A. S. Norov, who traveled in Egypt and Nubia in1834-1835, and physician A. A. Rafalovich, who visited the Nile Delta in 1846-1848.[3] However, the history of African people in Russia dates to more than a thousand years before Christ.[4]

The Black presence in Russia can be traced to Herodotus' account of the Colchis. According to the "Father of History", black people had settled in Colchis before the Iron Age and the naming of the people. Colchis was an area on the Black Sea's northern shore, between the Erytheran Sea on the South and the Phasis River on the North. The area led to the Caucasus Mountains what is now the small state of Abkhazia in parts of now Georgia, an area which became of the Russian Empire and later the FSU.[5]

The Colchis, whose name derived from the place, were descendants of Sesostris I, King of Egypt and Ethiopia's army. King Sesotris I (1980-1935 B.C.) had subdued the nations along the shores of the Erytheran Sea with his fleet of ships. He returned to Egypt, assembled a vast armament, and proceeded by land to conquer all of Asia, plus Scythia and Thrace in Europe. When Sesostris reached the northern slope of the Phasis River on his return home, he either detached a body of troops from his main army, leaving them to colonize the country or a group of soldiers, tired from travel and combat, deserted and established themselves along the banks of the river.[6] Since information about the African presence in Russia before the Bolshevik revolution is scanty, attempts by such historians as Holte to garner further empirical data about the Colchians have proven futile.

The African Caucasians

More recent accounts have either confirmed Herodotus' accounts or contradicted them. But what is remarkable about these "discoveries" is that they all were made in the early 20th century, several centuries after Herodotus had written about the presence of people of African origin in the region. Thus, these accounts remain largely inconclusive. When one considers the rugged terrain of this region, it is not surprising that these Black Caucasians remained isolated for centuries and were generally unknown to the Russian public.[7]

A letter by E. Lavrov to the KAVKAZ newspaper in 1913 and research by Patrick English and a century later corroborated the Herodotus account. In his letter, Lavrov had pointed out that the African Caucasians had lived in this area since antiquity. He said the Colchis were mentioned in Greek poetry as early as the 8th century B. Lavrov also alluded to Herodotus' historical writings about the Colchis. According to Blakely, Lavrov probably got this information from an 1884 compilation of classical writings mentioning the Caucasus, which had grown out of a an archeological congress held in Tiflis in 1881. Lavrov also observed that in the Bible, Moses describes the land settled by the House of Ham as a rich land far to the East and watered by the river Fisson. [8]

Half a century later, English pursued this line of investigation. Also beginning with Herodotus and other classical writers, English marshals an impressive array of contemporary scholarly data to support the plausibility of the hypothesis the Abhakhazian Blacks. Dismissing the argument that the Abhakhazian Blacks were imported slaves, English questions the likelihood that slaves would be imported to an area so famous for the export of slaves from its local population. He then presents linguistic and anthropological evidence supporting his theory that Abhkhazians had linguistic ties with the Bantu. To substantiate the historical continuity of a Black presence in the area, English relies upon such sources as the *Illiad,* the Bible, and the writings of the Church Fathers.[9]

But Soviet scholarship on this subject tends to refute the antiquity theory. According to Lily Golden-Hanga, a Russian-born African American, about 500 the African Abkhazians lived in the Caucasus at the beginning of the last century. They had been assimilated to a certain extent: they spoke the local languages and wore Caucasian dress, but differed sharply from the indigenous people by their features and dark skin.[10] People believed these African-Caucasians settled the Black Sea coast, particularly the Caucasus, first as traders, then as slaves. In Hanga's view, the Black Sea coast was at the crossroads of many land and sea routes. It was also the hub of international relations:

"Consequently there is nothing surprising in the fact that inhabitants of Africa came to live in the Caucasus. It is also possible that the ancient trade between Egypt and the Caucasus favored the settling of Africans on the Black Sea coast. Ancient Greece, the Roman Empire, the Arabs, and later the Genoese and Turks had colonies on the Black Sea coast, where the slave trade flourished. Naturally, Africans appeared on slave markets in the Caucasus and the Crimea. But probably the greatest flow of African slaves occurred during the 16-18th centuries, when the Black Sea coast was part of the Ottoman Empire."[11]

Hanga further notes that most of the Africans lived in Abkhazia. The Abkhazian sovereign, Prince Shervashidze, had many slaves of African origin. The Turks living along the Black Sea coast also had many African slaves. When Abkhazia was annexed to Russia in 1810, their masters took some of these slaves to Batumi and then to Turkey. Other accounts say they fled to Turkey. Concluding, Hanga observes that for almost a century afterwards, up to WWI, no one showed any interest in the Africans in Russia. Tsarist officials were completely indifferent to the fate of non-Russian peoples inhabiting Russia. Russian statistical data of that time referred to Africans as Arabs or Jews.

Imperial Russia

Yet Russian historians still stress that the first known Africans appeared in the country in the seventeenth century as slaves and pampered servants in the Tsars courts and aristocrats' mansions—a vogue which had become popular in Western Europe and Turkey. During the reign of Peter I, (the Great) (1682-1725), that destiny led the way for Africans to contribute to the culture of Russia, but then as individuals.

Abraham Hannibal (1697-1781) was the first of these individuals. There are contradictory accounts about how he came to Russia. One account had it that he was brought to the tsar from Amsterdam. The tsar's example was followed by many of the wealthy nobility.[12]

Yet another account indicated that at the age of eight, Hannibal was taken hostage from his parents in Northern Abyssinia and sold in Constantinople as a slave, then purchased from a Turkish seraglio and sent as a gift to the Peter the Great, who freed him. The Tsar, captivated by the boy's intelligence and personality, adopted him as a godson, with Queen Christina of Poland as the godmother. On being christened in 1707, his given name, Ibrahim, was anglicized to Abraham. His mother and father, a chieftain, learned of his whereabouts and went to see him. While there, the father said the family's surname was Hannibal, so Abraham was the descendant of the great Carthaginian general. Hence Hannibal became his.[13]

According to Holte, the Tsar became deeply impressed with Hannibal's talent for mathematics and engineering, and in 1717 sent him away to study in Paris. He returned to St Petersburg in 1723, after his studies and fighting for France against the Spanish, when he received a head wound. Back in Russia, he became an officer in the engineers' corps, rose in the rank on merit, and was appointed tutor in mathematics to the Crown Prince. After the death of Peter, his daughter, Empress Elizabeth, appointed Hannibal a commander in the Imperial Russian army. During her reign, Hannibal performed several feats recognized by the awards and ranks he held. Notable among his assignments were heading the Russian Commission to settle a border dispute with Sweden, and drawing plans for a canal to link St. Petersburg with Moscow.

Hannibal became a highly important figure in government and army circles. The Empress, before she died, conferred on him the title of General-in-Chief and the Order of St Alexander Nevski. Hannibal married twice, the first time to a Greek woman in 1731. She was unfaithful to him, and could not reconcile herself to the fact that Hannibal was not "of her kind." His second wife, Kristina Sherberkha, whom he married in 1736, was a Livonian. They were blessed with eleven children, of which nine survived—five sons and four daughters. His son Joseph was a navy commander and navigator. He married Nadezhda, the daughter of Count Pushkin, whose grandfather was privy counselor to Peter the Great. Her father carried the scepter at the coronation of Catherine the Great. Nadezhda's son, Alexander Pushkin, inheriting the pride and legacy of the two aristocratic families, became the nation's most celebrated person.[14]

Pushkin, whose birthday centenary Russia marked in 1998, is one of the few historical figures in Russia whose reputation remained untouched by the revolutionary hurricane and ideological alchemy that permeated Russian and Soviet history. Apart from being a revolutionary free thinker, he was the architect of modern Russian literary language. A humanitarian who regarded his African heritage as an honor, he not only created and elevated a great European language, but he lit the torch of emancipation for whites in Russia, just as Harriet Beecher Stowe did for Blacks in America.[15]

The last years of Pushkin were most tortuous. The secret police, on the Tsar's orders, followed and reported his every move. Reprimands by the Tsar, together with criticisms and rejections of his literary works, made his life very unpleasant. He wanted to leave Russia, but was denied permission to do so.

In 1831, Pushkin married a very beautiful girl of 16, Natasha Goncharov, as a way to attain happiness, and to deter his impulses for philandering and gambling. Pushkin's six years of marriage were filled with many problems stemming from financial worries and an incompatibility of interests. Natasha was concerned solely with social activities, which enabled her to parade her beauty and charm, while Pushkin's interests were wholly literary and intellectual. Natasha's flirtations and the attendant gossip caused Pushkin much anguish and frustration, which led to his untimely, tragic death. Pushkin had challenged to a duel Baron George d'Anthes, a Frenchman who was flirting with his wife. During the duel, he received a stomach wound and died.

Another black literary luminary in the annals of Russian history was Ira Frederick Aldridge (1807-1867). Aldridge was born in New York City to an African American woman and a native African man.[16] Aldridge introduced the dramatic art form to Russia. Until he began filling engagements in Russia in 1858, an actor devoting himself exclusively to plays by Shakespeare was unknown there.[17]

In his book on Aldridge, Sergei Durylin states: "The appearance of Aldridge was extraordinarily timely; the Russian actors awaited such a one in order to learn from him how to master their art, and the Russian spectators in order to delve into the mighty feelings and thoughts of Shakespeare.[18] According to Holte, Aldridge did not speak Russian, but his artistic ability to communicate enabled him to cast, produce, and direct plays with casts who did not speak English. From the reception the audience, actors, and the press gave him, Aldridge realized that Russia presented the best opportunities for him to work at his craft regularly, and that he could fulfil a need.[19]

In December, 1857 Alexander II published a declaration of intent for the abolition of serfdom. On February 19, 1861 the declaration became law, and some 22.1 million serfs were freed. Aldridge arrived in Russia in the midst of this euphoria. Since he symbolized liberation from slavery and backwardness, the serfs, and the radical intelligentsia eagerly supported him. During the year in St. Petersburg, he performed 71 times in the prestigious Imperial Theatre. With such unparalleled success he received extraordinary honors.

The summer of 1859 found Aldridge back in England, where he started his European career. But his reception there was so poor that in 1861, he returned to Russia for a long and extensive tour. He stayed in Russia for nearly ten years, working at his craft. He died at 60 on August 7, 1867 in Lodz, Poland, where he was acting. He was buried there. Aldridge was not the only African to live in 19th century Russia.[20]

Peter I's importation of black servants for his court was continued by his successors. Thus, from the reign of Alexander I in 1801 to the abdication of Nicholas II in 1917, as many as 20 Africans in Moorish dress—baggy red trousers, black jackets, white turbans and yellow boots—and labeled Abyssinians, Ethiopians, or Nubians became servants the Tsars' servants.

But ordinary Russians who had no access to the palace, where blacks worked and lived, did not know of their presence. So the news that broke in 1913 about blacks living in the Caucasus startled the country. In the late 18th and 19th centuries, the Black presence in Russia increased slightly thanks to Russia's participation in world trade Black seamen regularly visited the empire and some even stayed. Other Black visitors and immigrants came as well.[21]

Early Contacts With Black Africa

As mentioned above, the first contact between Imperial Russia and Africa was Abyssinia (or Ethiopia). Accounts of this were recorded in the *Primary Chronicles*, which date as far back as the eleventh century. Actual contacts and interactions, however, were much more recent. According to Blakely, from the 18th century to the end of the Russian empire, the tsarist regime, realized that it could set store by establishing religious, diplomatic, and economic ties with Ethiopia began to court the African empire. "In this process, at least part of the Russian public became knowledgeable about African and about [Africans]."[22]

But the idea of forging ties between Russia and Ethiopia did not originate in Russia or Africa. German Dukedom of Saxe-Gotha first raised the idea at the end of the seventeenth century. It proposed the creation of an anti-Turkish league to include Russia, the western European states, and Abyssinia. Although the plan did not materialize, it nevertheless became the basis of Russian attitude toward Ethiopia. The plan noted the similarity of their Orthodox religions, the military-strategic value of Ethiopian friendship and possible economic advantages. It took over two centuries before the ideas of promoting concrete ties between Russia and Ethiopia bore fruit and this was in the religious realm, although there was much coupling of religion and politics at the time. The chief proponent of Russian-Ethiopian Church alliance was Porfirii Uspensky, a monk. His proposal was contained in article he published under the broad title "Russia's Role in the Destiny of Ethiopia." His goal was to strengthen Ethiopia as a bridgehead from where to lead Africa to Orthodox Christianity and also to counteract activities of the Roman Catholic Church in Africa. At the same time, the impending construction of Suez Canal raised to a new level the strategic significance of Ethiopia's location[23] In fact, some scholars have strongly suggested that the opening of the Suez Canal in 1869 was the main factor prompting Russia to seek close ties with Ethiopia at the end of the century.[24]

Soviet Russia

Russian historical sources indicate that the first African students in Soviet Russia were from Ethiopia. These were all military students, six in number, who lived in Russia no more than two to three years at the end of the 19th century. [25]

Broader interaction with Africa began only after the Second World War. Although in the 1930s the Communist Party of the Soviet Union (CPSU) had invited some members of the South African Communist Party (SACP) to study at the Lenin Institute for the Peoples of the Orient, it was only after the death of Stalin that the largest number of Africans began to arrive in the Soviet Union.[26] These were mostly students, and diplomats and their families, who under Nikita Khrushchev's Third World policy came to the Soviet Union during the "thaw" years.

At the beginning of 1956, Ethiopia was the only black African country with which the FSU had diplomatic ties. By the time the Soviet Union disintegrated in 1991, there were more than 50. The approach chosen to establish these connections had followed the same pattern that had been set during the entire century of Russian ties with Africa: The FSU offered technical assistance in exchange for goodwill and the hope of future communist allies in world affairs. The impact of this strategy became ever broader under Leonid Brezhnev.[27] In the period from 1955 to 1978 an estimated number of 10,000 Africans, mainly from Somalia, Tanzania, and Ethiopia, received Russian military training.[28] But new configuration of post-World War II geopolitics dictated a radical shift in Soviet policy toward Africa. The direction of assistance changed from training communist cadres to the preparations of leaders for non-communist organizations, such as trade unions, student agencies, and professional academics. The main institutions founded to advance this approach the Friendship University established in Moscow in 1960 and named after the Congolese revolutionary, Patrice Lumumba. In the late Fifties and Sixties, the USSR offered liberal scholarships to thousands of Third World youths to enroll for higher education in Soviet universities and colleges.

The Patrice Lumumba Friendship University in Moscow was built for the express purpose of training Third World technocrats. Before the official collapse of Communism in 1991, there were over 50,000 African students in the FSU. By 1992, barely one year later, this number had whittled down to 12, 000 as the new leadership in the Commonwealth of Independent States, CIS stopped their generous scholarship programs to the developing countries. Recent reports indicate that there still is a sizeable number of Africans living more or less permanently in the FSU. According one report, Africans number about 12,000 in Russia, with thousands more Latin Americans, Middle Easterners and Asians living in the country. Many are settled and engaged in business, giving Moscow in particular a cosmopolitan air.[29]

In addition, the Soviet leadership devoted resources to the study and understanding of Africa. In 1959, the FSU established the African Institute within the Academy of Sciences. The creation of this special institute demonstrated Soviet awareness that FSU needed to learn more about the African continent if she (Russia) was to succeed in gaining dominant influence there. Soviet leaders, therefore, drew upon the tradition of African studies, which extended back to tsarist times and adapted it to new purposes. Leading Russian scholars, including N. V. Yushmanov and D. A. Olderoge, taught African Ethiopian linguistics, Hausa and Swahili at Leningrad University in the 1930s. Ivan Potekhin and his teacher, Olderoge edited an ethnographic survey, *Narody Afriki* (Peoples of Africa) published in 1954. This publication outlined the basic Soviet approach toward Africa in the Cold War era. It was anti-colonial and directed against "bourgeois" scholarship, which characterized African culture as inherently inferior.[30] The African Institute, according to Blakely, was very successful within the Soviet Union in training scores of specialists and spreading the awareness of Africa among the general public.

The African American Connection

If some African Americans saw Russia as land of promise in the 19th century, in the 1920s and 1930s other African Americans viewed the Soviet Union, and its idea of the "new society," as the Promised Land itself. The Soviet Union assumed the role of a kind of Mecca of human rights for some and an escape from the Great Depression for others.[31] Thus, individual African Americans made pilgrimages or settled permanently in Russia since the 19th century. Among them were actor Ira Aldridge mentioned above and George Thomas, who settled in St Petersburg in 1890. Thomas was said to have adopted the Russian name Fyodor and owned large amusement complex in Moscow called Aquarium. He fled possible reprisals from the Bolsheviks in 1917 and settled in Turkey. In addition, the famous African American jockey, Jimmy Winkfield also moved to Russia, where she married Russian noblewoman and they had one son. He fled Russia during the Civil War in 1919, after 15 years of residence in Russia. Other notable African Americans who lived in Russia were famous circus performers and singers, including Pearl Hobson who lived in Odessa in the decade prior to World War I. [32]

The Soviet Union became a kind of Mecca of human rights for some African Americans and an escape from the great Depression for others. Thus, a small community of African Americans fled Jim Crow racism and the Great Depression in the mid 1920s-1930s and made homes in the Stalinist Soviet Union. However, many of them were compelled to leave their newfound "safe haven," when they became victims of the Stalinist purge during the late 1930s and the early 1940s. It was estimated that by the early 1930s several hundreds of African Americans had visited the Soviet Union.[33] Of these visitors, a small segment remained for several years or permanently; others followed them in later decades—political activists, technicians, and artists.

Prominent among the black "pilgrims" to Soviet Russia in the 1920s and 1930s were writer Claude Mckay, George Padmore, W. E. Du Bois, William L. Patterson, and poet Langston Hughes, actors Paul Robeson, and Wayland Rudd. The majority of the early pilgrims paid glowing tribute to the Soviet for its lack of racism. For instance, Patterson wrote:

> It is as if one had suffered with a painful affliction for many years and had suddenly awakened to discover that the pain had gone.[34]

Writer Claude McKay was even more enthusiastic in his praise for the newly found home. He wrote in article:

> "...Russia is prepared and waiting to receive couriers and heralds of goodwill and interracial understanding from the Negro race. Her demonstration of friendliness and equality for Negroes may not conduce to promote healthy relations between Soviet Russia and democratic America, the anthropologists of

100 percent pure white Americanism may soon invoke Science to prove that Russians are not at all God's white people."[35]

The "Blind" Forces Of History, Culture, Prejudice, And Stereotypes In Intercultural Communication: An Attempt At A Conceptual Analysis

Intercultural perception depends largely on the subject of perception. Each participant strives to interpret the interlocutor's behavior, including his or her motives. Since in real life people are often unable to perceive others' motives correctly, or because they know them inadequately, interpretations depend on the strength of previous experiences or the analysis of one's own motives in a similar situation. A series of experimental studies[36] have shown that attitude plays a significant role in the process of interpersonal perception. This is especially so in forming first impressions about an unknown person based on previously acquired information.[37]

The Prejudice-Stereotype Dichotomy

Favorable or unfavorable prejudice concerns an unknown person or thing. It is not based on actual experience, attitude, or belief; it is antipathy based upon a faulty and inflexible generalization. In addition, prejudice is based on unsubstantiated data. Some psychological theories attribute individual, personal factors to prejudice. The frustration-aggression theory, for example, posits that prejudice stems from frustration. According to this theory, when people are unable to strike out at the real source of their frustration, they find scapegoats to blame unfairly.

The Authoritarian Personality theory postulated by Theodor Adorno and co. also sought to locate prejudice in personality characteristics. Thus people with what Adorno and his team of researchers described as the authoritarian personality tend to be highly prejudiced. Authoritarian people are usually intolerant, insecure. They are also said to be submissive to superiors, and they tend to be older, less educated, less intelligent, and belong to a lower social class.[38]

Sociological perspectives offer more plausible explanations for the emergence of prejudice than the psychological theories. Notable among them are the symbolic interactionist theory, which sees prejudice as a social construct learned in social interaction, and the conflict perspective, which locates prejudice in socio-economic praxis—the struggle over scarce resources.

The Symbolic Interactionist analysis of prejudice assumes that people learn prejudice from interactions with others. In other words, prejudice is a social construct. It derives from the concept of selective perception, positing that the labels people learn are essential ingredients of prejudice, leading them to see certain things and be blind to others. Racial and ethnic prejudices are mental shorthand. They constitute rules of thumb or mental shortcuts for emotionally laden stereotypes.

The conflict theory is rooted in the human tendency to seek to advance and protect self-interest. In our attempts to meet our basic needs of food, shelter, and clothing, we inevitably find ourselves locked in competition with others for the resources these needs demand, which are always relatively scarce. Winners in this struggle must create social institutions to protect their resources, so they develop ideologies to justify why they won and why the losers lost. Of course the winners portray the losers in dismissive, demeaning and degrading terms. They are dismissed as genetically inferior, lazy, deficiently endowed, etc. Whenever a crisis threatens the status quo, the winners must look for scapegoats.

The more powerful groups in a competitive environment resort to prejudice for preserving their privilege.[39] Individuals, of course, are responsible for harboring prejudice; they must be held accountable for actions that stem from prejudice.[40] However, these prejudgments do not originate in a vacuum. Nor can we separate them from the circumscriptions and choices within the broader social context. "Prejudicial judgments are a part and parcel of society, and failure to appreciate this social dimension is self-defeating."[41]

When prejudice is sufficiently widespread, it fosters a fertile ground for racial hatred and discrimination against identifiable groups under certain economic or social conditions.[42] Stereotyping reflects and reinforces this prejudice. So does ethnocentrism. Stereotypes, like prejudice, are socially learned. The stereotypes that people learn not only justify prejudice and discrimination; they also produce stereotypical behavior in those stereotyped, leading to a self-fulfilling prophecy.

Stereotypes—oversimplified, stable images of people—are based on limited previous experience and the desire or need to draw conclusions on the basis of such limited experience. Stereotyping has as its consequences two phenomena: on the one hand, an oversimplified process of mutual cognition, and on the other, the emergence of prejudices. If impressions are based on previous negative experiences, then they are inevitably negative. At a benign level, stereotypes help order our world and keep us from becoming overwhelmed by information. But this benefit comes at a cost.[43]

Racial stereotypes lead to racial and ethnic arrogance born of ignorance or incomplete knowledge, which may hamper healthy relationships. While prejudices often result from first impressions and may be transient, stereotypes form over a longer period of passive interaction or incomplete socialization.

Racial and ethnic stereotypes, like ethnocentrism, are universal phenomena. Limited information about individual representatives of a certain ethnic community gives rise to prejudiced opinions about an entire community, group or nation. Adequate and mutual understanding among people is hampered by stereotypes and prejudices. On the other hand, communication in groups united by their activities over a long period of time can contribute to a better mutual understanding, drawing people closer because of their similar "emotional background."[44]

Learning and Communicating Racial Attitudes, Prejudice, And Stereotypes

The impact of media-government symbiotic and adversarial relationships

The mass media's role in reproducing racial attitudes and stereotypes in contemporary Euro-American societies is as crucial as its general role in the political, social and ideological reproduction of modern societies.[45] The mediating and sometimes reinforcing function of the media is of paramount importance, especially in societies with advanced media systems. What most people know about other peoples and their cultures depends on their refracted picture constructed in the media.

Much research has assessed the influence of mass media on attitudes and opinions. Results have tended to show that social attitudes, including prejudice, are relatively resistant to influence by the media.[46] It appears that people select what they read and what they view, and they tend to avoid communications, which they consider unacceptable. Individuals are selective in what they perceive as well as what they remember. But people's selective perception does not happen in a vacuum. They are conditioned through socialization agents, prominent among which are the mass media.

According to Klapper, the mass media are much more likely to reinforce existing attitudes (whatever the attitude and whatever the "message") than to change them.[47] We may expect attitudes to resist change especially when they are supported by strong group norms or the prevailing cultural milieu. In particular, the mass media play a major role in defining the important issues and how to discuss them. This is the agenda-setting role of the mass media.[48] Lang and Lang (1966), focusing on this agenda-setting function, observed: "The mass media force attention to certain issues. They build up public images of political figures. They are constantly presenting objects that suggest what individuals should think about, have feelings about."[49]

Cohen (1963) noted that the press "may be successful much of the time in telling people to think, but it is stunningly successful in telling its readers what to think about."[50] While the mass media may have little influence on the direction or the intensity of attitudes, researchers have hypothesized that the mass media set the agenda for political campaigns, influencing the salience of attitudes toward political issues.[51] Soviet media coverage of Mandela's release as discussed in chapter one offers a good insight into the media's agenda setting. It also sheds light on the symbiotic relationship between the media and government. Politicians use journalists to "sell" their policies and programs to the citizenry and journalists need scoops, briefings, press releases, etc., from politicians to properly play their role as informers and educators of the public about the affairs of the state. In the FSU, this symbiotic relationship between the media and government was very crucial, since nearly all media outlets were owned, controlled and monitored by the communist party and state apparatchiks.

While Soviet journalists and politicians did not shy away from this symbiotic relationship, their Western counterparts acknowledge this relationship only to the extent of mutually beneficial exchange of information and service. Beyond that, media-government relationship is said to be adversarial. But contrary to the "fiercely independent" image of the Anglo-American media, they usually follow the lead set by their home governments.[52] Like the myth of objectivity, adversarial relationship is often circumscribed, or clouded by the national interest. As Baffour notes, the Western media are guided by four-point unwritten code:

(1)   National interest. This is by far, the most important of the four, in fact all the others revolve around it.

(2)   Government lead

(3)   Government leaning
(4)   Advertisers/readers power.[53]

Thus, what constitutes journalism in the West is not what the textbooks always say—an independent, privately owned, accurate, honest, unbiased and free to print whatever journalists want. Instead, journalism in the West is constantly dodged by a conspiracy of the four hidden codes, mentioned above. Cross-pressures from party politics, advertisers and readers, all seriously constrain the freedom of journalists in the West to write as they please. From Saddam Hussein to Malesovic, the national interest turned "the fiercely independent" Western journalists into cheerleaders, slavishly parroting government officials and military leaders. From Sierra-Leone to Zimbabwe, Western journalists take up the refrain from government officials. Writes Baffour:

> Western governments are known to set the lead for journalists to follow. "Mugabe is a bad guy", says the British government. And you would think that these "knowledgeable" and "independent-minded" Western journalists would not parrot the refrain. But they do. "Mugabe is a bad guy", they chant after the government...[54]

He adds:

> Another example is the reporting of Saddam Hussein. When Ayatollah Khomeni was leader of Iran and it served Western interests to use Saddam as a check on Iran, Saddam was a "very good guy" beloved by London and Washington...For the 10 years the Iran-Iraqi war lasted, Saddam's image as a "good guy" was trumpeted from the hallowed pages of the ...Western media—never mind the atrocities he committed against the Iraqi Kurds."[55]

In the case of media in the FSU, first code—the national interest—was the most important, since until 1989, private advertising was not part of the "media equation" and pressure from readers could conveniently be ignored since the government subsidized the media. The national interest dictated government lead, which journalists followed. Thus, when Nelson Mandela and his ANC were no longer of Soviet national interest, the government provided the lead and Soviet journalists followed. The national interest can best be seen within the framework of what I term the "*Nashi* ideology.

Courting And "Platonic Friendship" In The Prism Of Time: The "Nashi" Ideology

The Russian term "*Nashi*" roughly translates as "one of us" or "one of our kind." The Nashi mentality permeates the Russian attitude toward the "Other"; it has developed into a form of ideology itself. It reached its apogee in the war against Hitler and the Cold War. During the Cold War the *Nashi* ideology crystallized into the "Iron Curtain" mentality: an inordinate suspicion of the West. The *Nashi* ideology reflects the "Us Versus Them," In-group-Out-group mentality of ruling circles. It dominated Soviet official thinking, and formed the basis of ideological indoctrination, formal education, becoming the filter and agenda setting tool for the mass media. It also ties in with what I will term the ideological ethnocentrism of the Soviet years, which I will discuss in detail later in this study.

Over the years, Marxist-Leninist propagandists set the agenda for the mass media in the FSU. They projected Africa and the Third World generally as allies in the "struggle against Western domination." The apartheid issue fit well into the propaganda pattern, as long as the West appeared to provide the props for the South African racist regime. However, since the mid-1980s, when Gorbachev began his perestroika/ glasnost reforms, the old Marxist-Leninist state ideology gave way to "New Thinking," which saw a new rapprochement with the Western "imperialists." The favorable press the ANC and many progressive Third World movements enjoyed in the pre-glasnost Soviet Union did have a positive influence on Soviet public opinion, even if it was superficial and short-lived.

Since the Communist Party prohibited opinion surveys of political nature, the FSU produced no serious research to determine Soviet public opinion regarding the ANC and other Soviet-supported Third World liberation movements. However, stories by Third World students about their various encounters with Soviet citizens during the pre-Gorbachev era reveal that the Soviet public was at least tolerant of these movements and countries with a so-called socialist orientation.[56] Several African students have recounted incidents when they had to introduce themselves as Black Cubans in order to win the favor or friendship of Soviet acquaintances. Those who came from the so-called Capitalist Africa were treated like other foreigners from the West; Soviets saw them as spies or their potential enemies. Thus some of them had to introduce themselves to Soviet citizens as coming from friendly "socialist-oriented" countries, either to gain a favorable reception or to avoid hostile reactions.

For example, a Ghanaian student, confronted by a hostile Soviet youth-gang, identified himself as coming from Mozambique, which caused the gang leader to simply say: "*Nashi*," meaning "He is one of us." They left him unharmed. But luck did not smile on him later, when another gang confronted him. This time the student introduced himself as coming from Cuba; but when they asked him to speak Spanish, he began to stammer. The response was immediate; they beat him and stole his clothes. Even in lecture halls and classrooms, Third World students from "fraternal" countries or those belonging to "progressive" organizations and liberation movements, were treated differently from those from "reactionary, capitalist-oriented" states. It was common knowledge among Third World students that lecturers tended to be much more friendly to students considered as *Nashi*, i.e. coming from satellite states of the Soviet Union.[57]

There is little doubt that the *Nashi* perception, contrasted with the enemy or spy identification of African and other Third World students among the Soviets, mainly resulted from mass media messages. Various descriptive terms and stereotypes, the tone employed, and the significance the mass media attached to specific events and stories from various countries determined how the Soviets related to different countries and different citizens. The mass media's agenda setting was fairly easy, due to the party-controlled, monolithic press system. Since practically no alternative sources of information or media channels existed, the media gatekeepers could easily control the flow, quality, and quantity of information. They could also decide when and how to publicize news stories for the public.[58]

For example, stories about "socialist-oriented" African countries painted a picture of absolute agreement by the leaders of such countries with all the FSU's policies. As a rule, most stories included a quotation from an African statesman heaping praise on this or that Soviet policy.[59] This friendly image of the "African socialist" did not fail to register in the Soviet public's perceptions, even if the results were only momentary. At the same time, a different image, based on stereotypes recycled by the media, concerned Africans who did not fit the "Nashi description"; it was the image of real or potential enemies.

Carving Intercultural Images: The Role Of The Media In Communicating And Reinforcing Stereotypical Images

Any discussion of the roles and relationships of the mass media and intercultural communication inevitably links with peoples' attitudes and public opinion. If the media do influence events, they rarely do so directly, but rather through the way they encourage people to think.[60] Several factors condition this media-attitudes link, prominently socialization and hegemony. While socialization ensures that we internalize the socio-cultural norms of our societies and see social reality within prescriptive socio-cultural blinkers, hegemony forces us both directly and indirectly to stay the course of the ideological destination of nations. Hartman and Husband (1970) have pointed out that past research into attitudes commonly concentrated on differences in attitudes between people and groups.

The ruling elite teaches and enforces both socialization and hegemony. The interpretive frameworks within which such differences occur were either taken for granted or glossed over. Whenever racial or ethnic prejudice was involved, this emphasis often produced a tendency to root prejudice in the individual's personality or in the immediate social situation, not in the cultural or social framework.[61] Such an approach is evident in the so-called Color and Citizenship survey, which led to the misleading conclusion that intense prejudice roots in the individual personality.[62]Here lies one type of solution to the inadequacies of undetermined personality.[63]

But prejudice is often not merely the result of personal pathology or social strain; it may be built into a given culture. Hartman and Husband argue that British thinking about 'colored' people, influenced by that country's colonial past, constitutes a built-in predisposition to accept unfavorable beliefs about such individuals. The beliefs and values defining this thinking related to a particular social and industrial history, which is well-embedded in British culture. Only when we take into account such an underlying cultural predisposition to prejudice do variations in prejudice and how they relate to other factors make sense.[64]

The Russian Version Of Africa's "Tarzan" Image: From Tsarism To Communism

Considering the Hartman and Husband argument, it is tempting to say that because Russia has no colonial history in Africa, Russian thinking about Africans may differ from British thinking, since it bears no influence from a colonial past. It is equally tempting to conclude that Russian Orthodox religious ethics, as opposed to British Protestantism, may produce different thinking about 'colored' people. Indeed Tsarist Russia's imperial quest did not extend beyond its backyards in the Caucasus and Central Asia, and Imperial Russia did not participate in its Western counterparts' scramble for and partition of Africa. But Russian culture still shares many historical factors with British and European culture. In fact, as Likhachev (1991) notes, Russian culture has been greatly influenced by the West.

> From the beginnings of the three peoples possessing a common origin—Russians, Ukrainians and Byelorussians, their neighbors have played an enormous role. In the north there were the Scandinavian peoples, the Varangians: an entire conglomerate of peoples that included the future Danes, Swedes, Norse, and "English". South of the Rus the chief neighbors were the Greeks, who lived not only in Greece proper but also directly bordering on Rus, along the northern shores of the Black Sea. Then there was a separate conglomerate of peoples, among who were also Christians and Jews.[65]

More recently, Kingston-Mann arrived at the same conclusion when she observed that Russians may be "outsiders within Western culture," but their experience contributes to "a more inclusive picture of the West."[66] Kingston-Manning further states that in the second half of the nineteenth century, Russian thinkers were frontline participants in the European debate about economic development, who influenced the thinking of others just as they were shaped by them. Dismissing the argument that Russia borrowed Western thought, she emphatically declares: Russia was in the West, and the West was in Russia.[67] Peter the Great supposedly said that Russia was a kind of undeveloped Europe; "therefore I order us to be regarded as Europeans."[68]

Russian culture is a white culture. As in British and European culture, Russians have an endemic predisposition to accept unfavorable beliefs about colored people. In Russia they are its darker-skinned former subjects living south of the Russians in the Caucasus and Central Asia. Included are also a small number of African slaves brought to Abkhazia, on the Black Sea coast, by Turkish and Arab slave traders, plus individual Blacks including Abraham Hannibal, the great grandfather of Russia's greatest poet, Alexander Pushkin, actor

Aira Aldridge, and various sailors and ship captains, who lived in Imperial Russia at one time or another as mentioned above.

Some Soviet scholars have attempted to explain the Russian attitude towards Africans and people of African origin as more of a benevolent paternalism than racial prejudice.[69] But what these apologists for Russian racism tend to forget is that paternalism is merely the reverse side of the same racist coin. Racism is racism, no matter the name or guise it takes. Although anti-black sentiments in Imperial Russia did not reach the intensity of anti-Semitism, evident in various pogroms, the seeds of current anti-black hatred were sown long ago. Not even the Soviet Communist attempt to build a multi-racial society after the demise of the Tsarist Empire could wipe out racism among Russians. Russification of the southern subjects during the Tsars' times continued during the Communist era under the guise of sovietization. The "politics of internationalism" were the products of Russian racist thinking. The "Great Russian-nation's" chauvinistic attitude toward the Azeris, Armenians, Chechens, Ingush, Tartars, Tadjiks, Georgians, Uzbeks, and others, resulting in a reverse racism (Russophobia) from the former, has led to seemingly inexorable inter-ethnic vendettas plaguing the former Soviet empire since 1986.

The works of leading Russian writers and intelligentsia were replete with references to the black race as belonging to the lowest rung of the human ladder. Tracing the history of Russian attitudes towards blacks, Blakely notes that even among the radical intelligentsia one can find a total opposition to slavery accompanied by a general acceptance of racist theories denigrating blacks.[70] The following segment from an 1868 article by Nicholas Dobroliubov, Nikolas Chernyshevsky, the radical Russian publicist's young collaborator:

> We do not think it necessary to deal with the differences between the skulls of Negroes and of other lower races of man and the skulls of people among civilized nations. Who is not aware of the strange development of the upper part of the skull among these [lower] races..."

Emanating from the Russian Westernizer tradition and swept along by the reigning penchant for science among Western intellectuals, the Russian radicals of the 1860s dabbled in the prevalent racist theories, garbed as they were in the robes of scientific discourse. In this the radicals were in illustrious company. After all, most of the revered *philosophes* of the previous century had also opposed slavery while taking for granted that the slaves were of an inferior race.[71] Even more prominent Russian writers, including the great Nikolai Tolstoy could not resist social evolutionist views of the times. Thus, Alexander Girboedov wrote in his *Woe From Wit*:

> Out of the boredom I took with me
> A Negro girl and a doggie,
> Order them to be fed, my dear,
> Give them leftover from supper.
>
> ...Oh Sophie, my friend,
> What a Negress I have for a servant
> Wooly-haired! Humped-back!
> Angry! Cat-like in all her ways!
> And how black! And how frightful!
> How could God have created such a race?
> She is a real devil...[72]

Like in literature, Russian art denigrated blacks. Blacks were portrayed as subservient. Much like the characters described in Tolstoy and Griboedov's writings, Russian art of tsarist times portrayed blacks not only as servants, but infantile and diminutive.[73] Even Ira Aldridge who introduced the dramatic art form to Russia with his very successful tour of Russia in 1858 was not spared racist jibes. Racist comments appeared in the newspapers Syn *Otechestvo* (Son of the Fatherland), and in such periodicals as *Den'* (The Day) and *Nashe Vremia* [Our Time]. A letter to the editor of *Den'* by a writer N. S. Sokhanskaia and submitted under the pseudonym N. Kokhanovshaia described Aldridge in racist terms. The letter was littered with words and phrases as "savage," "thick blue lips," "leonine, animal cries," "revulsion," "African jungle," etc.[74]

Competition generated by large-scale immigration into an area leads to more negative attitudes. Competition, (real or imagined) may serve to activate or intensify the existing cultural tendency to view racial and ethnic minorities negatively.[75] Here again it is tempting to say that since Russia has never been known as a home for large numbers of African immigrants[76], attitudes towards Africans among the average Russian [Soviet] citizen may be less prejudiced than in the West. There has not been any serious extant research work on the level of Hartman and Husband (1974); work into Russian/Soviet attitudes towards Africans and coloured people in general. The data I do have are the results of opinion surveys conducted mainly during the first five years of Gorbachev's glasnost policy.

One such survey conducted in 1989 among Moscow school children revealed a high degree of prejudice towards Africans. Only 16 per cent of the children believed that "Africans are human beings like we are." Moreover, only one schoolboy said that Africans are good and kind. A year earlier, a similar poll conducted among 860 Moscow residents by the Moscow-based All-Union Centre for Public Opinion Studies showed the following: Only 37 per cent of Muscovites believe Africans are hard-working; As few as 23 per cent of the respondents considered Africans to be attractive; 65 per cent said Africans are poorly developed; only 15 per cent believed Africans are intelligent; 65 per cent said they would never approve of wedlock between their close relatives or friends and Africans; 55 per cent responded negatively to the question, "Would you like to get acquainted with and befriend a "dark-skinned African?"; 59 per cent of the Muscovites said they are indifferent to Africans, while only 25 per cent said they have any kind of sympathy for Africans, 12% harboured antipathy against Africans, yet only seven per cent of the respondents had ever had any interaction or contact with Africans. Nearly the same scores applied to perceptions of African Americans. The corresponding figures for the perception of Europeans were as follows: Hard-working-80 %; Attractive -74%; Developed -83%; Intelligent -66%; About wedlock, 66% Muscovites said they would give the nod to a marriage involving their close relatives or a friend with an European, and 67% would approve of acquaintanceship and friendship; 59% said they have sympathy for Europeans, 37% were indifferent while only 1% felt antipathy.[77]

Although the polls were conducted in the so-called prime years[78] of glasnost, they were not published in the Soviet press until 1990 when the new journal, *Respublika* printed a translated version of an article based on the polls in the French *Le nouvel Observateur*. The silence in the Soviet press over the path-breaking research is understandable. This period also coincided with the period when most Soviet media personnel were going through moments of introspection, and were agonizing over their gullibility and their slavish parroting of Communist Party propaganda; It was a period of rethinking party-fed theories and paradigms. One such theory claimed: "Socialism and racism are incompatible." Over the years, journalists and party propagandists had learned by rote the official dogma that "racism in the Soviet Union had dissolved in the new Soviet consciousness." Unable to recover completely from the stupor of indoctrination and the hangover following years of communist spoon-feeding and tutelage, many were then still adamantly holding on to this dogma in spite of the changes going on the Soviet Union.

Another survey I conducted in 1991 (see Chapter Four) among Russian students and professors, as well as Western exchange students at various St. Petersburg institutions of higher learning by this author produced similar results. Remarkable in these results was the fact that the majority of the polled Russian students said they had warmer feelings for white South Africans than black South Africans.[79]

The African/black experience represented in the Soviet media carried all the connotations of racism found in the "American West"[80] It depicted alien cultures and peoples who are less civilized than Russia's, people who "stand lower in the order of culture because somehow they are lower in the order of nature, defined by race, by colour, and sometimes by genetic inheritance."[81]

The prevalence of images and stereotypes about 'coloured' people in the Soviet/Russian mass media are at best implicitly derogatory. This may be gauged from the existence of a number of traditions in cartoons, jokes and photographs. Such themes and images are to be found in poetry, rhymes, idioms and literature. In Russia, early examples of images and stereotypes about Africans, and racial minorities in general, are to be found in travelogues and essays by explorers, historians and anthropologists. For example, a film produced by Lenfilm, the St Petersburg film board, based on the accounts of Russian/Soviet writer Vladimir Nabokov, portrays Africa as populated by wild, prowling man-eating beasts. Although the film purported to be about the bravery of Africans nothing in the film suggests that. Human beings are practically absent. The only Africans featured are a group of barefooted village women in a bamboo-thatched mud cottage.

Jokes and Russian/Soviet poetry include their share of derision and denigration of the African. A popular joke/riddle goes roughly like this:

> The Americans decided to send their best spy to Ryazan'. The spy, by name Smith knows the local dialect to a fault. Yet in his very first encounter with a babushka (old woman) he is exposed. How did the babushka know Smith is an American spy? Because there're no blacks in Ryazan'!

The joke, while it was meant to show the stupidity of American Intelligence officers, also ridicules black people. Another joke is about the dilemma of a Russian wife, who on delivery found out that her child was black. Fearing the reaction of the Russian husband, she asked the doctor to "invent" a reasonable explanation. The doctor, of course, could not come up with one. But as he was discussing the case with the *babushka* hospital cleaner, the woman's husband appeared in the hospital. The following conversation ensued: Babushka (Russian for granny or old woman): "Did you clean your chromosomes before having an affair with your wife?" Husband: "No." Babushka: You see, that's why your baby is black!"

Visual information plays a key role in helping people form ideas and perceptions about other people. Generally Russians, like other white people, perceive the African continent based on a narrow set of stereotypical ideas built up over a long period of time through photographic and other visual presentations in the media. A film shot in the thirties, called the "Circus", while meant to demonstrate the superiority of socialism over capitalism, also highlighted Soviet feelings of paternalism towards Africans. A section of the film includes the statement: "In our country we love all kids. Give birth to children of all shades of colour. They can be black, white, red, even blue, pink..." However, another segment goes as follows: "Inter-marriage between the black and white races is a racial crime." Significantly enough, the latter message did not fail to have an impact on the Soviet audience. In a 1992 Russian television talk show, a participant repeated that phrase. To show that the message was a result of seeing the "Circus" film, the show's producer used archival footage; specifying the segment of the film, which the woman participant was parroting. Textbooks used in the lower grades were written to infuse compassion for blacks in students, yet the racist undertones were clear. A textbook published in 1967 uses stories of racial abuse of African-Americans, claiming that a Soviet young pioneer saved a young black slave. She was said to have bought the slave for a mere five rubles from capitalist "sharks" at a slave auction in the United States. The paternalism is difficult to disguise. A white [Russian] girl infused with "communist compassion," and fired by the ideals of a Soviet civilizing mission, rescues a helpless black victim. A familiar picture is thus drawn: Blacks are the objects of infinite white benevolence, which is "the White man's burden."

Other messages were even more explicit. A poem by the popular Soviet poet, Chukovsky is one of the many examples, which could be cited. One stanza reads, "Kids, never on earth must you go to Africa/In Africa, there are gorillas/In Africa, there's huge crocodiles.../ They'll bite you./'" A television cartoon portrays the black man as being on the level of beasts of the jungle. Such truncated and stereotypical presentations of Africa have led to widespread prejudice. African students have complained that Soviet citizens often asked them questions like "Do you have houses in Africa?", "You must be brave to cohabitate with snakes and lions?" The students claimed that some who questioned them thought that they arrived in Russia half-naked in loincloths, only to be provided with clothing at Moscow's Sheremetyevo International Airport by compassionate communist party officials.[82]

The Soviet/Russian media portrayal of Africans and other 'coloured' people is no better. In the Cold War years, the Soviet media were saturated with images of poor, homeless and jobless blacks in London and Washington either begging for alms or queuing for the *dole*. Pictures emanating from Africa were predominantly those that reflected the seamy side of African life. The blame for Africa's *ostalost'* ("backwardness") was, as a rule, placed squarely on Western imperialist and neo-colonialist plunder. Where something positive was shown it was almost always to show the "positive" and modernizing effects of a Soviet "civilizing mission," such as the construction of Soviet-assisted projects in a "socialist-oriented" country.

In the pre-glasnost years, the Soviet media, while they painted a picture of a continent in permanent crisis, did so to show the negative influence of Western presence in Africa. Africans were often shown as "innocent" victims of Western capitalist exploitation and imperialist "blackmail," who needed the express and "selfless" assistance of the "big-hearted" Soviet Union. The USSR, it was proclaimed, "has always been on the side of the oppressed nations, giving moral and material aid to the national liberation movements"

Asoyan also quotes letters by African students to Moscow newspapers [the majority of which were not published] to demonstrate the psychological trauma students from sub-Saharan Africa[83] especially undergo while pursuing their studies. The letters complain of constant taunting, ridicule, humiliation and stigmatising. In the cafeterias, on the streets, in public transport, in the dormitories, they are jeered at, fingers are pointed at them and racist slurs like *obezyiana* ("monkey"), and of late *SPID* (AIDS) are hurled at them.

A Nigerian journalism student at Kazan University, (incidentally, a Lenin pioneer Soviet leader and ideological exponent of socialist internationalism received his undergraduate education at the same university) writes to a Moscow newspaper:

> One day I decided to have my lunch in a nearby cafe. As soon
> as I opened the door, I was met with jeers and catcalls by a

group of young girls sitting around a table. They were pointing
their fingers, laughing at me and cracking unfriendly jokes about
me.[84]

The student goes on to say that this was only one of the several moral
and psychological bruises he had received from a cross section of
Soviet citizens since he arrived in the country a year earlier. Another
letter quotes an African student as saying he had to play a curious
psychological game to save his skin when he was confronted by a
group of hostile Russian youngsters.   During the encounter, he
pretended he was an African American.   This resulted in milder
treatment from the youth gang, who soon began to ask questions about
Stevie Wonder, Michael Jackson, etc.

Asoyan also quotes the famous South African singer, Hughes
Masekela, who during a tour in Moscow happened to visit the Patrice
Lumumba Peoples' Friendship University in the Soviet capital: "The
chaps live under horrible conditions. They told me they are called
'monkeys'."   Another article captioned, "Johannesburg Moves To
Moscow," notes that Russia has become another South Africa. The
article, which I mentioned earlier on, was commenting on recent
opinion polls conducted among Muscovites about their attitude towards
various ethnic groups and races.

Soviet academia has its own share of anti-African prejudice and
discrimination.   In a three-year course in foreign literature for Soviet
and Third World students at the Department of Journalism of the
Leningrad State University, not a single African writer was mentioned
even though at the beginning of the course African writer Wole
Sonyika of Nigeria won the Nobel Prize in literature. The philosophy
course was taught as though Africa lies in a philosophical vacuum. Not
a single African or Third World thinker, for that matter, was
mentioned.

In the classrooms and lecture halls, African students have been at the
receiving end of both lecturers and fellow students' race prejudice.
Russian students and some lecturers avoid the company of African
students if they can. In the classrooms and lecture theatres students do
all they can to avoid sharing the same desk with African students.
Some lecturers and students, on encountering their (African) students
and mates on the streets look the other direction to avoid eye contact.

The (negative) attitude of Russian students towards their African and
Third World counterparts was not only acquired from their parents and
society as a whole - the Communist Party played an active part in
inculcating these attitudes. For example, first year Russian students

began to distance themselves after their first Komsomol (Young Communist League) briefing. Before then the majority of the students were eager to interact with their African hosts, even if merely to satisfy their curiosity. During the first few weeks prior to the Komsomol briefing the new Russian students freely mingle with African students, inviting them to social events. However, after the Komsomol briefing, where students were warned to stay away from foreign students, they begin to withdraw from foreign students in general and African students in particular. Although not all the students belonged to the Komsomol, other students behaved in the same way, for it was common knowledge that Komsomol and Communist Party agents always spied on "wayward" students.[85]

In certain cases, racial prejudice among Russians stems more from ignorance than ethnocentrism. A popular joke among the African student community in the former Soviet Union shows the extent of the ignorance:

> A Russian worker meets an African student in the coffee bar and the following conversation ensues between them.
> Vova: Where did you come from?
> Chike: I came from Nigeria.
> Vova: How did you come here?
> Chike: How did I come here? What do you mean? How do you think I came here?
> Vova: I mean did you...? Don't be offended, but we 're told you have no means of transport?
> Chike: Oh yes! I came on foot.
> Vova: Do you have houses in Nigeria?
> Chike: No. We live on trees. And your ambassador lives on the highest tree in Lagos, the capital of my country.[86]

Hartman and Husband have pointed out that the tendency may be seen most clearly in newspaper headlines and in cartoon captions, where the use of a phrase or images that will evoke a similar set of associations and meanings in virtually all members of the society to which it is directed enables a complex point to be crystallized *unambiguously* and memorably in a few words or a single picture.[87] For a long time, Soviet journalists have used the term *cherny continent* ("the Dark Continent") to qualify the African continent. In fact, hardly any article is written about Africa without the use of this most favourite term. Journalists accompanying former Soviet Foreign Affairs Minister Eduard Shevardnadze during his first ever visit to Africa filed reports without accompanying pictures. Moscow's Central TV coverage did not include a single shot of visits, which took him to countries like Nigeria, Angola and Namibia. Instead of photographs, a blank map of Africa appeared on the screen, as though to confirm the long-held Soviet view that "backward" Africa is nothing but sunshine and crocodiles; shots would have shown the foreign minister being welcomed at modern airports by African officials in limousines, or attending state banquets in high rise buildings which match or even beat similar ones in some Soviet cities in modernity and architectural beauty. The same attitude was repeated when Russian Federation Foreign Affairs Minister, Andrei Kozeryev was in Africa two years later in March 1992.

The examples offered above illustrate the way in which a cultural tradition may be at least partly self-sustaining. The image is used because it exists and is known to have wide currency and therefore enables easier communication. By virtue of being used it is kept alive and available for further use.[88] The nature of racial stereotyping, the negative imagery of Africans in the Soviet mass media is one aspect of the cultural parameters within which journalists and all media practitioners and propagandists operate. The other aspect is the repetition in the mass media of a very simplified and truncated way of representing blacks, as well as the absence of the black experience as any significant part of the Russian/Soviet story, although blacks have played vital roles in the history of that country as mentioned earlier on.

The lack of enthusiasm on the part of Russians to mention the contribution of blacks to Russia's socio-cultural development, as well as the African ancestry of their greatest poet, Alexander Pushkin, coupled with the plight of the new generation of African Russians is a further testimony to the culturally-ingrained non-acceptance or intolerance of black people by Russians. The life and plight of African Russians[89] and their mothers is proof of this fact. Several cases of racial stereotyping, abuse and threats were reported in an interview I conducted with African-Russians and their mothers for a video documentary film. To show the extent of the prejudice it is pertinent to examine the life and plight of African Russians and their mothers.[90]

An African Love Brewed In The Pot Of Russian Public Opinion?

The Life And Plight Of African Russians, Children Of The Cold War[91]

African Russians are the children of mainly African student fathers and Russian (Soviet) mothers. There are no official statistics on them, which explains the indifference of the authorities to their plight. In St Petersburg alone, it is believed, there are over one thousand Russian-born blacks. In the autumn of 1990, a dozen of them came together to form the African-Russian Society of St Petersburg. Joseph Okum, the organizing committee leader, whose late father was a Ghanaian, said at the launching ceremony: "We hope our association will unite all Soviets who have their roots in Africa. Many African-Soviets have never in their lives seen people of their like before. It's a delight for each of us to feel that he or she is not alone in this world."

The society was registered as a charitable organization, which aimed to attract world attention to "our perilous existence before we disappear like the dinosaurs", as the Ethiopian-Russian Mikhail Zayaistky put it. Okum, a high school graduate, says the society's immediate objective was to raise funds to set up an orphanage in St Petersburg for black Russian children. Later they planned a national hunt for abandoned black children in orphanages and baby homes if they could raise travel funds from abroad. The seeds of these youths' problems, the oldest of whom were 27 in 1992, were sown in the early 60s. The FSU, projecting itself as the leader of the worldwide anti-colonialist liberation movement, invited large numbers of African "youths dreaming about socialism" to take up university and college studies in the still closed society left by Josef Stalin.

The African student population was and still is predominantly male. For many a Soviet woman, marrying a foreigner provided a rare chance to escape the Iron Curtain. A spate of marriages—many of convenience—followed. In an apparent reaction to the Soviet media portrayal of Africans as *bednie rodstviniki* (poor relatives), some African men told tales of riches back home in their wooing of the largely ignorant, hence gullible Soviet women. Some said they were sons of millionaires or princes.

On graduation the young fathers, especially those from poor homes, faced a dilemma: take their wives back to a modest life, or leave their families behind. Russian officials did not allow foreign students to remain after their studies. Students were scared away by the militia (police) soon after completing their studies. Even students who had fallen out with their home governments were forced to leave, often to face persecution, although many such students managed to find their way to Western countries.

Concessions were not given, even to those who had Soviet wives. Soviet law did not allow for dual citizenship. The official explanation was that the young specialists must return to their various countries, to put their newly acquired skills at the service of their compatriots. Unlike the West, the FSU was unwilling to take part in the brain drain in the developing countries. This FSU policy sounds plausible and beneficent; but we must note that the Communist leadership was careful to avoid having a large population of Africans making Russia a permanent home, which might lead to the racial tensions felt in most Western countries. This partly explains why so many African men were compelled to leave their families behind. Many intended to return, but economic constraints at home meant few ever came back.

Martin Christoferovich Mikhailov was not yet born when his Nigerian father left the FSU for Africa, having completed his studies. His mother was barely three months pregnant. Martin was 16 in 1992. His mother, Galina Mikhailova, 39, met Christopher O. Beniju in 1972, while he was a student at an Energy College in then Leningrad, now St Petersburg. They lived together for four years before he left. He promised to return and continue his studies. In 1978, two years after his departure and one year after the birth of Martin, Galina received an invitation from her future husband (they were not legally married) to join him in his Apapa home in Lagos, the Nigerian capital. Beniju's attempt to return to Russia for his Master's program had fallen through.

However, her dream of a reunion with her loved one was aborted by what she termed "our monstrous and inhuman bureaucrats." They "tossed" her up and down, demanded document upon document after verbal and psychological drills by the KGB. Somewhere along the line she got fed up and gave it all up. She lamented: "They were set against my going to Africa to join my husband, and deliberately made it impossible for me to leave. I realized that and I said to myself enough is enough...I gave up." Ever since then, things have gone from bad to worse for Martin and his mother. But life became terrible after the demise of Communism. Anti-Black sentiment held in check by the old authoritarian system surged to the surface in the wake of Communism's collapse.

Ordinary Russians were now giving full rein to their subdued racist feelings in the best expression of glasnost. "They shouted at Martin: 'Negro go back to your African jungle. Your Communist godfathers who brought you here are no longer in power.' And I shouted back: 'He is not a Negro.' He has nowhere to go....'"[92] Galina recounted how she and Martin were confronted in the subway by a group of Russian youngsters a few days after the botched putsch of August 19, 1991. Galina says Martin cannot make friends among his peers or schoolmates. They keep on making derogatory remarks about Blacks.

Now he has made a new friend, but she is sure this one, like previous ones, will soon drift away. For a boy of his age, "it is too much of a psychological burden and mental agony to bear. I can manage to cope, although it is difficult when everyone, including your own relatives, have shunned you because they think it is only prostitutes who go out with blacks," Galina said.

Galina and her son Martin are not alone in their plight. Irina Yesina's husband Ferdinand Balige was expelled from his engineering institute for overstaying his vacation, and was to be deported to his homeland, Tanzania. But Irina was two months pregnant. He did not want to leave his future child behind. According to Irina Albertovna, a KGB man came to her flat and asked her to end the pregnancy, since she was, after all, not allowed to follow her husband to Africa. He said it was in her interest, as the child would be fatherless and a burden to her. Balige managed to slip back from Moscow airport to Leningrad, and went into hiding with his wife until Maria was born. However, after a year of hide-and-seek with the secret service, Ferdinand broke down under the psychological pressure, and attempted to take his own life. He was admitted to a hospital and soon deported.

Zhenia Limashevsky, whose father left the Soviet Union when he was barely three months old, had a harrowing experience at school. He said he was called names and made to feel unwanted. Fellow classmates obscenely cartooned his parents. He complained to his principal, who only told him to disregard his classmates' pranks. "How can I ignore such an insult? I did not offend anybody; I had done nothing wrong to deserve it. They were always provoking me, they cracked jokes and gossiped about me. There was an unbearable atmosphere surrounding me. I grabbed the cartoon and left the school," Zhenia said.

Looking for a day care center for black children was a big problem. Yelena, who adopted her Bulgarian girl friend's twins after she had abandoned them in a maternity ward and left for Bulgaria, said her search for a day care for the kids was painful and frustrating. When she finally found one, the kids were shabbily treated. One day, when she went to pick up the children, their caretaker was swearing at them. One of them, she complained, had bitten another child. She yelled and swore: "You wild kids; your only place is Africa!" According to Yelena, parents who heard about the incident began to withdraw their kids from the center. She was compelled to take the children away. Only later did she learn that another child had done the biting, for which her children were insulted.

Slava Dominikonovich is a highly gifted child who attends a special school for high IQ children. According to his mother, Nadezhda, Slava is very good at skiing, and she wanted him to join the national team. But when she approached the national coach, he told her bluntly: "Your son is surely excellent, but I'm afraid he cannot be accepted on the national team, since he is black, and our team is white. Nadezhda said because Slava has very prominent African features, schoolmates always say: "You are not one of us." In the first, second and third grades, Slava would return from school asking her mother: "Why do they regard me so lowly? I study well, at least not worse than the others. I do better in drawing, sing better than others. Why am I treated like an outcast?" When Nadezda and her son went out for a walk, he tried to keep a distance, either ahead or behind her. When she asked him why he did that, he said: "I don't want people to look at you and say you're a spoilt woman because of me. Let them look at me instead, and call me 'Negro'. I know you're a good woman."

Justina's father is from Zaire, where he works in the ministry of foreign affairs. He met her mother as a student in the FSU in the sixties. At school, Justina was made to feel different. "Sometimes I had to fight. But as a child, I was not bothered as much I am now. As a grown-up, I have become sensitive to racial remarks and attitudes. In food lines, I become depressed when I hear people grumbling about 'parasitic' aliens. She said someone in a line complained that they [Russians] must sacrifice to educate and feed 'these hordes.' And as if that was not enough, they continue to give birth to infants they must also feed, clothe and educate."

African Russians have had to put up with much racial intolerance, bigotry and hypocrisy. Neighbors scoff at their mothers for "shamelessness and debauchery." To Lena's neighbors she is a prostitute because her child is black and a black man comes to their communal flat. They don't want to clean the bathroom because they claim she has AIDS. "Because a black man comes here they claim I have AIDS. Morally it is difficult when everyday they tell you you're a prostitute just because you love someone with a different skin color," Lena said bitterly. "On the streets, they point fingers at my child, they call her names... baby Negro. I don't usually pay attention. It is my mother who sometimes explains to them that there is no difference between black and white people."

Yelena is a nurse living in a packed communal flat. She lives between the devil and the deep blue sea. At home she is an object of daily racial slurs from her neighbors, and at the hospital her boss ridicules her. "At the hospital, I 'm always made the scapegoat when something goes wrong. The head of my unit is Jewish, but she is a racist. At our usual morning briefings, she put one and the same question to me: 'What are the risk factors for catching AIDS?'" Her neighbors were always on her back. But when she could not endure their provocations any longer and contacted the militia, they were even more provocative than her neighbors. Yelena said: "The militia, even more than my neighbors, insulted and slighted me."

To protest the increasing racial abuse and discrimination against African-Russians and their mothers, Svieta and her colleagues arranged a radio interview with assistance from the local mayor's office. After the interview, Svieta's neighbor assaulted her and her mother because she claimed Svieta had caused her an embarrassment by publicly revealing that she shares a flat with the mother of a black child. Svieta recounts, as tears stream down her cheeks: "She yelled that she was going to teach me and my mulatto society a lesson. She claimed that I had no right to give the apartment's telephone number to the radio station, to make the entire city know that she lives with a mother of a black child; that I had caused her and other residents a moral damage. She was furious like a panther. She then picked up a telephone directory and hit me on my head. I tried to snatch the directory, but she grabbed me by my neck and began to strangle me."

Inna Limashevskaya and her son Zhenia Limashevsky sounded the bitterest. "We are isolated from the society. We are outcasts. The child is an outcast, and the person who gave birth to him is an outcast. This is not America. Not even South Africa. Here for centuries peoples' conscience has rotted away." Inna is now out of work due to failing eyesight and lives on her son's stipend of 300 rubles. In January 1992 this amount was only enough for two weeks' food for the two. Before now, she worked in eateries to procure food for Zhenia. She took up part time jobs to earn just enough money to buy clothes for herself and her son. She can't do all that now.

"The Russian psychology is that anyone who has dark skin or does not look like him or her should not live in this country. I am a single mother. They claim I parasite on them. I have Jewish blood in me. It is even worse. They claim Jews live off people the world over. And with my son Zhenia it is much worse." Her son chips in: "A Jewish woman lived in our old communal flat. Our neighbors subjected her to daily insults. They told her things like she was a glutton. And they insulted my mother also. They claimed she gave birth to me through prostitution. They had a whole pile of inhuman hatred and condescension against us." According to Zhenia, people told his mother to "'clear off with her Negro'"; that he was "'dirtying the city'" because of him.

Maria Balige was 14 in 1992. At 10 she was a promising gymnast, scoring second in the All-Leningrad championship. In 1991 her mother withdrew her from the gymnastics school because her classmates taunted her as soon as she started scoring at the top in many exercises. They called her names; called her "chocolate," and made uncomplimentary remarks and jokes about black people. Maria said she was treated better at school, where she was first in the class. But even there she had no friends. Not many kids wanted to hang around with her for long. Irina, Maria's mother says: "She has no close friends because they think as a black student she should perform worse than they do, yet the opposite is the case."

Gulnara Agossu also has a black child. She says the greatest problem for black children is at school. A colored child in a Russian school is still a sensation. "The school is the cruelest place for our children. Racism in our society begins at the schools and in infancy. Infants are weaned with racism," she said. Meanwhile, press campaigns have openly discouraged mixed marriages involving Russian women and Third World, particularly African, men. The media have carried reports of "terrible sufferings" of Soviet wives in Ethiopia, Mali, and Cuba. Some reports said Soviet wives were sold into slavery or forced into prostitution.

For example, in October 1987 the magazine RABOCHAYA SMENA carried a counseling interview between a psychologist/columnist and an expectant mother of 19. She was expecting a child fathered by an African. Her parents were against her entering wedlock with her lover. Her mother had been hospitalized, suffering from a heart attack triggered by the news that her daughter insisted she loved the African more than her former Russian boyfriend, whom her parents wanted her to marry. She had insisted she would marry Jozel, (her African fiancé,), even without her parents' blessing. She had unearthed a plot by her parents to have her child given away to a foster home on delivery.

She had telephoned the psychologist for counseling. He warned her against marrying the African, much less following him to Africa. He reasoned that the girl would be stressed by living in a "strange country, with different cultural norms, a different climate, a different life-style." But when she would not budge, he invoked familiar tales of "African husbands who traded away their Russian wives, and the others who gave their spouses to their fathers as presents."[93]

Although the Soviet and Russian constitutions made racial abuse or discrimination punishable by law, the courts hardly ever prosecuted offenders.[94] Marina Ngakutu, 19, whose father was a minister of state in Chad and whose mother sings at the Kirov Theatre in St Petersburg, says: "My only protector is myself. My tool is to pretend I don't see, don't hear, and don't care."

More difficult are the lives of African Russian men drafted into the ex-Red Army, where racial discrimination is severe. They are all, without exception, drafted into the civil units, where a good number of servicemen are ex-convicts and drug-addicts. Alex Mmzilangwe and Yevgeny Limashevsky, whose fathers came from Tanzania and Zambia respectively, spoke of their harrowing experiences during their service: "More often there is only one black in a whole detachment, and it is tempting not to make a scapegoat of him at the least pretext." Limashevsky said other draftees cracked jokes about him, "calling me names like 'black paint, "black sea,' 'monkey,' 'AIDS'." Alex said he was always given the hardest tasks to perform. He said African Russians were not allowed to serve in more sensitive units of the army, as the authorities feared they would one day join their fathers in Africa with military secrets.

The story of Molisa Seia in the MOSCOW TIMES[95] paints a similar picture of the products of a mixed-race love match at the height of the Cold War.[96] The emergence of yet another visible minority group does not appear to concern the leaders of the C.I.S. In the meantime, they have a grimmer task on hand, sorting out the seemingly inexorable inter-ethnic vendettas. Although Gorbachev's perestroika and glasnost reforms allowed for ethnic self-expression, and made it possible for African/Russians to form their association, they brought no improvements in their living conditions. In fact, like the growing army of Russia's poor, they live in despicable conditions. The speedy transition to a market economy has meant a further deterioration. As Limashevsky said, "We shall soon sink and disappear, and nobody will notice ... nobody will care."

But African Russians appear more worried about the rise of Russian Fascism. Although they have not been touched as a group yet, the prospects are that soon the Fascists will turn from Russian Jews to them. Nikolai Mikhailov, Director of the Institute of Ethnography at the St Petersburg State University, believes this may well happen in the not-too-distant future. "Although for now, the motley Fascist organizations appear to be more concerned with Zionists and Masons, with time they may remember others who spoil the purity of the Russian nation."[97]

That all this should happen in a country that was supposedly built on the most humanistic of all ideologies—that of the oppressed and downtrodden—goes to prove my argument that ethnocentric "blood" is thicker than ideological water. Soviet/Russian ethnocentrism, and not communist compassion for the racial and ethnic minorities guided interracial and interethnic discourse and relations in the FSU.

Russian Enthnocentric "Blood" Turns Out To Be Thicker Than Soviet-Communist Ideological "Water"

Ethnocentrism: The Mother Of All Sentiments

Ethnocentrism, the wellspring of all human sentiments both vile and noble, is both the balm and the bane of human societies. The tendency for people to put their groups at the center of the universe serves several useful purposes. It engenders collective self-assurance, collective solidarity, and a collective sense of worth. But ethnocentrism does have its negative side, which can have devastating consequences for both the in-group itself and the targeted out-group. Reverse ethnocentrism, i.e. denigrating or at best marginalizing or trivializing the out-group lies at the core of many inter-ethnic, inter-religious, inter-ideological wars and strife since the dawn of history.

For the in-group, ethnocentrism may breed collective ignorance and collective self-delusion, which may lead to a false sense of superiority and invincibility. Ethnocentrism can also impose on the in-group a collective tunnel vision and collective blinkers, which may prevent the group from seeing "beyond its nose." Ideology serves similar purposes, but it is more limited to public discourse than to an entire culture.

Ethnocentrism And Superpower Politics

Ethnocentrism and its canonical variants (nationalism, parochialism, patriotism, jingoism, etc) may be considered dominant characteristics of the human species, easily appealed to, easily surfacing...[98]

In his book, *Strategy and Ethnocentrism*, Ken Booth outlines several meanings of ethnocentrism. I offer a brief summary here. Ethnocentrism is used in the following closely related senses:

1. As a term to describe feelings of group centrality and superiority.
2. As a technical term to describe a faulty methodology in the social sciences.
3. As a synonym for being 'culture-bound'.[99]

For our purpose, the first definition, which was first introduced by W. G. Summer is more appropriate: ethnocentrism is the 'view of things in which one's own group is the center of everything, and all others are scaled and rated with reference to it'.[100] The characteristic features of ethnocentrism include: strong identification with one's own group and its culture, the tendency to see one's own group as the center of the universe, the tendency to perceive events in terms of one's own interests, the tendency to prefer one's own way of life (culture) over all others (seeing it has involving the best and the right ways of acting), and a general suspicion of foreigners, their modes of thought, action and motives.[101]

Also for our purpose, the cultural dimensions of ethnocentrism need to be explored. Here again, Booth's insights are important. He distinguishes several central propositions and discusses the pernicious effects of ethnocentrism. They include:

a.   Ethnocentrism is one of the factors, which can seriously interfere with rational strategic planning.
b.   Together with other mechanisms (psychological, historical, and bureaucratic) ethnocentrism can distort important aspects of strategic thinking, especially where problems of perception and prediction are involved.
c.   Ethnocentrism is one way in which individuals and groups evade reality.

As I have indicated earlier, at the root of media and political policy in Africa and the Third World is a deeply ingrained Euro-American and Soviet ethnocentrism, an inability and or an unwillingness to understand Africa in particular, and the Third World in general, on its own terms, an insistence on viewing it through the lenses of Euro-American and Soviet-Russian experience, and the condescending and patronizing attitudes that such ethnocentrism implies. Embedded deeply in the European ethos, this ethnocentrism was—and still is—

part of the educational systems of the competing ideological systems and is reflected in the social science literature on development.

It is ethnocentrism that made politicians and media practitioners in the FSU and the West believe that their institutions are the best and most developed that mankind has devised, that we can export their institutions to "backward" nations, and even that they have a moral duty to do so. In the American-led West, that missionary spirit of bringing the benefits of its civilization to the developing nations is very strong. It goes back to the Puritan and other Judeo-Christian traditions. In United States, it was known as Manifest Destiny and was "strong among the Founding Fathers who wanted to teach Latin America about electing good men, and it is expressed in Woodrow Wilson's naive faith that we could 'make the world safe for democracy:' That spirit is also reflected in John F. Kennedy's Peace Corps and Alliance for Progress, in Jimmy Carter's campaign for human rights, and in Ronald Reagan's effort to promote democracy and laissez-faire economic enterprise in Central America."[102] More recently, the Clinton Administration's zeal to push forward an American inspired and lead "Globalization's agenda is another manifestation of this ethos, which is deeply ingrained, it is of historic duration, and it crosses all partisan and ideological lines. In the FSU, the Soviet "internationalist mission" to build socialism around the globe was a continuation of Imperial Russia's "Great Russia" agenda, which was first directed at its southern neighbors in Central Asia and the Caucuses and then extended to other parts of the world during the Cold War era of "New Imperialism."

The educational systems both of the FSU and the "American-West," notwithstanding their ideological differences, were based almost exclusively on Eurocentric traditions, which treats other cultures and histories as peripheral, at best and inferior at worst. The education systems, in spite of their different ideological goals and orientations are essentially rooted in the Greco-Roman and Judeo-Christian traditions and European history, from which derive a set of concepts, ethics, and governing norms and experiences.

The concepts of justice, fair play, good government, progress, and development are similarly European concepts. They are all based on the mechanical, unilineal, dichotomies, European constructs postulated by social science and ideological stalwarts including, Hegel, Durkheim, Marx, Weber, and Lenin. Underlying these constructs is the assumption that the non-European world would inevitably follow the same developmental path as the American-West or the Soviet-East. In this tradition, Educators generally only touch in limited ways on the Third World.

The problem is not just an educational system that fails to equip to understand non-European areas; the problem lies deep in both the Soviet-East's and American-West's ethos and political culture. In the case of the American-West, the vast bulk of social science findings, models, and literature, which purport to be universal, are in fact biased, ethnocentric, and not universal at all. They are based on the narrow and rather particular experiences of Euro-American world and they may have little or no relevance to the rest of the world. The same can be said of the Soviet-East. As noted earlier, the Soviet educational system takes its source from the same Euro-American fountain. Thus, the self-same founders of Western social thought—Rousseau, Voltaire, Kant, Hegel, Comte, Durkheim and Marx—are considered the wellsprings of Russian intellectual heritage. The works of a substantial number of Russian thinkers, including both tsarist and post-tsarist luminaries such as, Radishchev, Chernychevsky, Herzen, Tolstoy, Mayakovsky, Gorky, etc., were watered by the wellspring of the common Western intellectual heritage. The new crop of political leaders and media practitioners during the communist era were all baptized, as it were, in the waters of this same intellectual fountain. It is therefore no wonder that, Soviet attitudes towards people of African origin mirrored the same social evolutionist and eurocentric thought systems of the Euro-American world.

Closely related to and indeed tied to this form of ethnocentrism is social evolutionism. Well before Darwin, theories of evolution began to add fuel to Western racism. Race logic in America and Europe was built on the notion that if humans had evolved, presumably from apes, some humans had evolved more than others. It presumed that the white race—especially upper-middle- and upper class white males—are furthest along the evolutionist line. Through the work of American anthropologist Lewis Morgan, social evolutionism influenced both conservative and radical European thinkers including Durkhiem and Marx.

In the evolutionist eye, others—including Africans—were less evolved.[103] As Keim notes, Africans were seen as "living ancestors" who were present in this time yet representatives of another time. Or they were "perpetual children, not yet adults and therefore only marginally significant in contemporary time"[104] Keim further notes:

"In the nineteenth century, the root cause of African backwardness was considered to be their race. Most whites, for example, believed that Africans lacked philosophy because they lacked the biological capacity to produce philosophy. Over time—a very long time—blacks would evolve the ability to philosophize like whites, to create real art and to rule themselves, but until that moment, the best that could be done was for white men to accept the burden of control and care as one might do for children. In practice, of course, the White Man's Burden of taking care of Africans turned into the Black Man's Burden of suffering exploitation. Because Africans were presumed to represent a more primitive time, most Westerners, including most Americans, could easily accept African subjugation and overlook African contributions to history."[105]

Keim's observation is also true of Russian attitudes toward Africans. Social evolutionism heavily influenced Engels and Marx, so it formed part of Marxist heritage. Marxist orthodoxy itself was framed as a theory of stages (primitive communism — slavery — feudalism — capitalism — communism). How deeply evolutionism is anchored in socialism is apparent, for instance, in the slogan, which from Karl Kautsky to Rosa Luxemburg, and later, sums up the socialist program: Socialism or Barbarism.[106] Although some writers, notably Allison Blakely and Paul Robeson had presented a rather benign view of Russian attitude towards Africans, a good number of Black scholars and even early communist activists such as James Ford and George Padmore have been critical of the condescending and racist attitudes of European communists in general, and Soviet Communists in particular toward people of African descent.

Both Ford and Padmore were unhappy that European-American communists had reduced the race question to class struggle and downplayed or even trivialized the "struggle for social equality of oppressed races."[107] Ford criticized the assumptions of racial and cultural superiority in certain socialist attitudes, for example those in the "renegade" Kautsky's notion that the proletariat in the "civilized" world has a mission to bring the "backward" colonized peoples up to their level. Ford who aired his criticism at Sixth Communist International (Comintern) Congress pointed out that he found this type of mindset even among members of the Comintern.

Ford's observation was corroborated by Padmore another prominent member of the Comintern. While Moscow had, in general supported the struggles of Blacks against colonialism, imperialism, and racial injustice, it refused to address the racial question independently. By its insistence that racism is essentially a capitalist creation, the Kremlin leadership and ideologues in the Communist Party misleadingly argued that the problem is a class one, not color one. Thus, the values and rights to self-determination were subordinated to a global communist revolution.

A good number of the early "Black Communists" and sympathizers of the Soviet cause were driven to one and the same conclusion about Soviet involvement in continental Africa, in particular and the African Diaspora, in general: Ideological expediency and ethnocentric, even racist motives informed Russian attitudes towards Africans. Backstabbing actions and imperialist maneuvers undertaken by the Russian leadership in both tsarist times and Soviet communist years increased the suspicion and distrust. For example, despite vigorous vocal support for Ethiopia against invasion by racist Italy, the Soviet Union sold fuels to Italy. The Soviet-Nazi pact of 1939 included plans to partition Africa. The Soviets were willing to agree to Hitler's control of Central Africa and Mussolini's territorial ambitions in the north and northeast in exchange for support of Soviet aspirations in the Indian Ocean.[108]

The tsarist Russia's contemplated plot with the Boers during the Boer War to expel the British and place the new Boer State under Russian protectorate is another graphic example of the willingness of the Russian leadership to use Africans to their advantage. Here again, the Blakely's observations deserve our attention:

> The Boer War had already been decided in favor of the British when a former Boer general, Pinaar-Joubert, sent a proposal to the Russian government outlining a plot to oust the British and place the new Boer State under Russia as a protectorate. The plan hinged on deliberately fomenting disturbances among Negroes in British African territories. British preoccupation with theses would allow the Boers eventually to mount force sufficient to drive the British out. The tsar would then proclaim himself ruler of South and Central Africa. Russian leaders discarded this proposal only after giving it a thorough consideration despite all the strain Russia was already experiencing at home and abroad from war and revolution.

Blakely notes further:

> Russia's objectives in this area would have been roughly the
> same as in Ethiopia: strategic location along vital sea routes,
> access to the riches of interior Africa; and a check of the world's
> greatest imperial power, Great Britain. This elaborate scheme,
> although inconsequential, shows that even though the Russian
> Empire never annexed a large Negro population, it was willing
> to consider the idea.

This attitude exhibited by both tsarist and soviet leaders was to be
repeated throughout the cold war years till the final collapse Soviet-
style communism in 1991. It is an attitude that is based on cold
ethnocentric calculations and ideological expediencies. The Soviets
also double-crossed even sympathetic and friendly African leaders such
as, Kwame Nkrumah of Ghana, Sekou Toure of Guinea, and traded
African regimes, including Somalia and Ethiopia on the platter of super
power politics. The Russians hoarded cocoa beans bought from Ghana
in their London warehouse and sold them when prices rose, glutting the
market. The result was that the price of cocoa steeply fell, seriously
affecting the Nkrumah regime's economic fortunes.   Soviet "experts"
and diplomats consistently smuggled diamonds from Sekou Toure's
Guinea until they were apprehended. As noted in chapter one, the
Soviet abandoned old African comrades for new ones as and when it
became ideologically expedient for them.

Ideology And Behavioral Bilingualism

Ideology –the fundamental principles, beliefs, ideas, and views of the
dominant segment of a society—serves as our mirror of our world.[109]
Ideology is the image-forming nexus of the observed, communicated,
accepted, desired, believed. It is the individual's eye upon society. An
ideology seeks specific order. It is a subtle and insidious means of
seeking order and discipline in public discourse.[110] The sermon in the
pulpit, the opprobrium inflicted by the press, the ridicule of friends, the
ostracism of colleagues, the sneer, the snub, and countless devices all
constitute non-statutory instruments by which societies exert coercion,
by which they achieve and preserve unity.[111] Like ethnocentrism, it is
emotionally charged, normative, value-laden, and self-righteous. It
dismisses other ideologies, and it is combative, fighting for and
protecting its territory.

While ethnocentrism may provide the rationale for a particular manner of discourse, ideology establishes a common public discourse. It is not understanding or belief that the propaganda system of a society aspires to achieve in its audience, but the standardization of public discourse. For example, Shlapentokh has advanced the notion of two levels of mentality: one "mythological"—the absorption of official ideology, governing verbal behavior, and the other pragmatic," regulating material behavior. In the latter area, Shlapentokh asserts, Soviet people behaved with such widespread disregard for official norms that they were "sliding into an abyss of complete demoralization." In Shlapentokh's view, the only official value that had achieved much real internalization was patriotism,[112] which I equate with ethnocentrism.

In the Soviet Union this led to the pervasiveness of behavioral bilingualism—the phenomena defined by Yuri Glazov as "that mode of behavior in accordance with which a member of a given society, while more or less soberly understanding the essence of what is going on around him, conducts himself with absolute conformism on the official level, whereas in a narrow circle of friends or among his own family members he expresses well-considered or even extremist viewpoints that refute the basic principles of the official outlook.... By language we assume a culture, a mode of behavior."[113]

An example of this phenomenon was the case involving the 19-year-old expectant mother, (noted above), whose parents would not allow her to marry her African fiancé. She said her father, a prominent party activist working in the Political Information section of Leningrad's office of the Communist Party, told her if she insisted on giving birth to a black child and brought it home he would shut himself in the washroom and vomit! His ethnocentric and racist instincts took over in the privacy of his home, away from the gaze of the party ideological machine.[114]

As Alexander Zinoviev argues, the crucial role played by the ideological apparatus is that it: "teaches and compels people in certain situations, which are vitally important in the life of society, to think, speak and behave alike and in a desired manner by their rulers.... People's acceptance of ideology is expressed by the fact that they will act as society demands."[115] Public officials, like the party activist mentioned above, suppress their ethnocentric and racist instincts while on official duty, but give vent to their real emotions once they are in "conducive" situations.

The Soviet press explained glasnost-era conflicts in several cities between Soviet youths and African students by citing competition for scarce resources.[116] However, Soviet reports about Africa had strong ethnocentric and paternalistic undertones, cast in "holier than thou," "God-like versus Satanic," "civil versus savage" images. Most of these reports were predominantly about the negative side of the African reality. Africa was painted as a continent in permanent crisis and Africans as desperately in need of Soviet assistance. The media and politicians never tired of portraying the USSR as a big-hearted "Big Brother," lavishing *besvosmezdnaya pomoshch* ("free or disinterested assistance"),[117] in line with Marxist-Leninist-humanitarianism, on "poor and defenseless peoples of the developing world struggling against capitalist subjugation and neo-colonialist blackmail."[118]

Historically, the Soviet media and political bureaucracy had painted a rather simplistic, idealistic, and exotic picture of Africa. A well-known poster, popular among Soviets before perestroika, summarizes it all: It depicts a muscular African man inside a map of Africa, who has broken a hefty chain fastened around his hands and feet. The poster's inscription read: "Svoboda Afrike" ("Freedom to Africa"). Ostensibly, this message was meant to elicit the sympathy of Soviet citizens for the African freedom-cause. But this mercy-eliciting and paternalistic propaganda appeared hand-in-hand with hate mongering. For instance, while kids were taught to have compassion for Africans, poetry and cartoons directed at young people featured the Soviet version of Tarzan images of Africa.

During the immediate pre-independence era in Africa in the late 1950s and early 1960s, the Soviet political bureaucracy preached that Africans would be better off by breaking the chains of colonial subjugation and western dependence. But they would be even better off if they chose the Soviet road to socialism.[119]

Images and propaganda replaced reality, and the media told Russians that with Soviet moral and material assistance Africans were breaking the fetters of imperialist domination and capitalist exploitation. However, not the destiny of the "exploited" and "subjugated" in Africa, but the scoring of ideological points in the Cold War primarily concerned the Kremlin. The net effect of this propaganda was the identification of Africans as part of today's problems in Russia and other member states of the C.I.S. The speed of the new Kremlin leaders' call for payment of what MOSCOW NEWS termed "Africa's secret debts" (*Sekretnie dolgi Afriki bivshemy Sovietskomy soyuzy*) as soon as Communism died indicates the spuriousness and shallowness of Moscow's commitment to the African cause.[120] The result—the boomerang effect of Moscow's paternalistic propaganda—is a backlash against Africans. It is easy to understand why, as Russia now finds itself in economic turmoil, Africans have become the convenient scapegoats.

To show the extent of the scapegoat-hunting syndrome in post-Communist Russia, we must consider a detailed account of the experiences of African students and diplomats in recent years.

Post-Communist Russia And The Scapegoat Syndrome

On August 11, 1992, Gideon Chimsuro, 24, a Zimbabwean law student at Patrice Lumumba People's Friendship University, was shot in the neck by a campus guard (militia), a fourth-year Russian law student at the same university, when Chimsuro attempted to drive away a dog that threatened to bite him. The dog allegedly belonged to a friend of the Russian student, who was also a militia (police) recruit.

This death yet again manifested the growing anti-African hysteria and hatred in the former Soviet Union. That his assailant was a fellow student is also symptomatic of the times. It clearly indicated how far a persistent and calculated scapegoating of Africans for the woes of Russia and other member states of the C.I.S. had gone. Killings of Africans on purely racial grounds are common occurrences. They did not start today. The first recorded murder of an African student occurred as far back as in 1963, when twenty-nine year-old Ghanaian medical student, Edmond Asare-Addo was found dead near a train track in sub-zero weather. His friends alleged that he was murdered by Russians who objected to his impending marriage to his Russian fiancé. Soviet authorities conjectured that he had been drinking and that had collapsed and frozen to death.[121] Other murders were to follow in other cities, including Baku, Kiev, etc.[122]

The Lumumba University incident was just one of many brutalities unleashed against black students in various parts of the former FSU that go unreported by both the local and international media. In the pre-glasnost, pre-perestroika past, the Azerbaijan capital of Baku in Central Asia and Rostov-on-Don in the Russian Federation were notorious for brutality against African students. However, since 1986 the wave of anti-black sentiment has spread to engulf all cities where foreign students are studying. Racially motivated attacks have been recorded in all parts of the FSU. Reports from different parts of the C.I.S. say that youth gangs have mounted a series of attacks on black students.

The Ukraine appears to be leading the anti-black campaign. Between October and November, 1989 four African students were killed in the Ukrainian capital, Kiev. A gang of *muzhiks* (robust-looking men, literally peasants) beat up three students, killing one, a Malagasy, on the spot. This triggered a sit-in protest by foreign students at Lomonosov University. In Kharkov, another Ukrainian town, a Ugandan student was murdered in cold blood in his room. The unknown murderers reportedly hammered nails into his skull. In February the following year, a Ghanaian student who had arrived in Kharkov for the annual congress of the National Union of Ghana Students, was assaulted by a youth gang and left unconscious in the snow.

A Zambian resting in a summer park with his white girlfriend in the Ukrainian mining city of Donetsk was shot in the thigh. Eyewitnesses said the gunman had aimed at his genitals, but the student jumped before the gun went off. Three years earlier in the same city, African students preparing to ship their personal belongings home, having completed their studies, had them set on fire by racists. The fire spread and destroyed the hostel, killing at least two students and wounding many others, including former Soviet citizens.

African students in then Leningrad, now St Petersburg, said to be the "most cultured city in the former USSR", have not been spared racist attacks either. In 1992 alone more than six African students were either killed or mercilessly beaten up, robbed, or had their cars set on fire. An Ethiopian post-graduate mining engineering student was murdered in his cubicle in the students' hostel. A Nigerian student woke up one morning to find his car burnt to ashes. Two Ghanaian students were beaten up by ambush-laying youth gangs near their hostel. Another was mugged in his hostel and all his personal effects stolen.

Militiamen assaulted another African when he was entering a hotel. They had called him *"obezyiana"* "monkey"); when he retorted by asking them whether "the monkey has offended the pig," they pounced on him, kicking and battering him with batons. Days later, another West African from Guinea-Bissau, was roughed up by the same militiamen. A Zambian student, who was being treated at the St. Petersburg Botkina Infectious Diseases Hospital, was beaten up after his Russian girlfriend had called to visit him. Although he had lied that she was his teacher, this did not save him. Hospital authorities described his attackers, also in-patients, as abnormal. But the Botkina Hospital is not a psychiatric treatment center. [123]

Between May and August, 1991 four Nigerians were beaten up, some very severely. Knife- and stick-wielding Azeri refugees in their dormitory attacked a group of African and Cuban students. They said they wanted to get rid of blacks because they were living off them. The picture is the same in Moscow and other cities. Although attacks may be aimed at "Third World" students in general, black students are the most conspicuous targets by virtue of their skin color. Thus all over the country, a black student is prone to attack or molestation, humiliation and stigmatizing, not only by youth ruffians, but even by law enforcement officers on the least pretext, and in most cases he/she remains defenseless.[124] To walk with a white woman on the streets of Moscow by day, or worse yet at night, requires extreme courage. The woman would be called a prostitute, while the man may be attacked.[125]

Nor have African diplomats in Moscow been saved by their diplomatic immunity. Not many have been physically assaulted yet, but a good number have been the objects of racist slurs, discrimination and humiliation. The wife of an East African diplomat shopping recently in St. Petersburg confessed: "In the shops in Moscow they refuse to sell items in the required quantity to me. Not even my diplomatic pass and my three children by my side are enough to persuade the salesgirls."[126] Another diplomat, a former student in the USSR confided: "The other day a militiaman hurled racist invectives at me. My diplomatic car number-plate was no security."[127]

In September 1997, during Moscow's 850th anniversary celebration, the daughter of a Kenyan diplomat said she was stopped, robbed, battered, and finally thrown into the Moscow River by the police, even though she had produced diplomatic credentials.[128] A black diplomat who recently arrived at the South African Embassy said he gets nervous on seeing skinheads approaching him. He said he was brutally molested by a group in broad daylight, just five months after taking up his diplomatic post.

In 1998 a Moscow-based Ghanaian researcher and writer on African affairs detailed a similar, if not more gruesome trend in Russian attitude and behavior toward Africans.[129] He describes in graphic detail several racially motivated assaults, insults, and murders. The victims include African students, refugees, and diplomats. The perpetrators of these acts run the gamut from ordinary Russians to law enforcement officers, the media, and government officials.

Beginning with his own experiences, Klomegah writes in an article, "Victims in New Russia Defenseless:" "While I was doing some final research on this essay... I was physically assaulted... The assailants were not skinheads, which is common enough in such circumstances, but the police, who seized my documents after beating me." "In October," he went on "I was thrown out of my apartment after arguing with my landlady over a racist song called "Black Skin Man," which her daughter and friends repeatedly played during a birthday party to tease me."[130] He goes on to describe how the virus of hatred has spread far and wide in Russia, particularly in Moscow. According to Klomegah, the new Russia has witnessed a sharp rise in the number of criminal gangs and racially motivated assaults. The increase in violent crime is a threat to all foreigners, but black people are the hardest hit. Each black person has his own experience with racial discrimination, but a shared theme is that the police are either unconcerned or part of the problem.[131]

According to the Helsinki Human Rights Watch report "Open Season, Closed Society," scores of similar complaints were recorded recently. Ugandan Paul Akera is believed to be the ninth victim of a racially motivated slaying in 1998 alone. Many live in perpetual fear. Derogatory names for blacks include: filthy nigger, chocolate, black monkey or ape, Snickers, Uncle Ben, and ____ing Negroes. Godfrey Chanetsa, the minister counselor at the Zimbabwe Embassy, has refused to learn Russian since he arrived here in 1991. His argument is simple: The more he learns the language, the easier it is to understand the racial insults. But despite Chanetsa's elementary understanding of Russian, the many verbal insults directed at him and his family when they shop at the market, are all too clear.

Michael Waganda, a Kenyan historian and researcher who has spent nearly 20 years in Russia, argues that neither the State Duma nor law enforcement agencies have done anything to address the racism problem. He still has a jackknife that a group of Russians tried to use on him recently. For him, the end of the Communist era also meant the end of protection for foreigners. A typical comment heard from Russians is: "Have you seen the hostels where blacks or Arabs live? If you haven't, then go to Miklukho Maklaya Ulitsa. They've just brought another group of African beasts who will be taught some manners." Miklukho Maklaya Ulitsa is the name of the street where the Patrice Lumumba Friendship University, now renamed Moscow Friendship University is located.

The university was built by the FSU in the 1960s expressly to train the future technocrats of the newly independent countries in Africa, Asia, and Latin America. Paul Charles Amara, a postgraduate student from Sierra Leone, described how police had arrived at his hostel unannounced, called his friends "banana-eating Africans," and mocked them while one policeman interrogated a female student about her documents. Paul, like many others, has nowhere to lodge a complaint or seek protection.

African refugees are also routinely confronted with racial discrimination. Many have fled political upheavals and ethnic persecution, or were simply seeking better living conditions in Europe. In 1999, there were about 200,000 asylum seekers in Russia; Africans constituted about 15 % of them. Somali Mohammed Tahir, 36, commented that, "when anything happens, from petty thefts to apartment raids, it is of no use to complain to the police. We're always wrong; the police are prejudiced, whatever the facts are."

The popular Russian-African-American television host of the midnight sex program for Russia's NTV channel, Yelena Khanga, wrote that she is irritated when asked about her skin color in the university libraries, airports, and public places.

"It's better when you're asked about your age or country of origin," she said. "You can obviously see the color of someone's skin. Even though people say it doesn't matter to them, it nevertheless interests everyone. Ignorance plays a large role in how Russians perceive the African community," she said. "Unlike other *foreigners* (read Europeans and Americans—addition and emphasis mine), whom Russians favor and treat with awe, African blacks are looked down upon. They don't spare me at all. The police have yet to make the transition to the new approaches required of a civilized democratic society."[132]

Officials in charge never investigate these cases, or accept such attacks, derogatory remarks, and inhuman treatment as racially motivated. Waganda attests to this fact: "Neither the State Duma (parliament) nor the law enforcement agencies have done anything to address the racism problem.[133] Typically for bureaucrats, they always wear a grim face, assigning the blame to ruffians, drunkards, and hooligans.

In one incident, an African student supposedly told his lecturer that there must be too many hooligans and drunkards in Russia. His lecturer had told him, replying to his complaint of constant heckling by racists, that his hecklers were hooligans and drunkards. But according to the student, his hecklers were not only hooligans and drunkards, but also apparently self-respecting citizens.

African students have been unable to form a strong organization to channel their grievances, due to official divide-and-rule tactics.

African diplomats in Moscow, who should speak on behalf of students or try to ensure the safety of their lives and property, find themselves seriously compromised and handicapped. Even before the dawn of glasnost, a few reports slipped into the mainstream media about African diplomats engaging in all types of shady market deals, ranging from currency trafficking to smuggling contraband goods. One case involved a West African diplomat who allegedly used a student as a cover, to smuggle several thousand US Dollars worth of Russian-made caviar into Germany. The student was apprehended in Berlin. The KGB, the Soviet secret police, has uncovered many such deals in the past. This evidently made diplomats powerless before the authorities to raise serious problems affecting African students. Thus when a student was murdered, molested, or victimized by educational authorities, the standard accusation heard from African diplomats was that the student was engaged in shady deals or was drinking or chasing women. They thus parroted charges made by school authorities and the militia.

No proper investigation was demanded from the authorities. Before perestroika Third World students were in a privileged class of their own. They were allowed to travel twice in the academic year to Western Europe, where they bought fashion goods and electronic appliances for sale on the booming Soviet shadow market. They enjoyed a virtual monopoly in this sphere, as Soviet citizens could not travel beyond the Communist community in Eastern Europe. Three pairs of jeans, a stereo, and five sweatshirts were enough to net the student sufficient rubles for comfortable living. He could buy a Soviet-made color television, a refrigerator, and still have extra money left for other luxuries.

But the life of foreign students, especially those brazen enough to flaunt their newly acquired riches, became the object of envy and anger from Soviet youths and an irritation to educational authorities and ideological guardians.[134] Educational authorities persuaded African embassies in Moscow not to pay their students extra allowances. They argued that the Soviet government stipend, 90 rubles ($90 then), sufficed if students lived frugally. In reality, however, the authorities worried that hard cash given by their home governments enabled Third World students to buy the "good things" of the "Wild West" "to spoil" Soviet youths.

Ideological watchers in the Kremlin alerted the KGB to flush out "extravagant" students. Many were expelled or jailed, especially during the brief Andropov anti-corruption campaign in 1983. Attempts were even made to close the Iron Curtain on foreign students too. Visa processing became unnecessarily time-consuming and cumbersome, with various conditions attached.[135] This is not to say that African students are angels either. A good number of them, until recently, smuggled icons, hard currency, and pornography. Many were caught and jailed. It is common knowledge that the KGB was well versed in the shady deals of students and diplomats, but only acted on big-time operators.

The chronic shortages of essential goods in the shops, coupled with the meager students' stipends, compelled nearly all foreign students, including those from the former communist countries, to engage in one deal or another—just to survive. Things became worse after 1989. Trade mafias and racketeers, taking advantage of the current economic crisis, hoarded all basic goods and resold them at cutthroat prices to foreigners.

It was the same at the country's ports of exit and railway stations. Sometimes students had to wait for three or four months before buying tickets home if they could not afford to pay twice the fare or freight. Africans have had much of their luggage rejected for no apparent reason by customs officials at the Moscow Airport. Special airport soldiers met protests by students with brute force.[136]

The End Of The Honeymoon: From Platonic Friendship To Progressive Disengagement

Many Russians, upset and threatened by the apparent economic dislocation in their country, began to find a scapegoat in the Kremlin's African policy. As the media and the apparatchiks continued to attack Soviet policy in Africa, ordinary Russians began to repeat a question the Deputy Director of the Moscow-based Africa Institute, Alexei Vasilyev, had posed in an article in IZVESTIYA, "Why Do We Need Africa?"[137] The major complaint carried by mainstream media with either left or right political trappings, as well as the neo-Communist press, was that scarce Soviet resources were "generously" thrown away in Africa and other parts of the developing world in the frenzied chase for ideological fraternity and spheres of influence during the Cold War era.

One critic said: "We gave to Africa without receiving anything in return." To him, Africa had nothing to offer Russia, so continued relations were unprofitable: "We have nothing to lose by cutting our ties with these backward countries but our chains of implacable aid."[138] In another IZVESTIYA article, "Africans Want to Work With Us But

We Do Not Need the Dark Continent," the author sums up these sentiments thus: "Enough is enough. After all, we saved them from starvation, we healed them, educated their military officers, bureaucrats, doctors, engineers and agronomists.[139]

In the late fifties and sixties, the USSR projected itself as a magnanimous do-gooder and godfather for newly liberated countries in the developing world. It offered liberal scholarships to thousands of Third World youths to enroll for higher education in Soviet universities and colleges. Soviet propaganda proclaimed that the USSR was offering humanitarian and "fraternal" assistance to eliminate the dire consequences of colonial rule, and save the peoples of the newly liberated countries from neo-colonialism. In reality, however the Soviet Union was busily recruiting future Communists. The Patrice Lumumba Friendship University in Moscow was built for the express purpose of training Third World technocrats, but the Kremlin knew it was also possible to groom there the future agents of socialism.

A West African journalism student once wrote in Leningrad's SMENA newspaper that he had arrived in the Soviet Union with a rather naive conception of Soviet people and their society. As an aspiring Marxist-Leninist, he had "swallowed every nice thing" [he] ever heard about the "friendly and compassionate Soviet people, their flourishing culture and their progressive, racism-free country." He said that back home in Africa, he had rejected off-hand any allusions to racism or xenophobia in the USSR as Western-orchestrated anti-Communist propaganda.[140] However, it did not take long for his illusions to be totally destroyed.

"During my early days, when I had yet to understand the Russian language, I mistook the invectives and catcalls shouted at me in the trams and other public transport as 'slogans of solidarity' in support of the oppressed peoples of South Africa, since in most cases their gestures were accompanied by a raised fist, something that looked like the victory salute of the ANC." However, soon it dawned on him that, "[he] was an object of ridicule and racial slurs, and not that of sympathy."[141]

In the heady years of revolutionary messianism, when Soviet propaganda told Russians they were performing a humanitarian duty by extending assistance to Africans in their just struggle against neo-colonialism and imperialism, solidarity slogans could indeed be heard from ordinary Russians.[142] The first batch of African students met cheers and slogans of solidarity on the streets of Moscow. The initial reaction of Soviets to what Leningrad University lecturer Valentine

Vydrin termed "the Black wave" was benevolent amazement.[143] A West African Minister of State, himself a former student in the USSR in the mid-1960s said elderly women who had read Harriet Beecham Stowe's UNCLE TOM'S CABIN openly wept when they first saw Black students in Moscow's streetcars and subways.[144]

That is no longer the case. The collapse of Communism changed the slogans of solidarity to cries of disenchantment; the cheers have changed to jeers at African "parasites" as living conditions deteriorate. A Ghanaian mining student in St Petersburg related an incident that took place in 1991, when he was physically prevented by an old woman from picking up a loaf of bread in a grocery store. He was standing behind the woman in a bread line. After she picked her own bread, she stood in front of the student with outstretched arms, preventing him from picking up his loaf of bread. At the same time she beckoned her compatriots standing behind the Ghanaian to move past him and take the bread.

Before glasnost, hatred for colored people was suppressed by the totalitarian system. The mass media were instructed to educate the masses that racism or ethnic hatred had dissolved as part of the "new socialist consciousness;" that only in the nespravdiliviy, dikiiy zapad ("unjust, wild West") black people were lynched.[145] To show the superiority of socialism over capitalism, Soviet television was saturated with images of homeless, unemployed Blacks lining up at soup kitchens or the dole in London or Washington. Meanwhile, the numerous cases of racially motivated attacks and murders of Africans in the FSU went unreported.

The tone of media reports about the plight of Africans at home and in the Diaspora expressed sympathy and solidarity. Deliberate efforts were made to solicit the mercy, good will, and support of the Soviet citizenry for the "defenseless victims of capitalist injustice" and "neo-colonial plunder."[146] But the truth was that it was not the miserable living conditions of Africans and people of African descent that concerned Soviet politicians and journalists. Their more important concern was scoring points in the East-West ideological confrontation during the Cold War.

Ironically, in the FSU's South-Central Asian and Caucasus regions, populated by non-white peoples or *Sovietskie negri* (Soviet Negroes) as Russians called them derogatively, the boomerang effect of the "mercy-soliciting" propaganda on behalf of Africans had a devastating effect. Anti-Black sentiments are stronger here than in the rest of the country. Armenians, Azeris, and Georgians, themselves looked down upon as "second-rate citizens", vent their spleen on Blacks to soothe their own feelings of inferiority. Their society has grown highly racist, in spite of 70-odd years of Communist rhetoric about racial harmony.[147] Black students in these republics have been sneered at, called names, abused, attacked, and even murdered on racial grounds. Following requests by Black students, African embassies prevailed upon the Russian educational authorities not to send their students to some of these former Soviet republics.

Among Russians the boomerang effect of Communist propaganda resulted in an aping of Western racists. With Soviet-style Communism discredited, many Russians have come to regard anything which Communist education taught them as lies or half-truths. Strange as it may sound, the new logic is: "If there is racism in the West, then racism is not as bad as Communist educators would want us to believe." Imitating Western examples is common today in an apparent effort to overcome a feeling that Russians are "second-rate" whites. Public ridicule of Africans by young and old alike serves not only as psychological relief, but also as an attempt to bolster their self-esteem.

After "Red" Racism, Back To "Basic Instincts"

Before Gorbachev, ideological and propaganda guardians rationalized racial discrimination meted out by Soviet citizens against African students as "vestiges of capitalism." When I interviewed the Chairman of the Leningrad City Council in charge of foreign nationals in 1984, he said, replying to African students' charges that Russians had hurled invectives at them, to disregard "the hooligans," whose behavior was one of "the vestiges of bourgeois thinking," and that the Communist Party was doing everything to wipe them out. According to him, the majority of Soviet people were imbued with "humanism, the respect for all races," ideals which the state ideology has imparted to everyone.[148]

The collapse of the ideology of "socialist internationalism" in the wake of ex-President Gorbachev's perestroika and glasnost reforms has led to the revival of nationalism, anti-Semitism, racism and extreme chauvinism all over the CIS. Consequently, there is intense mutual hatred among the ex-Soviet citizenry itself and resultant inter-ethnic clashes. The demise of Communism following the botched coup in 1991 added fuel to nationalistic passions.

There is a growing fear among Africans about the merging motley Fascist groups, notably the *Pamyat* (Memory), which make no bones about their commitment to "cleanse" Russia of Jews and other "bad-breeds." None of the early killings were directly linked to these groups, but Africans feel the upsurge of anti-black sentiments among a section of Russian youths may be blamed on the xenophobic propaganda launched by *Pamyat* and other groups and openly supported by the mainstream media, including former Communist Party publications like NASH SOVREMENNIK, SOVIETSKAYA ROSSIYA, MOLODAYA GVARDIYA, etc.[149] The number of new racist publications, according to one report, is about 150 with circulation throughout the FSU.[150] The daily MOSCOW KOMSOMOLETS, a carry-over from the Communist era, is one of the most virulently racist and anti-black. SPEED INFO, a Russian-language weekly and a model of post-perestroika yellow journalism, popular among ordinary Russians, has turned the Black man into an object of fun, in most cases, ridiculing his sexual behavior.[151]

Anti-black and other racist sentiments have long existed in the FSU. They were only suppressed by sporadic authoritarian measures. In fact, it was the Communist system itself that nurtured and propagated racist prejudice and hatred. Officials often hid behind such high-sounding slogans, as "Socialism and racism are incompatible" and pretended nothing was happening. But they actually allowed racism to find its own level in the society. What worsens the situation is the hypocrisy adopted by Russia's new leaders. They lead a national hate campaign against Africans, and then turn around to play the ostrich. Russian newspaper reports after the shooting death of the Zimbabwean student mentioned above, (the first murder case involving an African that merited any coverage by the mainstream media), [152] tended to question the existence of racism in Russia at all.

Newspaper titles like "Is There Racism in Russia?" [153] and "In Russia Too a White kills a Black,"[154] is nothing short of hypocrisy and arrant callousness. The day after the slaying, the popular daily MOSKOVSKY KOMSOMOLETS wrote that Patrice Lumumba University must be the ideal center for foreign language studies, as black monkeys have proved to learn Russian within months after their arrival from the African rain forest. It went on to say their tails had been chopped off at Sheremetyevo, and that medical doctors found these tails disease-ridden when the Africans were examined during quarantine.[155]

In early 1992, the first American-type television talk show in Russia, *TEMA* (Topic) had as its agenda racism in Russia. The program not only didn't show that people are now bold enough to openly vent their suppressed racist and anti-black sentiments; it also ignored the fact that Russia has become a country of racial intolerance. Let's hear what some of the participants said:

Journalist: Let's imagine your daughter comes home one day with a black person and says: "Daddy, meet my suitor"?

Man: This can't happen because she is a sensible girl... white!

Man: It's better for each person to live in his territory. I was in the US, and I saw the dirty, smelly, horrible black ghettos. In the nights they misbehave. Whites hide. I conversed with some. Excuse me for saying it, but their smell is different.

Journalist: But we are also different?

Man: We are. We are white!

Student: When two cultures intermix it leads to cultural miscegenation. The end result is negative.

Journalist: Let's suppose that in 10-15 years, the president of our country is a black person?

Man: I would never allow that to happen.

Journalist: Let's assume it did happen?

Man: Then I would migrate to South Africa.

Journalist: Why to South Africa?

Man: Because there it's possible to fight them.

Journalist: What of our country?

Man: We are soft. We are a soft nation...Russians!

Young Worker: Africans have no spiritual values, to which Russians must aspire.

These Russians did not acquire their racist and even Fascist views overnight. They harbored and nurtured them long ago. Like anti-

Semitism, racism has always existed in Russia in the form of pogroms against the Jews in tsarist times and the uprooting of ethnic minority groups like the Tartars under Stalin. It only underwent some form of mutation and took on a new coloring, becoming "red" racism during the communist era. With Soviet-style Communism gone, it has acquired new

Features—"red-brown"—as the new Russian neo-Fascist and national chauvinist alliance is called.

Glasnost-Era Confession And Self-Criticism

The extinction of Communism in Russia and Eastern Europe led to the appearance of extreme right-wing ideologies. Nationalistic, anti-Semitic, and even Fascist ideas hitherto suppressed by the authoritarian system are re-emerging. Their influence on both society and in the press is growing. In the FSU, the ideas of the national chauvinists and Fascists have been aired in mass media and in parliament.[156] They consistently fault the FSU's policies in the Third World in general and in Africa in particular. In several articles in the mainstream press, conservative politicians and journalists (on the left-right political and ideological spectrum) have found a scapegoat in the Kremlin's Africa policy.

For example, a member of the Russian Parliament complained in the newspaper LITERATOR that the former Communist leadership "wasted precious Soviet resources on peoples who have only begun to call themselves a people, who have just descended from the palm trees, and have only managed to pronounce the word 'socialism.'"[157] Of course the current mood could easily be explained away as a result of the economic crisis in the FSU, but there are deeper currents running far below the surface of economic distress and the resultant scapegoating. We may have to dig deeper to find the real causes.

For instance, what explains the Soviet/Russian media's propensity, during the Cold War era, to paint a picture of Africans as *bednie rodstvinki*, "poor cousins" exploited and subjugated by the imperialist and neo-colonialist west whom a magnanimous and compassionate USSR must salvage? What lies behind the Soviet/Russian version of the "White Man's burden"?   The media's portrayal of Africa as Communism's   burden   was   informed   more   by   ethnocentric, paternalistic, and even racist urges than by a Marxist-Leninist ideological inclination.

Even during the Cold War, the Soviet media were saturated with negative images of Africa. Those from the continent predominantly reflected the seamy side of African life. The blame for Africa's otsalost' ("backwardness") was, as a rule, placed squarely on Western imperialist and neo-colonialist plunder. Where something positive was shown, it was almost always to show the "positive" and modernizing effects of the Soviet "civilizing mission," such as the construction of Soviet-assisted projects in a "socialist-oriented" country.

During the pre-glasnost years, whenever the Soviet media painted a picture of a continent in permanent crisis, it was done to show the negative influence of the Western presence in Africa. Africans were often depicted as "innocent" victims of Western capitalist exploitation and imperialist "blackmail," who needed the express and "selfless" assistance of the "socialist-internationalist" Soviet Union. The USSR, it was proclaimed, has always been on the side of the oppressed nations, giving moral and material aid to the national liberation movements.[158] Yet despite several decades of Marxist-Leninist internationalist education based on racial harmony and the brotherhood of humanity, many Russians harbor racial antipathy against Africans.

In his article "About the Black Color without exaggeration,"[159] Asoyan recounted numerous incidents involving African students in the Soviet Union. He illustrated the abiding, antiquated stereotypes the average Soviet holds about Africans, their race, skin color and geographical origin. He writes:

> "In our age of cosmic means of information transmission, and moreover, when we have a correspondent in every African country, when we lead many countries in the volume of books and films about Africa, our internationalist education has practically not done away with our racist stereotypes.[160]

Asoyan blames the mass media for weaving a web of stereotypes around Africans. The mass media, even under perestroika and glasnost, he charges, continue to portray Africa as no more than an "exotic, undeveloped continent, which is struggling with superhuman strength against the forces of neo-colonialism, with our help." Asoyan contends that, "Under the conditions of our difficult existence, this generates anger and indignation" from the Soviet citizenry, who see Africans as lazy hangers-on, Asoyan contends.[161] Asoyan is a long-time Soviet journalist specializing in Africa and Russia's ambassador in Botswana. A physician complained to him, "It turns out that we continue to help build their countries, teach and clothe them. What compensation shall we get from them?"[162]

Asoyan attributes Soviet anti-African prejudice and dislike to "low levels of culture and a deficit of truthful information about the people of other nations."[163] The result is a clash of reality with distorted and idealistic views of Africa.

"Africans, after all, are not what we took them for—with all their drawbacks and stereotyped manners."[164] This also reflects our traditional relationship with foreigners. For those who are ahead of us, we use one yardstick; for those who are poor, another yardstick.[165]

In another article, "Red and Black," a Russian journalist agrees with the assertion that Russia is a country of racists. She recalls several incidents in Moscow when her compatriots cast aspersions on Africans simply because of their skin color. She recalls one such incident.

> " Recently, I saw in the metro a woman with her five-year old child. The kid was crying. The woman was trying to calm him down. Then she set eyes on "a dark-skinned uncle." Pointing at the African at the other end of the train, she told the child: 'You see, if you continue to cry this Black man will take you away.'"[166]

She went on:

> Several such scenes add some distractions to our lives. But behind the jokes and laughter, we think and forget that "the Black uncle" is by no means the cardboard placard depicting the typical [personalities/races], the chocolate-white-yellow trio. They [Africans, the subjects of the jokes and laughter] also think about us. Their opinion about us is: "The USSR is a country of racists."[167]

These examples are not of particular importance in themselves, but they indicate "an index of widespread familiarity with," if not acceptance of, the images of Africans they convey.[168] It does become disturbing to find this kind of image showing up in the media's handling of current events concerning Africans. As a result, elements of a cultural legacy that are "at best ethnocentric and at worst racist" come to influence reactions to and interpretations of events in Africa.[169]

Hartman and Husband pointed out that such a tendency emerges most clearly in newspaper-headlines and in editorial cartoons, "where the use of phrases or images will evoke a similar set of associations and meanings in virtually all members of the society to whom they are directed. Such usage makes it possible for a complex point to be crystallized unambiguously and memorably in a few words or a single picture." [170] For a long time Russian journalists have used the expression "the Dark Continent" to describe Africa. In fact, hardly any article is written about Africa without the use of this favorite term.

Journalists accompanying former Soviet Foreign Affairs Minister Eduard Shevardnadze during his first visit to Africa, filed reports without accompanying pictures. Moscow's Central TV coverage did not include a single shot of visits, which took him to countries like Nigeria, Angola and Namibia. Instead of photographs, a blank map of Africa appeared on the screen, as though to reaffirm the familiar picture of a "backward" Africa exemplified by sunshine and crocodiles. Pictures would have shown the Foreign Minister being welcomed at modern airports by African officials in limousines or attending state banquets in high-rise buildings which match or even exceed similar ones in Soviet cities in modernity and architectural beauty.[171]

"After All, We're Racists...."

Coverage of African news by the Russian mass media, like that of their western counterparts, has included more than its share of negativity, neglect and omission. Glasnost-era self-critical articles have thrown light on the sloppy and stereotypical character of Soviet journalism dealing with Africa. In the first article that appeared in the MOSCOW NEWS in 1986, Russian specialist on Africa A. B. Davidson noted: "Our journalists, more often than not, presented a one-sided picture of Africa. According to them, once Africa throws off the chains of colonialism, then everything will be fine. And should they decide on building socialism then all problems will be well nigh automatically solved.[172]

> "We know about the Flemings, the Welsh. The Scots number
> five million. We know about their epics, music, and their dress.
> Very few [Soviet] people know what ethnic groups live in
> Nigeria, a great African power with a population of nearly 100
> million.[173]

The second article, in LITERATURNAYA GAZETA, states that for most Soviet writers and journalists writing about Africa "is as easy now as it was 25 years ago." A common recipe exists for them.

> Mix a little bit of exoticism with the struggle against
> imperialism; add a few fine words by any African in praise of
> socialist countries, and presto! an article is ready.
> For those who have never visited Africa, there was a different
> recipe: "Describe the stormy continent from your Moscow
> office. Cut to the required size an article from a Western
> newspaper. Dilute the texture of a more successful article
> written by your compatriot. Add a quote from a mythical dark-
> skinned friend, and an article is born."[174]

The author adds,

> " To the overwhelming majority of Soviet journalists and
> writers, Africa today is still the Africa of the pre- independence
> era: the same myth-ridden, exotic Africa, with its awesome
> jungles populated by prowling, man-eating lions and
> crocodiles.[175]

Self-criticism by glasnost- and post-glasnost-era journalists does not
mean improved coverage of Africa. What has changed, though, is the
old Communist-style ideological "packaging" of the news. Some
Soviet commentators have faulted Stalinism and its latter-day
manifestation—neo-Stalinism or Brezhnevism—as the cause of the
poor Soviet coverage of Africa in the pre-glasnost years.[176] Nothing
can be further from the truth. The root of the problem lies elsewhere: in
the culture. Neither Stalinist nor Marxist-Leninist ideology can be
blamed for the stereotypical and one-dimensional presentation of the
African reality.

News from Africa came to be interpreted within the "old" familiar
framework, or in terms of the existing images, stereotypes and
expectations of the pre-revolutionary and pre-glasnost years. The
framework and expectations either, originated in Russian culture or in
the news, and passed from there into the culture. This situation creates
a "continuous interplay between events, cultural meanings and news
framework," despite the radical changes in ideological orientation and
expectations in Russia.[177]

The More Glasnost, The More "Glossovernost" Of Africa

The poor coverage given Mandela's release mentioned earlier was
not an isolated case; it exemplifies a common trend in glasnost-style
and post Cold-war era journalism in the FSU. This was evident in my
1991 survey of some FSU publications.[178] The survey showed that

marginalization of Africa during the glasnost and post-Gorbachev years had reached grotesque proportions. Perestroika and glasnost in international news coverage applied only to Europe, North America and some parts of Asia. In addition, the survey revealed that marginalization of Africa increased with the pace of glasnost.[179] The main stereotypes employed by Soviet journalists to describe issues involving Africans in the world context underwent drastic changes.

In 1985, Africa's problems were attributed to factors such as "birthmarks of capitalism", "imperialist intrigues", "hostile bourgeois propaganda", "U.S. expansionist policies", "a plot against Africa" and similar concepts. In 1990, these stereotypes disappeared from the lexicon of Soviet journalists. Terms like "solidarity", "disinterested aid", "proletarian internationalism", and "socialist fraternity," still employed in 1987 to describe Soviet-African relations understandably disappeared in later years.[180]

In their place, such new terms as "universal human values", "global cooperation", "deideologization of inter-state relations" came to be used. Yet another remarkable change during the period under review was the gradual toning down of paternalism in Russian writing on Africa. In addition, the "Soviet socialist experience" is no longer recommended as a recipe for good governance in Africa. It was clear from the survey[181] that the Soviet/Russian press' loss of interest in Africa coincided with the Kremlin's progressive disengagement from the continent. Not-surprisingly, this was also the period of East-West rapprochement and the eventual end of the Cold War. Ironically, however, the further the Soviet/Russian press trudged on the road to full-blown democracy, the less interest it showed in Africa.

All this is logical if one considers it from the point of view of the Gorbachev reforms inaugurated in Spring, 1985 to "give socialism a human face," which turned out to be an anti-Communist revolution. As the Soviet state-ideology fell apart under the "new-thinking" ideology, Soviet journalists, like the rest of the intelligentsia, appeared to grope for a different vision of the globe. Thus the old image of Africans had to be recast to suit the "non-ideological" new Russian vision.

Coverage of Africa now does no more than merely catalogue ad infinitum, the familiar banes and woes of the continent; the world's highest infant mortality and adult morbidity rates, the lowest life expectancy, the threats of a population explosion, AIDS, and famine. While past reports would surely have been spiced with accusations of western complicity or international finance capital pillage, recent reports do not look for external culprits.[182] Most articles now blame

Africans themselves. For instance, in the PRAVDA article "We are Africans in a European Home",[183] the author writes that Africans wasted the "solid" amount of Western credit through bad management and corruption, and that tiny Belgium produces more goods than the whole of Africa put together. Characteristically, other objective factors are glossed over –like the lopsided international economic order, skewed against most developing countries, or Belgian farmers receiving more than African farmers for the same amount of work.

But the new marginalization also has something to do with the new Eurocentrism engendered by Gorbachev's so-called "new-thinking." (Africa, of course, has always been marginalized and trivialized by the Soviet media.) "New thinking," which claims to root in "universal human values" has turned out to be rabid Eurocentrism and even racism for the political bureaucracy and the "new" media.[184] For journalists and politicians, "new thinking" and "universal human values" do not extend beyond the "Common European Home" and North America. (See Chapter Three for a more detailed analysis of Africa's marginalization by the Soviet/Russia media.)

Chapter Three
Africa In The Eyes Of The Northern Press: A Content Analysis Of Selected Russian And Western Publications

The African News Scene: The Positive Versus The Negative

Before proceeding with a survey of the press in the next chapter, it is expedient to look briefly at Africa's news "landscape" *vis-a`-vis* the "politics of news selection," and the North-South conceptual divide over what constitutes news about developing countries. During his nine-day tour of the continent in 1999, the first by a US President in 20 years, Bill Clinton declared that Africa must be seen "with a new eye." Clinton's message aimed at his home audience and perhaps the Western media is a classical example of agenda setting. But will this work for Africa? Will Clinton's clarion call sound the death knell of the marginalization and stereotyping of Africans and their continent?

President Clinton also made two other historic statements. He apologized for American proxy wars and interference in Africa during the Cold War, and declared that the slave trade was wrong. That these monumental statements hardly made it to headlines of the mainstream media in the Euro-American world is not surprising. It is even less surprising that news about the president's alleged philandering was rated higher than the historic statements he made on the iniquities of the trade and the use of Africans as pawns in the East-West ideological warfare during the Cold War era. It is also not surprising that the president's safari in a Botswana game reserve drew more media interest than all the statements mentioned above. Old habits indeed die hard. Old eyes see what old eyes want to see in Africa. Today the most primitive forms of the stereotypes of the "darkest" and "unknown" Africa are broken in the minds of Westerners, thanks to Africa's entrance into the world political arena after African countries gained independence from the colonial powers. However, Africa is still interpreted through the color-sensitive eyes of Western reporters. Although they have revised and refined the old image of savagery and heathenism to some extent, they have maintained the original "African story" as told by the early explorers, colonial masters and missionaries. According to this story, the African, like the grown infant or perpetual child has always needed European salvation and tutelage. The purpose of the original story was to prepare the minds of European citizens at home and to pave the way for the slave trade, colonization, partition and repartition of Africa. For how could the ruling elite in Europe explain the evil trilogy of their activities in Africa—enslavement, proselytizing, and the undemocratic practice of foreign domination—to their subjects at home, except to dehumanize and present Africans less than humans, heathenish, and unfit to rule themselves?

The current preoccupation of the western media with negative occurrences, which excludes news of African achievements, suggests the media are in line with the old story line. Like the old missionaries and colonialist, the Western media consciously and unconsciously, covertly and overtly emphasize the message that Africans cannot govern themselves; that the continent "is still stuck in its primitive, bloodthirsty past;" that nations have wasted the "golden opportunity" to build civilized statehood after attaining political independence.

Kwame Nkrumah offers a penetrating analysis of this position in HANDBOOK OF REVOLUTIONARY WARFARE.[1] After being forced to grant political independence to African countries after centuries of exploitation, the colonial masters were unwilling to cut their umbilical cords from the former colonies. To ensure that the old relationship remained intact, they established the myth with the help of the mass media of an affluent capitalist world promising abundance and prosperity for all. The aim, however, was the establishment of a "welfare state as the only safeguard against the threat of Communism."[2]

The mass media, private and government, were employed in the propaganda war. Massive brainwashing occurs through broadcasting stations like the BBC (British Broadcasting Corporation), Voice of Germany, Voice of America, and recently various satellite-hooked television stations like CNN (Cable News Network).

> This war of words and images is supplemented by written propaganda, embassy bulletins, and newspapers distributed by so-called independent and liberal publishers. The war of words penetrates into every town and village, and into the remotest parts of the "bush." It spreads in the form of freely distributed

propaganda films praising the qualities of Western civilization and culture.[3]

Thus, hegemony over truth and knowledge replaces troops and guns finally as the relevant tool of re-colonization. In this way the "psychological terrain" is prepared and the whole continent "is besieged without a single marine in sight."[4]

According to Nkrumah, "the most pernicious aspect of this psychological warfare" is the campaign to convince Africans and Western public opinion that Africans cannot govern themselves; that they are unworthy of real independence; and that foreign rule is the only cure for their wild, war-like and primitive way of life. Imperialism has done its utmost to brainwash Africans into thinking that they need the straightjacket of colonialism if they are to be saved from their retrogressive instincts. Such is the age-old racist justification for the economic exploitation of our continent. Now the recent military coups engineered by foreign reactionaries are also being used to corroborate imperialism's pet theory that Africans have shamelessly squandered the "golden opportunities" of independence, and that they have plunged their political kingdoms into blood and barbarism.[5]

Nkrumah continues: "Therefore, the imperialist mission: we must save them anew; the press, films and radio are fast spreading the myth of post-independence violence and chaos. Everywhere, the more or less covert implication is: Africa needs to be re-colonized. The fact that Africa has advanced politically more quickly than any continent of the world is ignored."[6]

Russian expert on Africa Evgeni Tarabrin expressed this fact a bit differently. He stated:

> "Imperialism's chief strategic objective is to draw the newly free countries into its political orbit, thus binding them to the world capitalist economy. Imperialism sees the attainment of this goal as an opportunity to secure its continued untrammeled exploitation of the developing countries, to establish and strengthen control over all spheres of their social, political and economic life, to weaken at their expense the world capitalism's crisis, and erode the acute economic contradictions between the developed capitalist states and the less developed newly free countries."[7]

But Tarabrin ignores the motivation behind the USSR's own penetration into Africa. My analysis has shown that the motives and strategies of the Kremlin in Africa were no different from those of

Western imperialists and neo-colonialists. Although, the USSR did not partake of the scramble for and partitioning of Africa in earlier centuries, it sought to gain what it had missed during the post-colonial ideological effort to re-partition Africa. While the Western media were busy presenting the western way of life as a model for their former colonies, the Soviet media were preoccupied with showing Africans the socialist alternative as the best way out of the "imperialist and neo-colonial trap."

The same imperialist methods and propaganda tools described by Nkrumah were employed by the Russians to capture the minds and souls of Africans, and to manipulate public opinion at home. This propaganda would assign legitimacy for their actions in Africa. The Russian media's message might have been different, but the result was the same. While the Western media's message aimed at re-colonization and continued dependency, the Russian media targeted wooing Africans away from Western dependency and into the Soviet orbit. Thus, the emergence of the USSR as a world power added a new dimension to the original African story. The media now had to add the cold war angle to make it complete. Thus the emphasis on alien values and the desire to see every African issue through the prism of the cold war ideological divide became the vogue of Western and Soviet reporting of African events in the Cold War years.

An African leader commented eloquently on this subject:

> "In the majority of cases, the world press is served by foreign journalists who pay short visits to the various parts of Africa, and on whom the world's verdict over Africa may rest. The news agencies are often relying on such journalists or reporters, who may not themselves know enough or physically be able to cover the area assigned to them to be able to interpret the African scene. The result is news coming out of Africa is often, if not always, related to an already biased and prejudiced mind that keeps asking such questions, as 'is this pro-East or pro-West?' Very few, if any, of the world's press organizations ask such logical and simple question as—'is this pro-African'?[8]

In the light of these developments, and realizing that the media are the most potent agents in building their emergent states, African governments, having wrestled independence from their colonial masters, began to create their own mass media infrastructure, to combat the biased reporting on their various countries. However, before they could establish their respective national media infrastructures, it became clear that the powerful world media dominated the information business so totally that little, if any, change could occur in the status quo. Five wire services controlled all news: Agence France Press (AFP), the Associated Press (AP), United Press International (UPI), Reuters, and TASS (*Telegrafnoe Agenstvo Sovietskaya Soyuza*).

The call for a new international economic and communication order begun by the group of 77 (now over 100) in the early sixties and championed by the United Nations through the seventies and eighties was meant to address this imbalance. Together with the struggle to fashion a new international communication order to replace the North-dominated, uni-directional—North-South—flow of information, African and other Third World theoreticians developed a new theory of the press. Hence, to counter the various concepts in the North, they created a novel concept of what constitutes news. This is called the development press theory.

This model advocates positive functions for the news media to further national development. Journalists, unlike their colleagues under the Western model, who are assigned the role of government watchdogs, must be partners with the government in progress. It is not within the purview of this study to expand on these theories. It suffices here to mention that Western mass communication scholars have identified five main press theories beside the development theory. These are: 1) The Authoritarian, 2) Libertarian, 3) Social Responsibility, 4) The Soviet, and 5) democratic/participant.

Like the debate over the New International Information and Communication Order (NIICO), this hybrid of theories has given rise to the on-going controversy over what constitutes "which news is fit to print." The controversy has revolved around fairness and balance in the international flow of news. As noted above, there is so much lack of balance and reciprocity of news flow worldwide. The controversy concerns not only the quantity of news flow; it also concerns fairness of content and "objectivity," or what is called the "topicality approach to news," or the "commonsense" means of categorizing news according to what it reflects—economics, energy, housing, national or international news, and so forth. The debate further concerns what the news means, its location, or the environment of a story.

Edelstein and co. captured the essence of this controversy when they wrote: "The quality of news will continue to be in the eye of the beholder."[9] This also captures the essence of the multi-cultural theory of news. Schudson and Schoenbach defined this cultural hypothesis of news in very concise terms. They saw news as a reflection of patterns of development and national character. Members of productive societies expected achievement, and failure was news, but in societies that experienced failure, achievement was news, failure was "olds."[10]

The Third World angle of this debate news was conceptualized as "little good news" by the dominant world press. They criticize the Northern media's propensity to report and dramatize bad rather than good news and their preoccupation with the coup-drought-famine syndrome in the South. Some Western scholars have sought to dismiss these Third World charges, saying that few stories in any country were explicitly negative or positive. Stevenson referred to an earlier study (Stevenson and Green, 1980), which concluded that most of what people saw as bias in the news was a function of the expectations they brought to it.[11]

This argument simply avoids the core of the problem, i.e. balance and fairness. Is the African or Third World reality a one-dimensional story of failure and perpetual chaos? And even if that were so, what are the roots of the problems? Are Africans mere passive bystanders in the midst of a chaos they themselves have created? A look at the national dailies of any country shows two scenes: the negative and the positive; chaos, destruction, and reconstruction, or at least efforts at rebuilding. So the question is: are Africans doing anything at all to improve their lot? Even a cursory glance at many African newspapers will show that Africa is not all chaos and helplessness, famine, and civil wars; that side by side with seemingly intractable problems, Africans are also trying hard under very difficult conditions to overcome at least some of their problems. They alone have not created these problems, and their solutions sometimes lie beyond the continent.

It is not that the media in the North do not see this aspect of the African reality; they simply do not want to see it. While media gatekeepers in the North are color-blind when it comes to selecting printable bad news about Africa, they are color-sensitive when it comes to good news. As I argued earlier, this goes beyond the realms of ideology and politics, although the two could be employed as yardsticks for news selectivity. The logic is not merely the propensity of the Western media to prefer "man-bite-dog" to "dog-bite-man" stories. Were it so, the ex-Soviet Marxist-Leninist press would publish entirely different stories about Africa than the Western press.

International News: Objectivity Verses Hegemony

Anglo-American journalistic theory and practice are predicated upon objectivity. However, media objectivity is non-existent. Objectivity in the media, as in real life, belongs in the graveyard. Only in the graveyard, where the dead cannot see, hear, and read, can one perhaps hope to find objectivity. Objectivity will continue to elude us as long as we breathe the culturally and ideologically polluted air of society.

The impossibility of media objectivity has been confirmed by a series of studies that date from the inception of communication research. Prominent in this seminal research are the newsroom and gatekeeper studies of Warren Breed, Edward Epstein, Herbert Gans, Leon Sigal, Gaye Tuchman, and David White.[12]

More recently, cultural/critical studies have given a hegemonic twist to the study of media objectivity. They emphasize examining media messages within the framework of ideological mobilization for public support in maintaining the values or policies of the status quo. According to this perspective, ideological mobilization happens when the news frame for presenting events gives one dominant or primary meaning or another.[13] Similarly, Hall has contended that particular news accounts may be ideological, "not because of the manifest bias or distortion of their surface contents, but because they were transformations based on a limited ideological matrix."[14]

For example, the cold war news frame organized virtually all foreign affairs coverage into a coherent ideological picture supporting American hegemony and the Soviet challenge to this hegemony. Hallin points out that cold war ideology is produced through a primarily "unconscious" process, employed by journalists not so much to make a political point as to "package" the representation of news in terms they assume the audience will find interesting and easy to understand.[15]

Although, Western journalists particularly insist that they exclude personal values in reporting, Gans posits that value-free reporting is impossible.[16] He contends that some "enduring values"—ethnocentrism, altruistic democracy, responsible capitalism, social order, small town pastoralism, among others—are "unconsciously" built into news judgment.[17] Similarly, McQuail proposes several possible appearances of bias in otherwise straight news reporting. Such bias includes explicit argument and compilation of evidence tilting in favor of one point of view; a tendentious use of facts and comments without any explicit statement of preference; language that makes a factual report implicitly value-loaded; and the omission of points favoring one side.[18]

News is socially constructed. What constitutes positive news, for instance, is actively filtered through mental templates that have long been made up and conditioned through repeated socialization. Thus the act of newsgathering and dissemination is not an innocent or neutral enterprise; it is also a social construct. What is more, far from being detached observers, the media actively construct social reality. Through newsgathering techniques, such as news presentation headlines, front-paging of news stories, and advertisement-news hole juxtaposition, journalists create the social world of their readers. The Mcbride Report puts it more succinctly: "...the act of selecting certain items for publication while rejecting others produces in the mind of the audience a picture of the world that may well be incomplete or distorted."[19]

Another aspect of newsgathering and dissemination is what Chomsky and Herman described as manufacturing consent about the status quo.[20] Newsgathering involves selecting codes that assign shared meanings to events in an attempt to create consensus. Transmitting or gaining information constitutes a portrayal and reinforcement of a particular view of the world. "What is arrayed before the reader is not pure information, but a portrayal of the contending forces in the world."[21] Essentially, the worldview portrayed and reinforced belongs to the ruling elite.

As "the principal means and channels for the production and distribution of culture," the mass media help "an alliance of the ruling class factions" maintain hegemony over society.[22] Yet this alliance is complex and in flux.[23] The entire process of "manufacturing consent," which involves subtle and refined means of coercion and persuasion, is broadly known as hegemony. The hegemony theory posits that media content is influenced by the ruling elite—cultural, ideological, political, military and economic—functioning to create public consent. For hegemony to be successful, it must be flexible and adaptable. Unlike the classical Marxist view of absolute control of ideological and cultural discourse, the Neo-Marxist hegemony theory posits more flexible, fluid, ongoing control and contest between superordinate and subordinate groups—between the rulers and the ruled.

In the end, though, the ruling elite controls media messages. They do so very successfully by being adaptable to the moods of both changing times and the temperament of the ruled. Through such flexibility the ruling elite acquires the oxygen needed to maintain its legitimacy. One may suggest that one of the several factors that accounted for the collapse of Soviet-style Communism was the inflexibility and non-responsiveness of its elite discourse. Lacking the much-needed oxygen from the subordinate classes in the form of participatory discourse, the system ossified and broke. It is understandable that the elite controls media messages in search of an enduring basis for legitimate authority.[24] Gitlin suggests that hegemony is a ruling class's domination of subordinate classes through the elaboration and penetration of ideology into their common sense and everyday practices."[25]

According to Hallin, the concept of hegemony plays a dual role in the study of the media. First, it is used to "conceptualize the political function of the media."[26] The media play the role of maintaining and servicing the dominant ideology: they glorify it, explain the world in its terms, and at the same time modify it to adapt to the demands of legitimation in a changing world.[27] At the same time, the concept of hegemony is employed to "explain the behavior of the media, the process of news production itself."[28] Hallin proposes that the media themselves are subject to the hegemonic process. The dominant ideology shapes and conditions the production of news. That is why the media can be expected to function as agents of legitimation, despite the fact that they are independent of direct political control.

Western media owners and party-appointed editors in the FSU have a vested interest in maintaining and servicing the status quo, since they belong to the power structures of their systems. The economic-ideological elite in the West and the ideological-cultural (and indirectly economic) elite in the FSU may hold different opinions on some issues, but maintain consensus after all. Consensus stems from the overriding interest in ensuring that the status quo remains; hence the unwillingness of the media elite and their brethren in the political and corporate realms to "rock the state boat" too much. Thus, although the media will criticize the status quo, establishing their own legitimacy as news organizations, the criticism will never be structural—against something that seriously threatens or changes it.[30]

The media-ruling elite alliance is even more manifest when it comes to foreign policy and international relations. Hallin argues that even in periods when the media do not support the foreign policy elite, they feel disinclined to support any attempts to challenge the establishment. In the context of foreign affairs coverage, the mass media contribute to maintaining consent for national systems of power, thus playing its role in the hegemony game. Elite ideology shapes and conditions news selection, so it represents a potent force in shaping both the kind of foreign news that the mass media in socialist systems project to their readers and the editorial decisions they make regarding the amount of Western-produced international news and information disseminated in the former Communist world.[31]

Much of foreign news coverage, both in the West and the FSU, is interplay of stereotypes and hegemony, power and prejudice. In this chapter I look at general coverage of African countries and the types of stereotypes the Russian and Western press employ to describe African events and Africans by analyzing the content of six Western and Russian publications. This analysis examines the images of Africa as conveyed in three Russian language publications and three Anglo-American newspapers and a magazine. For the Soviet side I chose:

1) PRAVDA, which closed for seven days in August 1991, due to its positive coverage of the abortive Communist comeback coup of that week. It re-emerged on August 31 as an independent paper with a print-run of 2.6 million copies.[32] The paper had a circulation of 11 million in 1985, but circulation has dropped drastically since 1989. In 1992, it had a total circulation of 1.3 million copies. In current terms, PRAVDA is regarded as rightist, conservative.

2) IZVESTIYA had a total circulation of 8 million in 1985.[33] Due to the current economic crisis in Russia, circulation has also fallen. This paper is regarded as liberal; in fact it acquired this status even under Communism.

3) NOVOE VREMYA (New Times) is published in Russian and seven foreign languages, including English.[34] Under perestroika and glasnost, it became one of the most respected publications in the country.

For the Western side, I selected:

1)   THE DAILY TELEGRAPH, generally regarded as a conservative, rightwing newspaper, published in London. Founded in 1855, it had a total circulation of 1.3 million in 1988.

2)   THE NEW YORK TIMES, the most influential and informative daily; formally independent but factually supports the Democratic Party of the USA. It was founded in 1851.

3)   NEWSWEEK, a weekly news and analysis magazine
first published in 1938. Total circulation is three million.

I limit analysis to these periods: February and October 1985;
December 1987; February 1990; January-March 1992 and March 1993.
This will enable us to chart the dynamics of the stereotyping of Africa
through the perestroika/glasnost/new thinking years and post-
Communist period. I start with 1985, because that year marked the
watershed of the old, cold-war thinking and the new, post-cold War
epoch of "New Thinking," "One Worldism," and post-Communist
unipolarism. I treat not only the problem of stereotyping; I also
consider to what extent Africa is marginalized or otherwise. By so
doing, I also attempt to determine how Gorbachev's "new political
thinking," with its philosophical linchpin of universal human values,
meets African interests and values.

These years were significant for Africa for two main reasons: (1)
they were characterized by liberation, counter-revolutionary struggles,
and continuing efforts to bring social change on the continent; (2)
Africa became the battleground where superpowers fought their
ideological and psychological war. It also became a testing ground for
the efficacy of their weapons of mass destruction, their ideologies of
cold-war mass indoctrination, and their post-cold war super-
cooperation.

Although, the USSR has ceased to exist, most reporters and staff of
the ex-Communist media are still at their posts, gathering and
processing news. They are likely to continue in their gate-keeping role,
contributing to what the media sees both within and outside the C.I.S.
Undoubtedly, under the new dispensation, the winds of change have
affected both the journalists and the press. Although, the dailies in this
study have survived as Russian papers, and are still published in
Russian, they have been adapting to the new market in Russia.[35]

Method
I analyzed three Soviet/Russian publications for frequency, and
value-loaded coverage of African events and issues for October 1985
and November-December 1987. The publications were chosen because
of their reputation as the major source of news for Soviet readers, not
as random samples. The publications analyzed included PRAVDA
(daily), IZVESTIYA (daily) and NOVOE VREMYA (weekly socio-
political magazine). By way of comparison, three Anglo-American

publications - THE DAILY TELEGRAPH, THE NEW YORK TIMES and the NEWSWEEK magazine were also coded.

All coverage of Africa was coded according to frequency, approximate number of words, and article subject. Frequency and approximate number of words determined the degree of Africa's marginalization, while article subject measured the extent of these publications' value-loaded treatment (stereotyping) of African issues. To determine the dynamics of marginalization, I analyzed the coverage of different world regions by NOVOE VREMYA and NEWSWEEK for 1985 and 1990. Since my prime focus is Africa's image in the Soviet/Russian press, I also surveyed IZVESTIYA (November-December 1987, February 1990 and March 1993) and NOVOE VREMYA[36] (January-March 1987 and October-December 1991) to determine post-cold War/post-Communist discourse *vis-à-vis* Africa.

I also conducted an opinion survey among Soviet students and lecturers, and Western students and research fellows in various St. Petersburg institutions of higher learning. This survey gave me information on their perception of the press' effect on the image of Africans. I used a structured questionnaire to gather the opinions of 200 Soviet students, 100 Soviet lecturers, and 200 Western students and research fellows.[37] I reasoned that because of the cosmopolitan nature of the St. Petersburg institutions, students and lecturers would have direct contact with Africans. Also, I considered that students, lecturers, and research fellows would obtain much of their information about Africa from the press and at least one of the analyzed publications. I use sociological and mass communication methods, not only for effect, but also for comprehensiveness and all-sided analysis. I interpolate my findings in tables and graphs.

The Soviet/Russian Press

1) On The Threshold: Between "Old" And "New" Thinking

Pravda (October 1985): Preliminary Review

For October 1985, Pravda carried 15 news items about eight countries in Western, Eastern, Northern and Southern Africa. As much as nine or 60% of the total news stories were about South Africa and apartheid. Ten news items (66.7%) were on the negative side of the African reality - violence, border conflicts, deaths. The captions of some news stories speak for themselves: "Aggression against Angola;"

"And a thunder is Roaring...Apartheid;" "Tension in Uganda—civil war;" "Sudan: a Difficult Stage—Civil War;" "Not Intimidated by the Bullets of the Racists—Apartheid;" "Seven more Anti-Apartheid Warriors Die in South Africa."

Five news stories were either neutral or positive. The paper covered: (1) presidential elections in Sao Tome; (2) The "Rape" of Nigeria's forests by Western transnational corporations; (3) An international conference of solidarity with the People of South Africa in Addis Ababa, Ethiopia; (4) Talks between President Mubarak of Egypt and the leader of the Supreme Military Council of Sudan, General Sinar ad-Dachab; and (5) The leader of the Libyan Revolution, Muamr Gadafi, accuses the Reagan administration of state terrorism. Six news items were news-briefs of approximately 30-40 words. Three stories were expanded non-analytical news-briefs of approximately 100-150 words. None of the remaining analytical articles exceeded approximately 500 words.

Although by October, 1985 Gorbachev had already spent seven months at the helm of affairs, and had outlined several policies that distanced him from his predecessors, perestroika was still in its embryonic stage, and did not seem to have any influence on press coverage of foreign news generally and news about Africa in particular. That explains the fact that the tone and ideological perspective of the articles in PRAVDA during the period under review reflected the East-West fission.

Table 3.1.

Total No. of Articles	Articles within the "coup-famine syndrome" framework	Articles of non-sensational character	Articles on apartheid	News briefs (20-100 words approx.[38]	Analytical articles (100-2,000 words approx)[39]
15	10 (66.7%)	5 (33.3%)	9 (60%)	6 (40%)	8 (53.3%)

Izvestiya (October, 1985)

This paper carried 34 news stories about 15 countries in October, 1985. It carried 10 stories, i.e. 29.4% of the total number, about apartheid. News stories that fell within the "coup-famine syndrome" totaled 23 (67.7%), while stories categorized as non-sensational, positive, or neutral numbered 11 (32.3%). News briefs (about 20-100 words) constituted 11.7% (4), whereas larger news stories of between 100-1,500 words constituted 88.3% (30).

Ten articles (29.4%) were about Soviet diplomatic overtures and friendly gestures toward various African countries. During this period, IZVESTIYA carried stories about a Soviet-built military hospital in Ethiopia (titled "A Humane Mission..."), the Moscow visits of heads of state in Madagascar and Libya, and a delegation of members of the Supreme Soviet to Algeria. Other stories touching on Soviet diplomatic and friendly activities in Africa covered activities marking the 25th anniversary of Soviet-Nigerian diplomatic relations in Lagos, Nigeria, and "Days of the USSR," an annual commemoration of the October Socialist Revolution in Mozambique.

These stories highlighted the dynamism and "friendliness" of Soviet diplomacy in these countries in particular and Africa generally. They showed how Africans were favorably reacting to the Soviet "humanistic" foreign policy actions and its assistance to African countries. Three front-page articles covered a Soviet-built military hospital in Addis Ababa, titled "Humanistic Mission in Ethiopia," (about 800 words): Gorbachev's speech at a Kremlin state dinner to honor Gadafi (about 1000 words); and a report from Tripoli, Libya on "the importance of strengthening USSR-Libyan ties" (about 600 words). These articles, like those on Soviet "humanistic" assistance and diplomacy, were couched in cold-war language, accentuating the achievements and positive image of the USSR and its allies, while ignoring or discounting the accomplishments of the "American-West" and denigrating the image of Western governments. Articles about apartheid stressed the atrocities of the white minority regime against the majority black population, and the collaboration of Western governments and institutions with the apartheid regime in perpetuating the racist system.

Table 3.2.

Total No. of Articles	Articles within the "coup-famine syndrome" framework	Articles of non-sensational character	Articles on apartheid	News briefs (20-100 words approx.)	Analytical articles (100-2,000 words approx.)
34	23 (67.7%)	11 (32.3%)	10 (29.4%)	4 (11.7%)	30 (88.3%)

2) In The Mid-Stream Of New Thinking And Glasnost

PRAVDA (November And December 1987)

In these two months the paper published 51 news stories about 18 African countries. Out of this total, 18 (35%) were about South Africa. Most of those articles were basically about the campaign against apartheid or the aggression of the South African regime against the Frontline states of Angola, Mozambique, Zimbabwe, and Zambia.

Generally, the articles about South Africa highlighted the ANC's struggle in a positive light, while they exposed the actions of the white racist regime in a bad light. The tone of the articles reflected the Soviet government's stance on the "apartheid question," which was sympathy and support for the ANC and the Black majority in the fight against the inhuman system. PRAVDA tried to attain a regional balance by covering events at all [cardinal] points on the African map. Its coverage extended to four West African countries (Chad, Ghana, Mali, Niger); five in East Africa (Ethiopia, Kenya, Rwanda, Sudan, and Uganda); and four in North Africa (Algeria, Egypt, Libya, and Tunisia). All the stories appeared on pages four and five under the rubrics "Foreign News," "The World of the Eighties," and "From the Pravda Teletype."

Out of all the articles PRAVDA published during the months under review, 19 (39%) were on the seamy side of African life; i.e. they covered themes on the coup-famine syndrome. Stories of this type filed by the paper's correspondents in Africa or culled from Western sources were basically about civil wars, famine, foreign debt and apartheid. Noteworthy are these facts: a complete absence of stories about (1) developmental activities in the various countries covered; (2) inter-African cooperation; (3) cultural life; (4) African unity; (5) rural life and (6) lives of ordinary people.

PRAVDA considered African events and news second-rate. My study revealed these tendencies: all the stories covered political personalities and leaders; they gave no space to other actors. The stories followed a predictable style, always praising friends and always condemning enemies. They did not show the relationship between politicians or statesmen and their subjects, such as workers, civil servants, and peasant farmers. Contrary to its masthead slogan: "Workers of the World, Unite!," PRAVDA did not cover the conditions of the working class, the proletariat, or the underprivileged. Instead, it devoted about 50% of its African stories to the highbrow: ambassadors, diplomats, and other government officials. Most articles—33 or 64.7%—were news briefs, giving the impression that African news is of little interest to the paper's readers. Furthermore, none of the stories were accompanied by illustrations such as photographs and sketch maps. Very few articles were analytical, and most were patronizing in tone.

Izvestiya (November-December 1987)

IZVESTIYA published 46 articles about 15 African countries. Coverage spread evenly throughout the continent, although West Africa was sparsely covered; the paper covered six countries in Southern Africa, five in North Africa, three in East-Central Africa, and one in West Africa. Thematic coverage of the continent was quite varied, touching on political, economic, ecological, trade, and cultural issues. Thirteen items (28.2%) were on the negative side of life— civil wars, border clashes, natural catastrophes, and apartheid. Almost half (45%) of the published materials were more or less analytical, ranging between 200 and 1800 words. On the whole, IZVESTIYA's coverage of Africa was fairly positive, and its tone was sympathetic. Although the paper published fewer articles than PRAVDA during the two months reviewed, most of IZVESTIYA's news items were more enlightening and informative.

However, as in PRAVDA, nothing appeared about the working class—urban workers and peasant farmers, the latter constituting the bulk of Africa's population. Analytical articles fell short of shedding light on what mistakes or progress African leaders were making in building the new societies. Less was written about "non-socialist Africa," and where "capitalist-oriented" countries were covered, it was almost invariably about problems these countries were facing: Kenya-Uganda border clashes, the activities and trials of Islamic fundamentalists/extremists in Egypt, etc. Most of the new stories had no illustrations. Although greater attention was paid to "socialist-oriented" African countries—Angola, Ethiopia, and Libya—the articles were full of praise and paternalistic in tone, while glossing over mistakes by leaders of these countries.

Furthermore, articles on regional conflicts were written with an obsessive over-cautiousness, so as not to offend either party involved, instead of enlightening readers matter-of-factly about the genesis of the conflict and who was at fault. As the government mouthpiece, the tone of IZVESTIYA's stories on internal and regional conflicts clearly reflected the regime's courting strategy and tactics, which writers coached in diplomatic clichés, to maintain cordial relations between the USSR and all African countries. This language reflects the sameness of journalistic and diplomatic discourse. Soviet journalism and diplomacy were, as it were, Siamese twins, one embedded in the other. Only the scalpel of glasnost began to separate the two.

Novoe Vremya (January-March 1987)

This publication published 13 journalistic pieces on Africa in January, February, and March, 1987. Almost half (46%) of the coverage went to the anti-apartheid campaign in South Africa. While most articles were positive and sympathized with the African cause, 39.4% reflected the negative side of the African reality. Some articles were written through the prism of the East-West confrontation. In all, five African countries—Central African Republic, South Africa, Tunisia, Zambia, and Libya were covered during the period under review. Two articles were on US-African relations. Most articles were large and analytical (200-2000 words), with illustrations, mostly photographs. On the whole, NOVOE VREMYA's coverage of Africa was informative and fairly enlightening

The Western (Anglo-American) Press: A Preliminary Review

New York Times (February 1985)

In February 1985, the paper published 115 news stories about 23 countries in Africa. Forty-one-news stories (41.7%) concerned apartheid. Only 20 articles (17.3%) were non-sensational, neutral, or touched on the bright side of African life; thus as many as 95 (83.7%) touched on issues within the framework of the coup-famine syndrome. The majority of the articles (109 or 94.7%) were detailed and analytical, ranging between 100 and 2,000 words. Six stories (5.2%) were news-briefs of between 20 and 90 words.

Apart from one editorial comment and four news items appearing on the front page, nearly all news stories were published on "Foreign News" pages. Most articles on apartheid took the white minority South African regime to task for perpetuating the racist system, although some expressed levels of cynicism over the ANC's role in the anti-apartheid struggle—for example, "The Truth and Cynicism," "A Vicious Circle in South Africa". Nearly all articles were written in the traditional Anglo-American style of dispassionate "objectivity."

But a closer look shows they reflected the journalist's point of view, which usually coincided more with the liberal-democratic position of the Democratic Party than with the conservative view of the Reagan administration. The distribution of news stories coincided with the East-West confrontation over Africa during the cold war era. Thus, over 80% of the news stories covered events in Southern Africa, South-Western Africa, and the Horn of Africa, plus the conflicts in South Africa, Angola, Mozambique, Ethiopia, and, Eritrea. Nearly all articles had a tinge of anti-Communism.

Table 3.3.

Total No. of Articles	Articles within the "coup-famine syndrome" framework	Articles of non-sensational character	Articles on apartheid	News-briefs (20-100 words approx.)	Analytical articles (100-2,000 words approx.)
115	95 (82.7%)	20 (17.3%)	48 (41.7%)	6(5.2%)	109 (94.7%)

The Daily Telegraph (November-December 1987)

This paper carried 107 news items, editorial comments, "photo-news", analytical articles, and commentaries for November and December 1987. They covered 18 African countries—four in East Africa, six in West Africa, three in North Africa, five in Southern Africa. Among them, 35 items (32.6%) were devoted to the anti-apartheid campaign. About the same number, 40 (37.4%) were on the darker side of African life. On the other hand, 45 news stories (42.5%) were on issues that could be viewed, in one way another, as devoid of sensationalism. A greater proportion (just over 70%) of stories was analytical and research journalism. While 28.97% or 31 pieces were news-briefs of between 25 and 60 words, 70.03% were fairly long, ranging between 150 and 1000 words.

Most news items were accompanied by illustrations (mostly photographs), and appeared in the foreign news column on pages 6- 11. A few items got front-page coverage. The November 16 issue of the D.T. devoted the entire foreign news column (page 9) to African news. THE DAILY TELEGRAPH, for the months reviewed, attempted to cover a broad range of events and issues in Africa. Apart from apartheid, border disputes, civil wars, coups and hunger, it also touched on African music, sports, economic issues (such as the discovery of oil deposits in Gabon), plus the winning of a French literary award by a Moroccan writer.

Most articles on the struggle against apartheid were positive in exposing the system's atrocities. However, writers adopted such a positive attitude only to send warning signals to Western investors in South Africa, who wanted to know of the dangers the struggle against apartheid posed to their business interests. So these articles reflected no true love for the ANC or other groups fighting to end apartheid. This explains why the paper described ANC members not as freedom fighters, but as guerillas and rebels. I also observed the following while analyzing the contents of THE DAILY TELEGRAPH for the two months under review:

1)   A complete absence of news on development—inventions, the commissioning of new projects, or the life of ordinary African people;

2)   News on culture and sports was scanty, compared to news on border clashes, civil wars, accidents—both man-made and natural, and famine.

The New York Times (November-December, 1987)

In this period the paper published 90 articles about 15 African countries. Of them, more than half—48 (52.7%) were on apartheid, border conflicts, famine, natural catastrophes, and civil wars. Only 22 stories (22.1%) fell outside the "coup-famine" bracket. Nineteen articles were more or less development news, reflecting the economic and cultural lives of African countries. The articles were mainly devoted to Western aid to specific African countries; but they devoted no room to Africans talking about problems they encounter in carrying out Western-designed development projects. This gave the rather misleading impression that Africans are just observers in the center of a chaos they themselves have created.

On the other hand, many articles were notable for their distinctive broadness and all-sidedness, touching on all major "news-making" events in various African countries. More than 86 news stories were long (from 200 to 2,500 words), and were analytical and research journalism. Most were accompanied by illustrations (maps, photographs, sketches). Coverage demonstrated a high standard of journalism. Readers of THE TIMES probably have a better view of

African countries than those of THE DAILY TELEGRAPH and other Western publications.

In spite of the predominance of sensational news, the paper adopted a serious approach to its coverage of African news. For instance, sometimes the whole "Foreign News" page carries only news from Africa. A few articles, such as one about the freeing of ANC leader Govan Mbeki from apartheid detention, appeared on the front page. For THE TIMES, this news was sensational—if not monumental— enough to win front-page placement.

Newsweek (January-March, 1987)

Newsweek published 15 news items about various events in Africa in this period. Five (33.3%) were on apartheid. Out of those five stories, only one was negative toward the struggle against apartheid, doubting the ability of the ANC to dislodge the apartheid system through force. The other four articles sought to expose the atrocities of the apartheid system or problems the South African racist regime was facing. More than half the published articles—9 (60%)—were on the seamy side of life in Africa: death in South African mines, AIDS, civil wars in Angola and Mozambique, apartheid, etc.

Only 33% of the coverage could be considered more or less positive: exposés of African culture, the popularity of African music in the West, gains in the struggle against apartheid. A series of feature articles on AIDS sought to corroborate the racist and pseudo-scientific "theory" that the disease originated in Africa. However, in a subsequent edition, NEWSWEEK offered an African editor the opportunity to refute the "green monkey" theory, which claimed that the deadly disease was transmitted from African monkeys to man. Although NEWSWEEK attempted to widen its coverage of African themes, it failed to report on events that had a direct effect on the ordinary people of Africa. Development news was absolutely absent. One would have expected stories about economic projects, rural life, and the effects of western-sponsored projects on the life of African peoples.

Table 3.4.

Comparative Table Showing Coverage of Africa by Soviet/Russian and Western Publications For November-December 1987 and January-March 1987

Press System	Total No. of Articles	No. of Articles Between 100-2,500 words	No. Of News briefs (30-90 words)	No. of Articles Reflecting the "coup-famine syndrome"	No. Of Sensational Articles
Soviet	107	43 (40.2%)	49 (45.9%)	58 (54.2%)	27[40] (25.2%)
Western	213	70 (81.7%)	43 (19.3%)	107 (50.2%)	106 (49.7%)

Africa, The Kremlin, And The Press: An Unholy Trinity Generalized Analysis Of The Soviet/Russian Publications
(November-December, 1987)

The three Russian publications published among them 107 journalistic pieces about 23 African countries. Their coverage extended to all the cardinal points on the continent. Between IZVESTIYA and PRAVDA, nearly half the published material (49 or 45.8%) was news-briefs of between 25 and 60 words. Only 27 items (25.2%) were devoted to non- sensational or positive occurrences in Africa; 25 news stories were banal, official information, or diplomatic news, mostly announcing the arrivals and departures of Soviet and African delegations to one African capital or another. Most such "diplomatic news" was written in a drab monotone, and in only one genre, *zametka* (brief notes).

Another outstanding feature of the Soviet press coverage of Africa was a manifestly conscious attempt to inform the Russian audience how much assistance the Kremlin was giving African countries, and how African leaders were praising Soviet peace initiatives, perestroika and new thinking. The overall impression is that all African leaders and peoples were united, in sharing a common view with or supporting the USSR on all international issues.

Secondly, analytical articles woefully failed to produce a complete picture of the African reality. Correspondents failed to provide the Russian reader with information on how opposition parties or groups (which exist in almost every African country) react to the policies of the ruling governments. In fact, apart from war-torn countries like Mozambique and Angola, where the press mentioned the rebels, the impression conveyed by reading PRAVDA and IZVESTIYA is that there were no opposition groups or parties in most of Africa. This created the false impression that African leaders rule their countries in absolute harmony with all sections of society.

Thirdly, there was an apparent effort by the three publications not to offend the sensibilities of African governments by publishing "unpleasant" information or the "bitter truth" about these regimes, especially information concerning human rights abuses. Unless there was evidence that an opposition group was being sponsored by the West to overthrow an African government, Soviet press references to human rights abuses against opposition members by African governments were either glossed over or trivialized. For example, the Russian press virtually ignored Morocco's expansionist policies in Western Sahara, the late Samuel Doe's repression against the opposition in Liberia, and Arap Moi's crackdown on students and political dissidents in Kenya.

This is understandable. Journalism and diplomacy, as noted above, were two sides of the same coin in Soviet Russia. Unless the hand of the White House or the C.I.A. was seen in an internal political crisis in an African country, it was always prudent for Russian journalists to "let sleeping dogs lie." Such crises were seen as purely internal matters of sovereign states, and if they merited coverage, it was safe to steer away from criticism of the government. This policy also ties in both with the "courtship theory" and orthodox Marxist-Leninist press theory. For a long time, Russia had tried to court the friendship of as many African countries as possible in its competition with the US for spheres of influence in Africa. Although, Doe's Liberia was anti-Soviet, and Kenya under Moi was firmly in the embrace of the "American-West," Russian journalists were cautious not to tread on the toes of these countries leaders, so as not to block chances for rapprochement in the future.

According to the Leninist [press] theory, the government/party and the people are one. Anyone who goes against the party or government is an enemy of the people, and must be either eliminated, sidelined, or ignored. The absence or rather the stifling of an organized opposition in the Soviet Union, coupled with a Soviet journalistic tradition that did not tolerate "washing the dirty linen of comrades in public," must have influenced press coverage of Africa. For the two months under review, only one news item was important enough to occupy PRAVDA's front page—a telegram sent aboard an aircraft by the former Ethiopian leader, Mengistu Haile Mariam, to his Soviet counterpart, Gorbachev.

Not even the release of Govan Mbeki was monumental enough to win front-page placement in PRAVDA or IZVESTIYA, much less to attract an editorial comment.

As noted above, nearly half of the stories (45.8 %) were news—briefs of 30-90 words, mostly culled from the main western wire services—the Associated Press, Reuters, Agence France Presse and the United Press International. Apart from presenting an incomplete and superficial picture of Africa, the gatekeepers of the FSU publications ostensibly sought, by using western sources, to absolve themselves from blame for the predominantly negative information. "After all, we are not saying so. They say so." A graphic example of this blame-shifting approach was PRAVDA's coverage of the debate over the origin of the AIDS.

After its initial claim that the disease was artificially manufactured in a military laboratory in Fort Derricks, USA, was vehemently protested by the American government with threats of suspending bilateral talks with the USSR, Pravda was compelled to revert to the "African- (Green Monkey) origin of AIDS" version propagated in some western publications. Thus under the heading "It Originated...It's Not a Mutant" Pravda culled an article from NEWSWEEK that claimed AIDS originated in Africa. [41] But unlike NEWSWEEK, which, even if only in the name of fair play and journalistic objectivity, published a rejoinder from a Kenyan journalist to contest the "Green monkey" theory, Pravda only published a 30-word summary of the NEWSWEEK story. By publishing the article without any commentary or follow-up, PRAVDA sought to tell its readers that NEWSWEEK said the disease originated in Africa.

At a time when African governments and intellectuals were fighting against attempts by part of the right-wing Western press to "racialize" the AIDS "question," one finds it confounding, if not disconcerting, that PRAVDA's coverage of the issue tended to affirm the discredited racist theory. It is pertinent to note that even a right-wing magazine like NEWSWEEK, after its features that suggested the disease originated in Africa, offered an African publicist the chance to rebut the unscientific and purely racist theory. (Newsweek, March 23, 1987 No. 12.)

Although, the three Soviet publications adopted a friendly and sympathetic tone to Africa's many problems, the preponderance of news-briefs (45.8%) gives the impression that African issues were of secondary importance. This tendency was even more glaring in PRAVDA. Considering that this paper played a cardinal role in the formulation, shaping, and dissemination of Soviet policy in Africa, it is safe to surmise that whatever it said about Africa had a significant impact, not only on policy makers, but also on its readers. Furthermore, sympathy and solidarity were demonstrated at the expense of an all-sided, professional, and critical analysis of African problems and issues.

With so many news-briefs lacking illustrations and background information, the educational function of PRAVDA and IZVESTIYA were largely sacrificed. Soviet readers received a confused, muddled, incomplete picture of Africa. The dilemma of the Soviet reader was further complicated by the absence of follow-up stories concerning events reported earlier in these media. An example is the release of Govan Mbeki from apartheid jail. Soviet readers were informed briefly that the South African government had freed the ANC activist. But that was all they learned. No more was written about him, as he was pushed into complete oblivion.

Here are further observations I made about the Soviet publications:

(a) Socialist-oriented [read pro-Soviet] African countries were given more and better publicity than "non-socialist Africa"[read pro-Western]. Most information about countries like Angola, Ethiopia, Mozambique, Libya, and Zimbabwe was more positive than news about Kenya, Central African Republic, for instance. While "socialist-oriented" African countries were portrayed as trying hard to overcome their internal political and economic crises, albeit with Soviet help, news about "capitalist-oriented" African states was mostly "border-clashes," "trials of extremists," etc.

(b) Egypt was covered more frequently than any single "non-socialist" African state. In both PRAVDA and IZVESTIYA Egypt appeared eight times during the period under review. This can be explained by Egypt's crucial role in the Middle East. Soviet interest in that part of the world was a strong factor in the press focus. Growing trade links with Egypt is another factor.

(c) A great deal of emphasis was placed on negative occurrences.

(d) Very scanty attention was paid to cultural and sporting life in Africa. So was the life of ordinary people totally ignored. The Soviet Union's overriding concern for such diplomatic "offensives" like a "nuclear free world," "a Common European Home," and bettering its relations with its former rival, the USA, appeared more newsworthy than living conditions of refugees in the horn of Africa, for instance.

Lenin had instructed the Soviet press "to write this history of contemporariness" and to be truthful. "We should do the constant work of the publicist, write the history of contemporariness, and write in such a manner that our mode of writing could help the participants in the movement and heroic workers at the local levels, the places of action—write in such manner as to promote the expansion of the [proletarian] movement."[42]

Next to this Leninist behest, both PRAVDA and IZVESTIYA, like many other Soviet publications, carried the rather flamboyant slogan "[Proletariat] Workers of the World Unite!" This suggests, as Soviet mass media theorists loudly claimed, that the media in Russia was the tribune of workers and peasants, reflecting their hopes and aspirations, and addressing their immediate and future problems. Before the demise of communism in the USSR, PRAVDA and IZVESTIYA celebrated the Russian worker by frequently featuring "*peredovie*" (advanced) workers, state farmers, and winners of "socialist competitions" on the front pages. The media was also charged to be internationalist in its perspectives, and in performing its Leninist internationalist duty, should cater to the interests and defend the rights of not only the local working class, but also workers and peasants worldwide.

However, as my analysis has shown, these Leninist precepts were ignored when Soviet journalists covered the African continent. The lives of Africa's working class was absolutely ignored. Instead, the publications adopted an elitist stance, covering the activities of diplomats, statesmen and other members of the ruling classes in African countries. The press failed to provide its readers with a clear picture of life in Africa, to enable them to overcome stereotypes and prejudices. Even otherwise competent Soviet journalists writing about Africa often could not rise above Soviet propaganda in the coverage and evaluation of events in Africa.

In spite of the fact that Soviet journalists writing about Africa adopted a more sympathetic and friendly stance than their western counterparts, they often appeared to be driven by habit to portray events in Africa routinely, according to a predictable, well-rehearsed formula. A few of them, following their western colleagues, could not help writing sob stories about political violence, poverty and "crocodiles in the Nile."[43] Of course Africans have plenty of difficulties, and it would be ridiculous and dishonest to portray life in Africa as prosperous and steadily advancing. However, in human history there are examples of despair existing side by side with hope and the desire for change, submission side by side with resolution.

Common to the three Soviet publications was the absence of development news, based on personal observation and research by journalists. A good number of African events were highlighted without any analysis or commentary whatsoever. Almost all the articles made no attempt to explain the genesis of the event. What is more, the lack of analytical articles gave the impression that a disinterested observer disseminated news coming from Africa. These publications also paid particular attention to Soviet-African cooperation, covering every single event, but generally ignored the issues and problems involving intra-African cooperation.

Evidently, such scanty attention paid by the Soviet press to the pressing problems facing African countries did not reflect the much vaunted "principled and consistent" policy of the USSR in support of Africans in their efforts to build independent and viable societies after centuries of colonial and neo-colonial plunder and subjugation. So did the press' paucity of news and analysis of economic and cultural life in African countries not tally with the Soviet leadership's proclamation that the USSR stood on the side of Africans in the struggle for a more just international economic and information order.

Spared of the necessity for advertisement [during the period under review], the Soviet press had more space and leeway to concentrate on the problems of war and peace, the anti-armament campaign, and other issues posing a real danger to the existence of the human race generally and African and Third World countries in particular. Yet PRAVDA, IZVESTIYA and NOVOE VREMYA hardly touched on the dangers posed to African countries by the arms race, imperialism, and neo-colonialism. Although in 1985 the Soviet press often, not without justification, charged Western imperialism and its transnational corporations for siphoning away African resources (hence the continent's backwardness), recently accusing fingers were pointed at the West less often. This created the impression that, if it was not Western imperialism and neo-colonialism, then Africans themselves are responsible for their "backwardness."

This was bound to lead to mislead Russian readers into seeing Africans as lazy hangers-on and parasites, and consequently calling on their government to cut its support to African states. Only a small percentage of Soviets could travel outside the USSR or have broad and regular access to foreign publications during the period under review; most did not have personal experience or knowledge to enable them to make independent or alternative judgments. Indeed, this tendency was discernible in the press a few years after perestroika was launched.

Countless articles and readers' letters to the editors of the mainstream press either questioned or called for the complete stoppage of aid to African countries. Even parliamentarians successfully agitated for a substantial cut in aid to Third World countries. The economic rationale behind the cut is indisputable.   However, the ethnocentric and apparently racist hysteria ignited by powerful opinion leaders via the mass media did play its part.   One clear example was the Russian parliamentarian who called for the immediate stoppage of Soviet assistance to "people who have just descended from the palm trees, just begun to call themselves a people, and have just learned to pronounce the word 'socialism."

The role of the three Russian publications in the strengthening of the international campaign against apartheid is hardly disputable. The frequent appearance of apartheid stories in the publications itself indicates the Soviet resolve to see the end of the evil system. Having said that, however, it came as a big surprise that press coverage of the activities of the ANC gradually took on an air of negativity and indifference during the perestroika/glasnost years. The dramatic release of Mandela in February 1990, received less than enthusiastic coverage in the media. One can only come to one logical conclusion: the Kremlin's "disinterested" assistance to the ANC in the fight to end apartheid was not really disinterested; the country used the apartheid question as a chip in its propaganda war against the West.

Finally, as I argued in Chapter One, despite their manifest ideological slogan-mongering about solidarity and support for Africa's economic development, the powers-that-be had a latently different agenda in the international political arena: namely, to maintain the status quo and the East-West economic and ideological equilibrium. The coverage of the three Soviet publications reflected this double agenda.

Africa, the White House, and the Press: The Tainted Triangle
The Western Publications Taken Together

Let us now take a quick glance at the background of the relationship between the "American-West" and Africa over the years, and how this relationship has taken shape, particularly through the years of Soviet power to the end of Communism.

The "American-West" Connection: The Politics Of The Cold War And Beyond

"Collective imperialism" is the most appropriate term to describe the relationship that has developed between African and Western countries during the past three decades. With most African countries attaining independence by the late '60s, classical imperialism gradually changed its strategy and tactics in the former colonies. "National" imperialism was superseded by collective imperialism, in which the USA began to play the leading role. The roots of this process date back to the period after WWII. The war had sapped the political and economic strength of Europe.[44] Having assisted the allies in winning the war, the USA from then on could retain its preeminent position, and to acquire increasing clout in the economic life of the exhausted European countries. Through its Marshall Plan the USA "was able to internationalize or syndicalize its own imperialism" throughout Western Europe.[45]

The US-Western Europe alliance opened up new vistas in Africa, Asia and Latin America for the "American-West's" supremacy and the formation of its neo-colonial domination. Through the principle of mutual inter-imperialist cooperation and help, American, British, French, and West German monopoly capital extended joint control over the natural resources of the developing countries, particularly Africa, by forming interlocked financial institutions and bodies of credit. Involved were the International Monetary Fund (IMF), International Bank for Reconstruction and Development (IBRD), and the International Development Association (IDA).

On a more modest scale, Europe as a whole found profitable outlets for big business in Africa through the agencies of such organizations as the European Common Market (EEC) and the Lome Convention. There is more than enough documented evidence showing that the "American-West" relied and continues to rely extensively on Africa's raw materials, fuel and other energy sources.[46] The growing economic importance of trade with African States and the growing share of the major capitalist countries' imports of all types of raw materials, especially during the 1970s, led the "American-West" to jealously guard its relations with Africa. West German Minister for Economic Cooperation Dr. Jurgen Warnke expressed the sentiments of the entire "American-West" when he stated: "It is in our interest that Africa should develop and find a way out of its deep economic crisis. Only when Africa has recovered her economic strength, can she again become for us, the attractive partner for trade and private investment so important for us...[47]

By 1969, Southern Africa alone (including Zaire) accounted for 69% of the world's gold production, 64% of the world's gem and industrial diamond production, 32% of its chromite production, 22% of its copper, and 28% of its antimony and platinum. Additionally, 57% of the world's known cobalt resources and 17% of the known uranium resources were in this region.[48] More specifically, Africa supplies the West with 20% of its oil needs, 30% of its uranium, 15% of its iron ore, 25% cent of its copper, and 75% of its phosphorites.[49]

Through neocolonialist methods of economic exploitation, military and economic assistance and propaganda, the "American-West" has maintained its stranglehold on African economies. Kwame Nkrumah offers insight into how this is done in his book REVOLUTIONARY PATH. After being compelled to grant political independence to African countries, the colonial powers resorted to a "containment" policy to stop any further progress, and to deaden the impact of the liberation process in the young African states. To achieve this objective, the colonial powers have used their "arsenal of alliances, network of military bases, economic devices such as corruption, sabotage and blackmail."[50]

President Harry S. Truman's policy of containing the FSU provided the justification for the USA to assume the role of self-appointed policeman of Africa in particular and the developing world in general. As early as 1947, Truman had outlined the philosophy of containment that was to guide US policy through the post-war and Cold War years.

> At the present moment in world history, nearly every nation must choose between alternative ways of life. The choice is too often not a free one. I believe it must be the policy of the USA to support free peoples who are resisting attempted subjugation by armed minorities or by outside pressure.[51]

To justify intervention, successive US leaders from Truman through Lyndon Johnson down to Ronald Reagan and George Bush were obliged to link national liberation struggles to a mythical Soviet threat. In 1966, Johnson's justification for allowing the CIA to overthrow the government of Kwame Nkrumah in Ghana followed the pattern set by Truman.[52] According to Johnson, revolution in any country is a matter for it to deal with; but it becomes a matter for hemispheric action when the object is the establishment of a Communist dictatorship.[53]

The traditional approach of US diplomacy was to deploy military force and *force majeure*. A network of US bases in Africa were set up in Ethiopia, Libya, Kenya, Somalia, etc. In some of these countries—Libya, for instance—popular pressure forced the US to evacuate its military bases. US gunboat diplomacy reached its first peak in the 1960s and then in the 1980s. The US became directly and indirectly involved in the overthrow of radical African regimes in Zaire (then Congo) and Ghana.[54] Under Reagan's presidency, Libya was the victim of US gunboat diplomacy and state terrorism in response to alleged Libyan-sponsored terrorist attack on a night bar in West Berlin. One major innovation of the Reagan presidency was the deployment of local "freedom fighters" such as the Union for the Total Liberation of Angola (UNITA), and the National Resistance of Mozambique (MNR) in an attempt to overthrow radical African regimes.

In all this, America's allies either, tacitly or openly, supported and collaborated with the various US administrations. Collaboration in the "American-West" reached its highest ever during the Gulf crisis in 1990. The world saw the entire Western Hemisphere rally under the Bush administration to "punish" Iraq for invading Kuwait, the same crime the US had committed in Cuba under J.F. Kennedy, in Grenada and in Libya under Reagan and in Serbia under Clinton. What was remarkable about the latest invasion was how America managed—using the United Nations as a Platform—to win almost unanimous support from a good number of Third World countries to invade one of their member states.

Behind The Facade Of The Soviet Threat

From the beginning of the Reagan presidency, the US administration adopted an increasingly interventionist posture, accompanied by military aggression overseas on a scale not witnessed since the 1960s. This stance, codified in the 1985 Reagan doctrine, had been justified as the only way to meet the threat of the Soviet "Evil Empire." But the question that begs answering is: why did the US launch a new *brinksmanship* when the "Soviet-East" had long begun to pull back from its involvement in Africa and other Third World countries? It is difficult to attribute the new anti-Soviet shift in US foreign policy during the Reaganite years to changes in Soviet policy in the developing world. In fact, the Soviet Union had by this time lost much of its political impetus in the Third World, and its army became heavily bogged down in Afghanistan. The main motive behind Reagan's new cold war was to prevent the decline of the USA as the dominant global capitalist power. Within the "American-West" the USA had begun to lose ground to Japan and West Germany.

In the developing world, the *pax Americana* had to confront a number of challenges. Reagan had hoped that by militarizing US diplomacy, he could reverse the trends towards decline.[55] The decline of US hegemony in Africa and the Third World in general resulted from internal stagnation in the USA and anti-imperialist revolt in the developing world, not the rise of Soviet power. But it had been more convenient for Reagan to tackle the difficulties in the western camp under the guise of countering Soviet subversion.[56] Later in the mid-1980s, US propaganda added to the "roll back Communism" rhetoric the bogey of "international terrorism."

The Reagan doctrine developed the previous doctrines of containment by widening the range of targets. The USA was still committed to "rolling back" allegedly Marxist regimes through techniques of "low intensity warfare" and covert action. By using rapid military strikes and promoting local right-wing resistance movements, Washington hoped to minimize direct US involvement. By sponsoring guerrilla organizations such as UNITA in Angola and the MNR in Mozambique, the Reagan administration aimed to legitimize US intervention in key African trouble spots. Where it was impossible to sustain the myth of Soviet expansionism, the USA played the terrorist card. This is far from a recent technique: the need to rescue "women and children" provided the pretext for military intervention in the Congo in the 1960s. The menace of international terrorism became the standard justification for the bombardment of Libyan cities by US air fire in 1986.

When Bush took over from his former boss, Reagan, he added a drug card to the "Evil Empire" and "international terrorism" cards. The first victim of Bush's anti-drug *brinksmanship* was Panama. In December 1989, under the pretext of fighting international drug racketeers, the US invaded Panama and arrested its President, General Manuel Noriega, until then a collaborator of the CIA. Although, the Bush administration coincided with the collapse of the Soviet Union and the demise of Communism, it adopted its own doctrine along the lines of Truman. In the absence of the "red threat," the Bush administration invoked the fear of Communism's ghost. Bush thereby invoked both a possible nuclear war among the former republics of the FSU Empire and the danger of the former Communist republics selling their nuclear weapons to "enemies" of the West.

Very instructive is the attitude of the Bush and Clinton administrations toward the Castro regime in Cuba. Although the Soviet threat no longer exists in Cuba, Washington is still intent on subverting the Castro regime, not only because Castro is hanging on to his Communist ideas, but also because of the fear of a possible resurgence of Communism, if not now perhaps in the future in the FSU or some of its former satellite states in Eastern Europe. That explains the hysteria in the White House over power struggles between Yeltsin and so-called hard-line Communists, and the Clinton administration's haste to pledge $1.6 billion "to support the historic movement toward democracy in Russia."[57]

The current Democratic administration differs very little from the preceding Bush government concerning the legacy of the Truman doctrine; it would be a miracle to see any dramatic shift in US foreign policy toward the Third World generally, and Africa in particular, in the near future. A miracle is unlikely because what the "American-West" sees as "threat factors" endangering its affluence—AIDS, terrorism, or the drug problem—are not going anywhere and have not disappeared with the Cold War.

So is it less likely that the change of guard in Washington will lead to American disengagement from Africa and the rest of the Third World. In fact, Clinton's statements during the 1992 election campaign shows that the end of the Cold War has actually led to a renewed determination to use American military power to safeguard Western interests.[58] Clinton's Georgetown University speech in December 1991 contains several passages showing that his view of the post-Cold War world is much the same as Bush's:

> "I have agreed with President Bush on a number of foreign policy questions: ...that retreating from the world or discounting its dangers is wrong for this country; that the collapse of Communism does not mean the end of danger. A new set of threats in an even less stable world will force us, even as we restructure our defenses, to keep our guard up. To protect our interests and values, we are sometimes obliged to stand and fight. We must maintain military forces strong enough to deter, and when necessary, to defeat any threat to our essential interests."[59]

Making clear the Third World focus of the US's post-Cold War self-imposed role as the world's policeman, Clinton said, "we should end or reduce programs intended to meet the Soviet threat. Our conventional programs, like the new Air Force fighter and the Army's new armored systems, should be redesigned to meet new regional threats...to combating terrorism and drug trafficking."[60] Retaliating for an alleged plot by Saddam Hussein to assassinate Bush during a visit to Kuwait, Clinton's bombing of Iraqi military facilities, killing civilians in June, 1993 indicates his determination to continue the traditional US role as global policeman, even after the "Communist bogey" has been confined to the garbage bin of history. So do two other US-led allied bombings: the one in Iraq, to punish its UN ceasefire violations, the bombing of Somali warlord General Faraah Aideed's headquarters in retaliation for the killing of 20 Pakistani peacekeepers in Mogadishu, the bombing of Sudanese pharmaceutical plant to "flush out" suspected Iranian terrorist Usman bin Laden, and US-led NATO attack on Serbia all in 1999.

Now back to the generalized analysis of the Western publications. For November and December, 1987, the DAILY TELEGRAPH, THE NEW YORK TIMES and NEWSWEEK published 213 journalistic pieces concerning 22 African countries. Southern Africa was paid the most attention, with nearly half (96 items, 45%) coming from that part of the continent. This is explained by the fact that the struggle against apartheid and civil wars in Angola and Mozambique made Southern Africa not only the "hottest spot" of Africa; it also provided a strategic terrain for superpower machinations and maneuvers. In both the civil wars in Angola and Mozambique, pro-Moscow Marxist regimes were fighting anti-Marxist pro-Western rebels. The white minority regime in South Africa supported and armed the rebels in both countries, and even conducted raids into the two neighboring states in pursuit of ANC activists.

Slightly over half (107, 50.2%;) of the news items highlighted the seamy side of life in African countries. But about the same number (106, 49.7%) were non-sensational. Less than 20% were news briefs of between 30 and 60 words approximately, and as many as 170 items (81.7%) were large (100-2,500 words) and analytical. Most articles were accompanied by illustrations. The NEW YORK TIMES had the most illustrations, making liberal use of sketch maps. Although the publications covered all regions on the continent, Central Africa and Namibia were practically glossed over. THE TIMES and THE DAILY TELEGRAPH covered a broad range of topics—from economics, politics, deaths, and culture to sports, although the last two were scantily covered. There was no information about the lives of ordinary Africans. Newsweek in particular gave the impression that the only problem in Africa worthy of attention is apartheid.

I also made these observations:

- The three periodicals gave adequate space to the anti-apartheid campaign. Aside from an article in the DAILY TELEGRAPH, which doubted the ability of the ANC to end apartheid, all the remaining articles were favorable to the ANC and the oppressed black majority. Some also showed the apartheid regime in crisis in the face of a mounting international outcry, economic sanctions, and division within the ruling Nationalist Party.
- NEWSWEEK and THE TIMES placed too great a premium on sensation. News about apartheid in South Africa, famine in Ethiopia, border disputes in Kenya and Uganda overshadowed information on development issues.
- Most news stories were written with a detached, western-style "objectivity," i.e. reporters attempted to provide the raw facts without opinionizing, leaving the reader to make his/her own judgment. But in most cases, the bias of the reporter is seen through his/her "objectivity."
- African problems and issues were analyzed through western value-orientation.
- Nothing was said about efforts by African governments and peoples to overcome the difficulties in nation building. News about foreign aid, for instance, was not analyzed against the background of attempts by these governments and peoples to help themselves.
- THE DAILY TELEGRAPH was hypocritical in its coverage of the apartheid story. Rallying against apartheid and the South African racist regime, the paper also supported the Tory government of Margaret Thatcher, which openly supported the white minority regime and refused to impose economic sanctions as demanded by the United Nations.

It was clear from the tone of articles in the Western publications, especially THE DAILY TELEGRAPH and NEWSWEEK that behind the screen of objectivity lay their desire to see the continent remain dependent on the West. Behind the facade of objectivity lurks the insidious propaganda couched in these imperialist dogmas and stereotypes:

- That Western democracy and the parliamentary system are the only valid ways of governing;
- That capitalism, free enterprise, free competition, etc. are the only economic systems capable of promoting development;

that the newly independent African states should become an economic satellite in their own interests; that there is no reason to end the policy of "cooperation" pursued during the colonial period, and that any attempt to break away would be suicidal, since the colonial powers are always ready to give "aid."

- That the slightest "lapse" on the part of African leaders could push their countries into the grip of "Communism" and totalitarian dictatorship.
- Analytical articles were mostly value-loaded. Western standards and the capitalist ideology were suggested, albeit subtly, as the best alternatives.
- Much of the coverage was done through the prism of the East-West confrontation. Thus like the Soviet publications, the DAILY TELEGRAPH, THE NEW YORK TIMES and NEWSWEEK were prompt to report military activities, talks or agreement between African governments and the FSU. However, the Soviet reporters did this more often than their western counterparts.
- Like the Soviet press, the Western Publications maintained what looked like a conspiracy of silence over Namibia. The atrocities perpetrated against innocent civilians by the South African occupation forces were ignored during the period under review.
- Quite unlike the Soviet publictions under review, the Western press were ethnocentric and even racist in their coverage of Africa; they used blatant and insidious methods of dis-information to reinforce already held notions about Africa and Africans.

To prove my point I analyze the coverage of AIDS in Africa by both the Soviet and western press. According to an article in the London-based newsmagazine AFRICAN CONCORD[61], several British newspapers and the Independent Television News (ITN) sounded the alarm on Africa's probable destroyer—AIDS—out of proportion to the real danger.

In 1987 A London-based Ghanaian doctor, a Consultant Physician at the Upmarket Cromwell Hospital in London, embarked on a fact-finding tour of sixteen African countries in 1987, to acquaint himself with the true AIDS situation in Africa. According to his findings "AIDS is not uniform over the 50 countries in Africa. In most it is now in the introductory phase. In five or six countries AIDS is in the propagation phase, with the highest incidence in some French-speaking (but not necessarily French-related) regions and countries bordering them." Judging by the misinformation about AIDS in Africa, the physician said, if one were to assess the extent of AIDS in Africa on an arbitrary scale from grade one (not much of a problem) to grade five (a catastrophe), the epidemic is a problem (grade two) in only five of the countries where AIDS has occurred.

"Information I received from the World Health Organization (WHO) and from doctors I wrote to in other countries enabled me to grade the continent's problem in 1987," said Dr. Konotey-Ahulu. "In no country is the AIDS problem consistently grade three (a great problem), and in none can it be called a catastrophe (grade five). In Kenya, for instance, contrary to widespread reports, I would rate AIDS in 1987 as grade one."

Referring to a dossier compiled by the Panos Institute in London, parts of which appeared in the British press, Dr. Konotey-Ahulu said two maps showed Ghana striped with AIDS while neighboring Cote d'Ivoire was recorded as free of the disease. Said Dr Konotey-Ahulu: "At that time it was common knowledge that two of the AIDS patients in Ghana were prostitutes who had been working in Cote d'Ivoire and had been sent home to die. The two non-prostitutes were a Ghanaian and his German wife, who had previously lived in Germany for 15 years. Nigeria, which had no AIDS patients and remained without clinical AIDS in February, 1987, was included among the AIDS affected countries—but with the comment 'no cases reported to WHO.'" According to Dr. Konotey-Ahulu, the total population of the African countries with an AIDS problem was less than 10 per cent of the total population. Yet the headlines scream "Africa Faces Devastation from AIDS"[62] and "Sickening of a Continent...AIDS[63]" With justifiable indignation, Dr. Konotey-Ahulu asked: "When a nuclear reactor explodes in the Soviet Union, no journalist worth his salt wrote about the 'European explosion.' Why, when five or six contagious African countries have a problem, are the remaining forty-five blanketed with them?"

The American press was no different in covering AIDS in Africa. NEWSWEEK's cover story for March 16, 1984 was devoted to the subject. In fact, the pivot around which the cover story revolved was Africa as the origin of the so-far incurable disease. Africa was portrayed as the nemesis of the white race: a scourge, the source of danger to world civilization. The impression one gets from the series of feature articles on "African AIDS" is that the disease would decimate Africa before the turn of the century.

The tone of articles in the Soviet press about AIDS in Africa was no different from the Anglo-American press. Apart from the publications under review, AIDS has been widely reported in the Soviet press and electronic media. Papers like LITERATURNAYA GAZETA, TRUD, KOMSOMOL'SKAYA, PRAVDA, etc., have systematically reported AIDS in Africa with the same approach: Africa is in danger of extermination by AIDS; Africans are a danger to the white race. A documentary film shown in St. Petersburg cinema houses had a Congolese student, allegedly infected by the disease, as the chief protagonist. However, there were Soviet AIDS patients when the documentary was shot!

The first AIDS victim in the USSR was said to have been a Homosexual who worked for several years in Tanzania. The Soviet press claimed he contracted the disease while there. The first AIDS patient to die in 1988 was reported in LENINGRADSKAYA PRAVDA as having had her "first sexual contact with Africans 10 years ago," although other press reports added that the deceased had contacts with other foreigners, mainly Finns. However, they stressed that 10 years was the time span within which AIDS was likely to become full-blown.

Sensational press reports about 27 Soviet babies infected by AIDS via non-sterilized syringes in the hospital in Elitsa, added that the mother of one baby had had an affair with an African. KOMSOMOL'SKAYA PRAVDA carried a lengthy interview with a leading Moscow physician in its August 1, 1987, issue. The interview, while trying to project socialist countries as more morally upright, hence less affected by the deadly disease, also suggested that Africa, especially Central Africa, is the home of AIDS. It enlarged upon the now discredited hypothesis that the HIV virus crossed over from a green monkey, which is found in Africa. The physician interviewed, Dr Vadim Pokrovsky, suggested the disease is widespread in Africa because of large-scale prostitution among poverty-ridden African women. He charged the Soviet media for shying away from writing about the origin of the AIDS virus, for fear of offending the sensibilities of Africans, urging greater glasnost about AIDS. "After all," he added apologetically, "Africans are not to blame for AIDS."

But Pokrovsky's main message—Africa originated AIDS—did not fail to register in the minds of the general public and the rest of the media. Since that interview, a barrage of newspaper reports attributing the origins of AIDS to Africa followed, after an initial report that the virus was artificially manufactured in a US military laboratory. A

USSR Ministry of Health brochure on AIDS prevention warned Soviet citizens to beware of foreigners, particularly Africans and Americans. Starting from September 1987, mandatory screening of foreign students were conducted annually. African students testing positive for the AIDS virus, mainly from East Africa, were deported.

The AIDS issue became so prejudiced in the USSR that Russians, known for their knack for catchphrases, coined various acronyms and abbreviations to match the original Russian abbreviation for AIDS, *SPID*. Two examples show the extent of prejudice: Africans are *SPIDonosetsiy*, carriers of AIDS. *SPID* is *sotsial'noe nosledstvie international'noi druzhbi*—loosely translated, AIDS is the social consequence of international friendship. Another saying goes: *Spestial'ny podarok inostrannikh druziei*, meaning AIDS is "a gift from foreign friends."

Empirical research conducted by Jenny Kitzinger and D. Miller for the Medical Research Council of Britain in association with the Glasgow University Media Group found that most popular beliefs about the origin of HIV claimed it came from Africa and Africa had a particularly high incidence of AIDS. Many research participants said the media was their source of information, and recalled ways that early reporting of AIDS linked it with Africa or the Third World. The researchers argued that statements about "African AIDS" is not "simply due to the direct influence of media AIDS reporting, but is partly dependent on widespread pre-existing ideas about Africa; it is easy for white people in Britain to believe that Africa is a reservoir of HIV infection because 'it fits'."[64]

More recently, other scientists, tagged "dissident" by the mainstream Western media have added their voice to that of Dr. Konotey-Ahulu's. These scientists have not only questioned the "orthodox" view that the HIV virus caused the AIDS disease, they have expressed serious doubts about the "astronomical figures" of AIDS patients in Africa. For example, Professor Sam Mhlongo, chief family practitioner and head of South Africa's Department of Family Medicine and Primary Care told the NEW AFRICAN magazine on the eve of the International Aids Conference 2000 in South Africa:

> " I would like the 'orthodox' scientists to begin to acknowledge that there are diseases—29 or 30 diseases—which mimic AIDS. They must really begin to acknowledge this, including hypoprotinaemia, which is related to poverty. But they will not accept that because poverty does not make big money; HIV does make them money."

Professor Mhlongo became convinced that the AIDS figures in Africa reported in the Western media were exaggerations after his 11 "AIDS patients" from Uganda in London office (he had practiced in London for 17 years until he returned home in 1999) tested negative. The eleven had tested positive in Uganda. When they arrived in London, they presented documents attesting that they had the disease. According to Professor Mhlongo, the "patients" had probably learned that they had better chances of acquiring government housing if they proved that they were ill.

It was the views of scientist, such as Professor Mhlongo, that prompted South African president Thabo Mbeki to set up International Aids Panel to discuss both sides of the Aids debate. The South African president who apparently supports the "dissident" side of the Aids controversy, has been heavily criticized by the mainstream white-owned media in South Africa.[65]

From the above analysis it is easy to see the role of the media in changing, reinforcing, or contributing to ideas about AIDS, Africa and race. The press, whether in the "American-West" or in the "Soviet-East" tended to racialize AIDS. Abundant evidence says the disease is now a pandemic, affecting nearly all parts of the globe, and that there is no scientific proof yet of the origin or cause of AIDS. But the Russian and Western press both claim it is an African scourge.

In the same light, we can see the strands that run through value-loaded news coverage of Africa generally in both Russia and Western media. Dominant social values, tempered by ethnocentrism rather than the flow of events or the psyches of editors, determine what becomes news.

What makes the editor of THE NEW YORK TIMES, for example, decide to report the death of AIDS victims in Kampala but fail to report the commissioning of a new hospital there? Or what prompts the editor of PRAVDA to publish a story about crocodiles in the Nile or Egyptian mummies instead of news about the leaders of Ghana and Burkina Faso signing a protocol to unite their two countries?

News content, like journalistic consciousness, is the product of a social process resulting in some information being published, while other information is ignored or discarded. Some information gets prominence, and some is trivialized when reported at all. The ideological "seasoning" of news is also a very crucial factor. By that phrase I don't mean the classical Communism versus Capitalism flavor; from the point of Marxian social stratification and class struggle, there is little difference between the worldview of the Russian apparatchik and the American corporate businessman. I have in mind the ideology of the ruling elites of the dominant, white societies in Russia and the West, which filter the raw news in the press.

Thus the similarities between press coverage of Africa by the Russian and Western publications substantiate my thesis that white culture has a built-in predisposition to accept unfavorable beliefs about Africans.

Hartman and Husband attributed historical and cultural factors to British attitudes towards Africans and all colored peoples. However, despite the different historical and cultural environments, Russian attitude towards non-whites, particularly Africans, is hardly different from British attitudes.

In both the Western and Russian press, the Africans appear as a permanently stagnating human species with little or no hope of ever disentangling themselves from gloom, squalor, poverty, and self-imposed internecine "tribal" feuds and combats. Remember Bush's "operation restore hope" in Somalia and Clinton's "operation consolidate hope." The image of the African personality as the "white man's burden" runs like a red thread through both Russian and Western press coverage. The African is presented as hopeless and helpless—in fact, an endangered species, which would actually perish if denied the paternalistic protection of his white master.

The press, as in Russia and the West, has reduced Africa to the Bokassas and Amins. Yet, Africa is a diversity and unity of cultures and civilizations. The reality of Africa is the aspiration of tens of thousands of people to decide their own destiny; it is the reality of daily struggles by the masses to overcome the vestiges of centuries of colonial and neo-colonial plunder, as well as the current misrule of their rulers. The press may not be wholly responsible for the stereotyping of Africans; but there is little doubt that the images they project help reinforce stereotypes, prejudicing citizens' views of Africans and other non-white people(s).

The same pertains to the six publications under review. The perception of Africans was on the edge of reality; they often appeared as a "problem" or an "issue" that confirmed the reader's thought. This misinformation linked to the press' search for spectacular and monumental events[66], which would attract the public's attention, and reporting of some extremist groups' positions further reinforced the negative image.

Where East Met West: "Points Of Accord" (1985-1987)

My examination of the six publications in both the "Soviet-East" and "American-West" revealed the following similarities in their coverage of the African continent:

- A tilt towards sensationalism and a disinclination to report events and issues relating to developmental issues.

- The press of both systems reported the same accidents, coups, border clashes in Africa, although the Soviet press glossed over the coup in Transkei.

- They shared an elitist style of journalism; News tended to revolve around prominent personalities as against ordinary people.

- "The Apartheid Story" was given due attention. It served as the centrifugal force drawing the press under both systems together. By systematically exposing the cruelty of the apartheid system, the press in both camps helped to marshall worldwide support for the anti-apartheid campaign.

Points Of Departure

The coverage of Africa by the press of the two systems differed on the following scores:

- The American publications were more comprehensive, more analytical, and more illustrative and thus more educative. The Soviet/Russian publications preferred brief news to research journalism. The three Western publications carried 50% more material about African countries than the Soviet/Russian publications.
- PRAVDA, IZVBESTIYA and NOVOE VREMYA remained silent on several events were reported by the Western publications, including a French literary award to a Moroccan writer, and demonstrations by African students in China against racial discrimination there. The reason for ignoring the latter incident is understandable. African students in the FSU Union similarly face extreme racial abuse.
- The several cases of beatings, even murders, on purely racial grounds, were never reported by the Soviet media.[67] This ties in with the tradition of Communist media practice and

journalistic training. Soviet journalists were instructed to write that "socialism and racism are incompatible"[68], and that "racism has dissolved in the new socialist consciousness; " it is only in the "unjust" "wild" West where blacks are lynched.[69]

- Contrary to their avowed commitment to the famous Marxist slogan of "Workers of all countries unite"[70] displayed on their mastheads, these publications were elitist in their coverage of the continent, reporting the activities of statesmen, diplomats, and big shots to the exclusion of ordinary peasants and workers in Africa.

- By contrast, while about half the Western media's stories reflected negative aspects of African life, more than four out of five were analytical and comprehensive, giving a fuller picture of the African reality.

- Notably, THE DAILY TELEGRAPH and THE NEW YORK TIMES devoted the whole foreign page to African news and analyses. That the three Western publications carried twice as many articles as their Soviet counterparts cannot be explained by their sizes or news hole for international news. News hole for foreign news is about the same in all the publications. While the Western publications carry advertisements, PRAVDA, IZVESTIYA and NOVOE VREMYA did not do so until 1990. Before then, it was considered against Marxist-Leninist ethics to advertise.

- In the western media, news originating from Africa was rated equal to news coming from other parts of the world when selected for placement by gatekeepers; if sensational or monumental enough, it was put on the front pages. For example, the release of Mbeki from jail captured the front pages of THE DAILY TELEGRAPH and THE NEW YORK TIMES, and NEWSWEEK ran several column-inch features on the event.

- But the Soviet press treated news coming from Africa as second rate. It hardly ever attracted front-page treatment, not to mention editorial comment. For the period under review, only a telegram sent on board a plane to Gorbachev by former Ethiopian dictator Mengistu Haile Mariam appeared on the front page of IZVESTIYA.[71] Front-page placement of foreign news appeared more often in PRAVDA, since IZVESTIYA did not usually carry foreign news there.

- Analytical articles remained largely moralising and paternalistic. Journalists who tended to sympathize with Africa consistently leaned towards writing sob stories about famine, AIDS[72] in Africa, "the debt trap", crocodiles in the Nile river, and Egyptian mummies. Some wrote with racist undertones. For example, one time prominent *Izvestiya* columnist Alexander Bovin (then Russia's ambassador to Israel) wrote with "concern" that the continent could have a population explosion if efforts were made to check the effects of the AIDS disease. To him the disease appeared to be playing a positive role in Africa by keeping the population down!

• Soviet analyses on apartheid almost invariably accused the Western powers - USA and Britain - and rightly so, of condoning and abetting the racist regime in South Africa. The Western publications for their part, refrained from wholesale condemnation of the Thatcher and Reagan governments for their support for white minority regime.

• THE NEW YORK TIMES, DAILY TELEGRAPH and NEWSWEEK wittingly exhibited a greater capacity to ignore the crucial issue concerning the efficacy of sanctions in expediting the dismantling of apartheid by focusing their attention on irrelevant issues such as whether or not the Black majority in South Africa and the Frontline States were ready to suffer the consequences of imposing sanctions.

• This was done not only for the political convenience of Western governments, which were opposed to sanctions, but more important, for the economic convenience of Western multinational corporations operating in South Africa.

• This is borne out by the fact that a great number of multi-nationals with investments in South Africa also own and control, directly or indirectly, the Western press. For example, the International Business Machines (IBM), which has a place on the board of directors of the NEW YORK TIMES, is the biggest supplier of computer technology to the Pretoria regime.

• But there is another dimension, which supplements the economic factor. At the ideological level, the apartheid regime and right-wing elements of the Western ruling class shared a common interest in fighting communism. Yet to them communism was not a distinct social order but a loose category defined in terms of anything that threatened western capital and apartheid. From this perverted conception of communism, the liberation movements fighting to dismantle the evil apartheid system were seen, both in the West and Pretoria, as constituting part of the "communist threat, which had to be fought."

Another essential difference noted is that the long and detailed accounts of African events that appeared in the Western newspapers

(THE TIMES and THE DAILY TELEGRAPH) were practically absent in PRAVDA and IZVESTIYA. The reasons for brief and shallow reporting as contrasted to interpretation and commentary, was simply to withhold the full range of facts and opinions from the population, for without the raw data of events, it is difficult for anyone to reach conclusions of his or her own or at least question the conclusions of the leading newspapers.

By and large, the survey showed that marginalization of Africa during the past seven years or so has reached grotesque proportions. Perestroika and glasnost in international news coverage went only as far as Europe, North America and some parts of Asia see fig. 3.2 p. 163. To Russian journalists Africa still lies in the darkness of the pre-glasnost, (*zastoi*)[73] stagnation years of the seventies. That perhaps explains why hardly any report about Africa is complete without their favourite qualification *"cherny"*[74] *kontinent* (the dark continent). The survey further revealed that contrary to popular belief, the ex-Soviet press built on the principles of Marxist-Leninist proletarian internationalism,[75] and "natural solidarity with the oppressed peoples of the developing world"[76], fell far behind a number of western publications in depth, frequency and "objectivity," even given the latter's extremely miserly and sensationalized coverage of Africa.

As a supplement to our analysis, I shall attempt to compare the level of marginalization or otherwise of Africa by NOVOE VREMYA and NEWSWEEK in a five-year interval (1985 and 1990); and *Izvestiya* and *The New York Times* for November-December 1987 and November-December 1992. Our aim is to find out how frequently Africa is reported by these publications in relation to other regions - Europe, Asia and Latin America. See Figure 3.1, p. 160.

Here too, as Figure 3.1, p. 160 shows, notable differences are observed. While *Newsweek*'s coverage of Africa remained stable (21:21), *Novoe Vremya*'s coverage dropped by more than half (32:13). The reason behind this development lies in the growing disinterest in Africa by the Soviet media during the perestroika years, which coincided with the receding of the Cold War and the new rapprochement between Washington and Moscow. During this period, a number of articles appeared in the Soviet press, which corroborate our findings. One such article, captioned "Why Do We Need Africa?[77], attempted to warn the Soviet public against the growing anti-African mood in the country. NOVOE VREMYA and the two other Soviet publications reflected this drop in interest in Africa in the manner in which the release of Mandela from prison was reported.

In contrast to the euphoric coverage given by all three Western publications, the Soviet publications showed a marked disinterest in the freeing of the man whom the entire Soviet propaganda machine in the pre-glasnost period had projected as a comrade and ally, whose ANC was financed and armed by the Soviet Union. The ensuing inter-ethnic wars and deepening economic crisis have been cited as accounting for the flagging interest of the Soviet press in Africa. This excuse hardly holds water considering the fact that coverage of other regions did not suffer as a result of the crisis.

Yet another noted change was that IZVESTIYA, whose liberal position allowed for more or less better coverage of Africa than PRAVDA, drastically changed in the first five perestroika years. Less was reported on Africa and news selection tilted more towards the seamy side of African life. Like PRAVDA, a good number of the news stories were provided by Western agencies, namely Reuters, The Associated Press (AP) and Agence France Press (AFP). This perhaps also explains the predominance of news briefs in the Soviet publications.

Marginalization Proceeds Apace With Glasnost

As figure one shows (p.160), marginalization of Africa advanced with the pace of glasnost. Similarly, the main stereotypes employed by Soviet journalists to describe issues involving Africans in the world context underwent drastic changes. In 1985, Africa's problems were attributed to factors such as, "birthmarks of capitalism," "imperialist intrigues" and exploitation," "hostile bourgeois propaganda," "U.S. expansionist policies," "a plot against Africa" and many more. In 1990, these stereotypes disappeared from the lexicon of Russian journalists. Terms like "solidarity," "disinterested aid," "proletarian internationalism," "socialist solidarity" and "socialist fraternity,"[78] still employed in 1987 to describe Soviet-African relations, understandably disappeared in later years. In their place new terms such as "universal human values," "global cooperation," "deideologization of inter-state relations" came to be used. At the same time, Africa began to be increasingly described as "*cherny kontinent*".

Sometimes Russian journalists appeared to have difficulty deciding how to describe Africans. Thus, the African is variously referred to as "N*egro*", "*cherny*". But the former is the most often used, although it is offensive now to call Africans and African Americans "Negroes."[79] Yet another remarkable change during the period under review was the gradual toning down of paternalism in Soviet writing on Africa. The "Soviet socialist experience" is no more recommended as a recipe for good governance in Africa.

All this is logical, from the point of view of the Gorbachev reforms which he inaugurated in the spring of 1985 to "give socialism a human face" but which turned out to be an anti-communist revolution. As the Marxist-Leninist state ideology fell asunder under the "new thinking" ideology, Russian journalists, like the rest of the intelligentsia, appeared to be groping for a different vision of the world as a whole. Thus the old image of Africans had to be recast to suit the "non-ideological" new Russian vision. Western journalists need not recreate a new image of Africans, because although during the period under review, the United States, for instance, saw a change in leadership (Ronald Reagan was replaced by George Bush and the opposition Democratic Party controlled both the Senate and Congress) the basic underpinnings of the Western system and capitalist ideology did not suffer any discernible change.

Coverage of Africa by the Soviet/Russian press now does no more than merely catalogue the familiar banes and woes of the continent - the world's highest infant mortality and adult morbidity rates, the lowest life expectancy, the threats of a population explosion, AIDS, famine, ad infinitum.

While in the past such reports would surely have been spiced with accusations of "western complicity" or "international finance capital pillage,"[80] recent reports do not look for external culprits. Most articles now put the blame on Africans themselves. For instance, *Pravda* in an article captioned "*We are Africans in a European Home*"[81] writes that Africans wasted the "solid" amounts of western credits through bad management and corruption, and that tiny Belgium produces more goods than the whole of Africa taken together. Characteristically, other objective factors like the lopsided international economic order, which is so skewed against most developing countries or the fact that the Belgium farmer receives more than the African farmer for the same amount of work are glossed over.

As I noted above, the economic crisis and political uproar in the disintegrated Soviet Union has been blamed for the "*glossovernost*" of the ex-Soviet "glasnost" media of Africa. In fact, the standard reply often heard when the question of Africa's marginalization by the new media in Russia is raised is that domestic problems have shifted media focus from the continent.

However, our study of the "glasnost" press showed that coverage of foreign news did not decrease during the six Gorbachev perestroika years. On the contrary more countries and regions left out of the orbit of Soviet press coverage suddenly came to be covered regularly. Coverage of the countries of South-East Asia, the so-called tigers, has more than trebled. It must be noted here that foreign news in general was very much restricted in the pre-glasnost era.[81] The study also showed that while *Newsweek*'s[82] coverage of Africa and Latin America remained more or less stable in 1985 and 1990, *Novoe Vremya*'s coverage of the two continents dropped to less than half for the same period (Fig.1).   Thus, the "domestic crisis" argument does not adequately answer the question mentioned above. The real reason may be found in the boomerang effect of decades of paternalistic communist propaganda[84], which portrayed the ex-USSR as a big-hearted Big Brother lavishing free *besvosmezdnaya pomosh* ("disinterested assistance")[85] in line with Marxist-Leninist-humanitarianism on "poor and defenceless peoples of the developing world struggling against capitalist subjugation and neo-colonialist blackmail."[86]

Figure 3.1.

Frequency of Coverage of Regions by New Times and Newsweek for 1985 and 1990

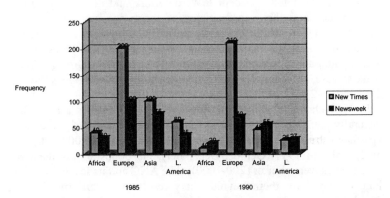

In conclusion, it must be noted that the main difference between Western press coverage and the ex-Soviet approach to African news coverage may be explained more by professional and dogmatic ideological factors than ethical or ethnocentric considerations. The authoritarian legacy of the Soviet state has left its marks on Russian journalism on Africa. Thus as Gorbachev decreed a change of vision the entire press uncritically fell in line. Although there was a significant qualitative change in Soviet international journalism, this extended only to coverage of Western Europe, North America and parts of Asia. Africa still lies in the darkness of the pre-glasnost era.

3)Post-communist Glasnost and New Thinking

To determine if there have been any significant changes in press coverage of Africa after the August 1991 aborted coup, which signalled the extinction of Soviet-style communism and the disintegration of the Soviet Union, I surveyed two of the three ex-Soviet publications, *Izvestiya* (March 1993) and *Novoe Vremya* (October-December 1991) for both value-loaded coverage and frequency.

For October-December 1991, *Novoe Vremya* carried 12 stories about Africa. Out of this total, as many as 9 or 75 per cent were about South Africa. Two articles were positive; the first positive one was brief article under the rubric "*Lyudi*," "People" about the Kenyan environmentalist, Mangari Maathi and the second was about the political transition process in Zambia. Four articles were negative, reflecting the "coup-famine syndrome."

In one of the South African stories, the reporter, while declaring personal support for President F.W. de Klerk and describing him as "reasonable" and the sole "initiator of the peace conference," saw Mandela and Chief Buthelezi as the main trouble-makers, and therefore responsible for civilian causalities, including victims of "white attacks." The reporter also described former Minister of Law and Order, Adriaan Vlok as wise, someone he would "stand up for" (*Novoe Vremya*, No.40, 1991, pp.26-27).

In 1987-(January-March), the tone of *Novoe Vremya*'s articles was generally sympathetic to the African cause, particularly the anti-apartheid struggle. Most of the articles were long (200-2000) and analytical. In 1991-(October-December), the opposite was the case. The articles were shorter (200-1000). The ANC and its leaders were no longer praised for their "revolutionary resolve to overthrow the evil apartheid system." Instead, the ANC was seen as being part of the problem in South Africa. In 1987-(January-March) only 46 per cent of the stories came from South Africa, but in 1991-(October-December) as much as 75 per cent were devoted to South Africa alone. Only three other African countries - Kenya, Zambia and Egypt - were covered.

A similar scenario was obtained from the survey of *Izvestiya* for March 1993. The paper carried twenty-one stories during this period. Only one article was positive—oil export earnings for the Egyptian economy - and one neutral. This was about Algeria severing diplomatic relations with Iran. Over 57% (12) of the total number of stories was on the seamy side of the African reality. Over 70% of the total number of articles emanated from Southern Africa and North Africa. No stories came from West Africa at all, while one was about the political turmoil in Zaire in Central Africa.

In 1987- (November-December) and 1990 - (February) *Izvestiya* published 46 articles about 15 countries and 38 articles about 14 countries in Africa respectively. In 1987-(November-December), 45% of the total number of stories published was long and analytical, non-sensational articles constituted 56.5% and 28.2% were negative. The remaining was mostly diplomatic news announcing the arrivals or departures of Soviet or African delegations. The corresponding figures for 1990 (February) were as follows: 28.9%, 26.3% and 73% stories about South Africa constituted 31.5%

Thus, it is clear from the above survey that the loss of interest in Africa by the Soviet/Russian press coincided with the period of the Kremlin's progressive disengagement from the continent. Non-surprisingly, this was also the period of East-West rapprochement and the eventual ending of the Cold War. Ironically, however, the further the Soviet/Russian press trudged on the road to full-blown democracy, the less interest it showed in Africa.

Are the newspapers and journals reviewed racist or ethnocentric? The publications, like other mass media, may genuinely be the "mirror" of society as a whole. But to paraphrase Leon Trostky, it is not the world of the newspaperman that interests us; it is the workings of deep social forces that appear in the crooked mirror of the press that concern us. The media are not the only ones to create positive and negative images; the family, the school, the church, peer groups, etc. each play a role. In the long run, however, what really matters is which members of society's views get the most widespread circulation and through which media?

It is true the media are not the only ones to create positive or negative images, but since they are by far the most effective means of communication in a given society, their role in relation to any expression of prejudice about other ethnic groups or races is fundamental.   As I have argued all along, the press [used inter-changeably for mass media] is a powerful medium through which the dominant group defines society's values.   It is a tool with which the dominant group "defines the situation" for the rest of society. Whatever "definition of the situation" the press carries may not necessarily be the true or the most representative of society as a whole. But the press plays a crucial role in "making-believe" the particular definition of the situation is the "normal look of things"

Thus the six publications could, by "defining the situation" of Africans, create false images or stereotypes that become real in their consequences.   Readers of these publications might respond to these stereotypes and act on them, with the result that false definitions become accurate or a self-fulfilling prophecy. Self-fulfilling prophecies can be especially devastating for minority and disadvantaged groups or races.

Whether or not the "definition of the African situation" by the publications under review had any influence on the perceptions of Africans and their continent in the minds of Russians and Westerners will be my next task.   An analysis of an opinion survey of Russian students and professors, as well as Western students and research fellows in various Leningrad educational establishments will the subject of the next chapter.

Figure 3.2.
Frequency of Coverage of Regions by (*Novoe Vremya*) *New Times* for 1985, 1990, 1991

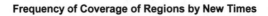

Frequency of Coverage of Regions by New Times

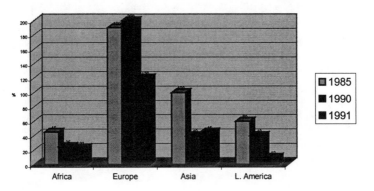

Chapter Four

Is Russian Public Opinion Harsher Than The Truth?

The preceding chapter looked at Soviet/Russian press coverage of Africa. For comparison, the Western [Anglo-American] press was also surveyed. Press coverage of Africa in the "American-West" often resembles that of Soviet/Russia –in spite of differences in their socio-cultural and political systems, at least until the collapse of Soviet-style Communism. Differences in coverage were more of a professional nature and journalistic tradition, rather than ideological or socio-cultural.

This chapter determines whether the press coverage of Africa in Russia and the West does indeed influence Russians' and Westerners' perceptions of Africans and their continent. The best way to tap reliable public opinion among large groups in society is the public opinion poll.[1] The observations and experiences of African and other Third World students, plus my own experiences and observations in the FSU regarding Russian attitudes toward Africans, gain usefulness when we compare them with the benchmarks, or parameters, provided by public opinion data among broader elements of society. Beyond helping to flesh out my conclusions in the preceding chapters, public opinion research offers "some insight into the functioning of the everyday, 'normal' communication process."[2]

I. Sampling, respondents, questionnaire

I polled 200 Soviet students and 100 Soviet professors at St. Petersburg State University and 200 Western students and research fellows who had come there for short-term studies from Western

Europe, the USA and Canada. I chose members of academia for these reasons:

- Previous studies in both Russia and the USA suggested that readers of the national newspapers—PRAVDA and IZVESTIYA and THE NEW YORK TIMES—are much better educated than the population at large.

- One of the most important and complex determinants of media attitudes and exposure is education. The college-educated are the most intensely interested in political and news analysis programs. College-educated Russians are avid consumers of newsprint. The higher the level of education, the greater the demand for more information about foreign countries.[3] Whereas in 1970 roughly 6.4 % of Soviets over 20 had incomplete or complete college education, that percentage for the PRAVDA readership was 39 %; for the IZVESTIYA readership it was 47 %.

- For American surveys, according to Ellen P. Mickiewizc, the same relationship obtains for newspaper reading, even though the percentage base of the well-educated in the Soviet Union is much larger in the USA than in the FSU[4]. "As education goes up, so does the reading of the daily newspaper."[5]

I based the sampling of students on information about the number of students at the various faculties and departments of the university. Using a two-level sampling approach, departments and faculties were first selected. Then questionnaires were distributed among the sampled groups within each department and faculty. At this level I secured equal representation of students at different stages of their studies.

I used the same sampling for professors (lecturers) in various departments and faculties. The interviewed professors and students agreed to complete questionnaires. The research was conducted when most lecturers were in their departments/faculties and most students were in their lecture halls. I did not use necessary sampling procedures when selecting Western students and scholars [I call them all students], as their numbers were too small to sample. With fewer than the required number of Western students at the university, I included Western students studying at other institutions of higher learning in the city. Even then, I could not reach the target of 200 students.

I prepared questionnaire files for analysis after discarding damaged questionnaire forms. The returns were: Soviet students - 193; Soviet lecturers - 98; Western students - 166. Here are the general characteristics of those polled:

1. Sex: Soviet students
   male -34.2%
   female -65.8%

Professors:
   male -70.4%
   female -29.6%

Western students:
   male -51.8%
   female -48.2%

2. Age:
All students under 30;
   Professors: under 30 - 13.4%;
                31-40 -34%;
                41-50 - 23%;
                51-60 - 24%;
                above 60 - 4.1%

3. **Nationality or citizenship:**
   Soviet students - Russians - 81.2%
   Professors - 86.5%.

*The percentage of other nationalities among Soviet students and professors is too small to merit any statistical analysis.

Western students - Citizens of the United States constitute the majority - 81.0%

4. **Political leanings (bias).** Most of those polled (only Soviet respondents were classified: students - 71.7%; professors - 52 %. They said they were either indifferent to politics, or did not sympathize with any socio-political organizations. About 17.3% of Soviet students and 32.7% of professors had democratic views. Communist Party and Komsomol adherents turned out to be few; among student respondents

—1.6%; among professors—11.2%. "Greens" were 7.9% and 4.1% respectively, and "Rightists" - 1.6% (students only.)

The Logic Of The Questionnaire

Questions aimed to discover the main source of information about Africa, the level of interest respondents showed in African events and cultures. Then I defined these levels. I also aimed questions at determining respondents' knowledge of different African styles of life. Several questions were meant to discover the respondent's image of a "dark-skinned" African—namely, the degree of his/her sympathy or antipathy.

"Dark-skinned" was added to African deliberately. In Russia North Africans are perceived differently from Africans south of the Sahara, who are considered specifically so—*temnokozhny*, "dark-skinned." Moreover, Soviet/Russian minds seem to perceive commonality between North Africans and citizens of the FSU in Central Asia and the Caucasus. Finally, I tried to define the position of "dark-skinned" Africans in the hierarchy of sympathy of the different groups polled. I prepared an English version of the questionnaire (a translation of the Russian version) for Western participants, since the Westerners had different levels of ability in Russian. The poll was conducted in March 1991, five months before the aborted coup, which led to the end of the 70-year old Communist regime and the disintegration of the FSU

II. Source of information, interest, knowledge

1. Soviet students

a) The interest of Soviet students in African events was low. 48% of the respondents were not interested in them. Women's interest was 1.5 times greater than males'—54.3% and 36.4% respectively. Interest in African culture among Soviet students was greater. Three-quarters of them confirmed this interest. Only 23.3% showed no interest. Men and women scored equally in this regard.

b) Questions testing respondents' knowledge about Africa proved too difficult for many participants. The question about the so-called Frontline States—countries involved in the anti-apartheid struggle in Southern Africa—asked respondents to identify two out of three countries among a list of six. Only 31.6% of the students could answer correctly. Female respondents fared worse than their male counterparts. Respondents whose sources of information were newspapers and magazines scored highest -41.3%. And readers of PRAVDA, IZVESTIYA, KOMSOMOL'SKAYA PRAVDA[6], and NOVOE VREMYA were about equally successful in answering this question.

Another multiple-choice question—"what is Bantu?"— required choosing one of several answers. Correct answers were a bit more than half - 53.4%. Again, men proved more knowledgeable than women; men scored 60% of the correct answers. More than 60% of those who knew the correct answer had obtained their information from newspapers or books and from Africans they knew. Among those who had their information from periodicals, readers of PRAVDA and especially of NOVOE VREMYA were better informed than others— 64.3% and 75.9% respectively.

The other multiple-choice question was aimed at finding out whether respondents knew, who the famous African statesman, writer, and philosopher Leopold Senghor was. Students woefully failed the test. Only 5.2% of the answers were correct. NOVOE VREMYA readers performed slightly better, with 13.8% of the scores made by readers of the magazine.

c) The main sources of information informing students about Africa were: television and radio—76.2%; newspapers and magazines— 47.7%; friends and acquaintances—17.6%; personal communication with Africans—16.6%. Other sources were insignificant. Books were twice as important to men as sources of information as they were to women. But films were three times as important to women as they were to men.

Which periodicals were the main sources of information about Africa for students? KOMSOMOL'SKAYA PRAVDA stands first: 51.8% of respondents read the paper more or less regularly. Every sixth student read IZVESTIYA more or less regularly: 16.6% and 15% are regular readers of NOVOE VREMYA. PRAVDA readers were only 7.3%. Gender differences were not great here.

d) Interpersonal (direct) communication with Africans as a source of information about Africans was rare among the students polled. Half had never communicated with Africans. Only one-fourth had ever communicated with Africans on a regular basis and by sheer chance. And only 6.8% of the respondents said they had met Africans

frequently enough. Men met Africans twice as often as women.
Consequently, there were twice as many women as men who had never
communicated with Africans: 54.8% and 38.5% respectively.

e) A desire to work in Africa for two or three years, given the chance,
was considerable 13% of students wanted to work in Africa. Half were
ready to think over such a proposal: 52.3%. Only 9.3% rejected the
proposal flatly. Answers to this question were not influenced by
interest the respondents showed in Africa in general.

2. Soviet professors

a) The percentage of professors interested in Africa was quite high.
Only 22.4% indicated disinterest. Women showed much less interest
than men: 31% and 18.8% respectively showed no interest in African
events. Professors of all age groups showed equally high interest. The
figure rose sharply after age 50: only 8.3% in this group were
indifferent to African events. Interest in African culture was at about
the same level—18.4% were indifferent. Interest depended on the
professors' age, rising from 61.5% among the young (under 30) to up to
95.8% in the oldest group.

b) The professors scored high in the "what do you know about Africa?"
test. Nearly half (46.9%) correctly named two countries out of three
involved in the anti-apartheid struggle in Southern Africa (6 countries
in the multiple choices). Female lecturers were less successful than
their male counterparts. The figures were almost the same for all age
groups, except for those ages 31-40. Among them, two-thirds gave
correct answers; the figure was twice as high as those for other age
groups. Those who fared well received their information about Africa
from books and periodicals, and had communicated with Africans
directly. PRAVDA readers and especially NOVOE VREMYA readers
were among those scoring highest: 64.7% and 72.0% respectively.
Three-quarters of all lecturers (74.5%) answered the Bantu question
correctly. Women respondents scored the lowest. Age distinctions
were irrelevant, although the figure was slightly higher for the 41-50
age-group. Those well informed had obtained their information from
books and through inter-personal communication with Africans.
IZVESTIYA and NOVOE VREMYA readers were the best informed.
   Only 27% of the lecturers knew the name Leopold Senghor. Here
scores for both men and women differed greatly. 37.1% of male

lecturers answered correctly, as opposed to 3.5% of female lecturers. The younger professors were the best-informed, with the 31-40 age group scoring highest. Those who obtained information from books were among the best-informed. Compared with others, readers of PRAVDA, IZVESTIYA and NOVOE VREMYA gave the best answers—40% of correct answers.

c) The most important sources of information about Africa for lecturers were periodicals -71.4%; television and radio - 63.3%; and books - 25.5%. Friends and acquaintances were fairly less important as sources of information - 18.4%; inter-personal communication with Africans - 17.3% - was also insignificant. Television and radio were more important sources of information for women. Age difference was irrelevant for information sources. Books were less used, while direct communication with Africans as one of the most important sources of information increased with age. Thus the older the respondent, the more personal communication became a source of information.

Periodicals were the most important source of information about Africa for professors. Two newspapers stood out -- IZVESTIYA (42.9%) and KOMSOMOL'SKAYA PRAVDA (38.8%). Every fourth lecturer indicated N.V. and every sixth PRAVDA. There were nearly no differences in male and female preferences in publications. Younger lecturers read less, although they topped the list of K. P. readers.

d) Lecturers had considerable experience in interpersonal communication with Africans. Every sixth lecturer had met and interacted with Africans fairly frequently. Only 27.1% of lecturers had never had any such experience. Nearly all male and female respondents had the same answer. Naturally, older respondents had more such experience than younger ones. Thus, more than half the young lecturers and only every eighth one above 50 had never communicated directly with Africans.

e) Forty per cent would like to work in Africa, though the degree of desire differed; 45% refused (13.3% of this number flatly—under any conditions). Enthusiasm fell with age. 30% of young respondents would be happy to take the offer. Only 15% of young respondents did not want to work in Africa. Up to two-thirds of senior respondents above 50 would reject the offer. There was a connection between interest in Africa and desire to work there.

3. Western students

a) Western students studying in St Petersburg showed great interest in African events. Only every 10th student had no interest at all. The percentage of women interested in events happening in Africa was quite high (97.5%). Male respondents were much fewer (83.7%) African culture evoked less interest. Every fourth student had a negative answer. Gender distinction here was even greater than in the answers to the question regarding interest in African events. Only 7.5% of female respondents said they were indifferent, as against 41.8% of their male counterparts.

b) Students' knowledge about the Frontline states was fairly low; only 29.8% answered correctly. Female respondents were less knowledgeable than their male counterparts. Those who obtained information about Africa from books or lectures proved more knowledgeable. The question on Bantu was answered by equal numbers of men and women (about 60%). Among the best-informed were also those who had read books on Africa and listened to lectures on the subject. But respondents who had obtained most of their information through interpersonal communication with Africans were unrivalled. All of them gave the correct answer. The percentage of those who knew about Leopold Senghor was fairly high—23.8%. Women proved to be 1.5 times as informed as men. Respondents who had communicated with Africans knew about Leopold Senghor best of all (54.5%). Those who had obtained information from books and lectures were above average.

c) Most Western students (83.3%) pointed to newspapers and magazines as the main sources of information about Africa. Radio and television came second (70.2%), then friends (31.0%), books (23.8%), lectures (15.5%), films (24.3%), and interpersonal communication with Africans (13.1%). Male respondents were twice as likely as female respondents to indicate inter-personal communication as a source of information, while twice as many females mentioned lectures.

d) Only 17.9% of Westerners had never communicated with Africans. About 60% had met and interacted with Africans; such meetings were far from chance ones. Women's experience of this kind was twice as great as men's, who usually met Africans by chance and briefly.

e) More than half (56.6%) would like to work in Africa for 2-3 years. Every sixth would rather not. Women were more enthusiastic about an opportunity to work in Africa. Women not desiring to do so were 3.5 times fewer than men. A moderate correlation was noted between interest in African culture and the desire to work in Africa.

4. Comparative analysis

Interpersonal communication with Africans was an important factor in shattering respondents' stereotypes about Africans and evoking their interest in Africa as a whole. In this respect, the opinion of Western participants was based on their own direct experience than other respondents. Only every sixth had not communicated directly with Africans; among Soviet lecturers every fourth, and among Soviet students every second. About 60% of Western students/scholars and Soviet professors had some experience of interpersonal communication that was not by chance. By contrast, only one-fourth of Soviet students had had some long-term interaction with Africans. Whereas professors' communication experience with Africans did not depend on the respondents' gender, it did among Soviet students. Soviet male students had more contact with Africans than their female counterparts. The opposite was true among Western respondents.

b) The mass media was the second most important factor in image formation about Africans. The hierarchy of information sources about Africa differed from one group to another. The table below shows the degree of importance of various information sources for different groups.

Table 4.1

	Soviet students	Soviet professors	Western students
Newspapers & magazines	2	1	1
Television & radio	1	2	2
Books	6	3	4
Friends	3	4	3
Interpersonal communication with Africans	4	5	7
Films	5	6	6
Lectures	7	-	5

The structure of information sources used by Soviet lecturers resembled the one used by Western respondents (with the exception of lectures). Information consumption was much lower among Soviet students than among the other two groups of participants, and this was true in nearly all the items [information sources]. Although interpersonal communication with Africans was an important information source for Soviet students (it stood fourth), the number of those who referred to it was not larger than the respective percentages in other groups, which was about every sixth respondent. Another notable difference: Soviet students half as often as Western students indicated newspapers and magazines among other information sources. Unlike Western students of the same age group, Soviet students took very minimal interest in lectures in gleaning information about Africa.

Gender distinctions in the structure of information source are relevant enough for all groups. Both men and women read periodicals to the same degree. This was also true for information obtained from radio and television. Books were more important sources of information regarding Africans for Soviet men than for women. There were no differences among Western students. Female lecturers tended to rely more on interpersonal communication, whereas among foreign students it was the opposite. Finally, female students tended to have an inclination for films as a source of information about Africans, although among lecturers there was no discernible distinction. Since the study did not determine statistically significant groups of this or that periodical readers among Western students, only the preferences for various media among Soviet respondents, were analyzed. With a certain degree of confidence, one can speak of the influence of certain periodicals on the formation of notions about the image of the African in the minds of Russian people.

Undoubtedly, KOMSOMOL'SKAYA PRAVDA stood first among the most influential media. The youth newspaper guided 40% of Soviet students and 40% of Soviet lecturers. But among professors, IZVESTIYA ranked lower, providing less guidance for opinion formation about Africans. NOVOE VREMYA was at par with IZVESTIYA in this regard.

PRAVDA came fourth on the list for both groups. With the exception of K. P., the other publications were much less influential among students than among lecturers. Gender was irrelevant for the influence-rate of the enumerated periodicals although K. P. is evidently much more popular among female students.

c) Respondents' nationality, gender and age group differed greatly in their interest in Africa. Thus Soviet and Western students stood furthest from each other here. Among the latter, 90% more or less followed events in Africa with varying degrees of interest. Among Soviet students: only about half. Soviet lecturers stood in between. Mostly women among Soviet respondents were disinterested in Africa, and mostly men among Western students.

Differences in interest in African culture are not significant. The number of those who showed no interest was almost the same in all the groups. Here again, 38.1% of Western students were actively interested in African culture, while only 7.3% of Soviet students and 14.3% of Soviet professors showed interest. Unlike African events, the culture of the peoples of the continent was of more interest to female respondents among both Westerners and Soviets.

d) Lecturers naturally know more than students. Thus they scored 1.5 higher points than students for the question regarding the Frontline states in Southern Africa. Scores by both Soviet and Western students differed very little. In all the groups, women scored lower than men. The better informed respondents read periodicals (Soviets), and lecturers and Western students read books on the subject. Interpersonal communication with Africans helped Soviet respondents to acquire better knowledge about them. Finally, while among Soviet students readers' knowledge depended less on their preferred periodical, those professors guided by PRAVDA and especially NOVOE VREMYA were better informed than others.

The distribution of those who gave the correct answer to the "Bantu" question was similar to the distribution vis-a-vis the previous question. Here again, women were less informed. There were no differences among Western students, though. On the whole, those who had communicated with Africans before gave mostly correct answers. For lecturers and Western students, books as sources of information about Africans were highly significant. The best-informed among readers of Soviet periodicals were those who read N.V. and IZVESTIYA [for lecturers].

The question about Senghor was the most difficult for all groups. Disgraceful were the answers given by Soviet students. Their Western counterparts performed better. Lecturers also performed better. Only 1/4 of the answers by Soviet students were correct. Hardly any Soviet woman could answer the question. On the contrary, Western women scored higher. Again, N.V. readers were in a favorable position, although PRAVDA and IZVESTIYA readers among lecturers tended to be more knowledgeable. Those who had read books relating to the subject and had communicated with Africans were better able to answer.

e) Though it is difficult to interpret the question regarding the opportunity to work in Africa in one way only, it did provide clues to respondents' general attitudes towards Africans. Most students and young lecturers would like to go to Africa to work. About half of the lecturers and only 1/5 of the students (both Soviet and Western) said they would not. Men among Soviet students and women among Western respondents were more interested in the prospect of working in Africa. There was nearly no correlation between the wish to go to Africa and interest in the continent among students, although teachers showed this connection.

Table 4.2.
Percentage distribution of answers to specific questions by the groups of respondents [SS - Soviet students, SP - Soviet professors, WS - Western students]

1. Interest in African events

	SS	SP	WS
I endeavour not to miss press reports about Africa.	3.1	9.2	6.2
I sometimes read specific articles about events taking place in Africa.	47.7	68.4	82.1
I'm absolutely not interested in whatever is happening in Africa.	48.2	22.4	9.5
Other answers	1.0	-	2.4

2. Interest in African culture

	SS	SP	WS
I am interested. I try to learn something new in the culture of African peoples.	7.3	14.3	38.1
I read some articles about African culture when I come across them.	67.4	67.3	21.4
I'm not interested in African culture.	23.3	18.4	25.0
Other answers	2.1	-	15.5

3. Knowledge about the "Frontline states" involved in the anti-apartheid struggle in Southern Africa.

SS	SP	WS
Correct answers	31.6	46.9	29.8
Incorrect answers	68.4	53.1	70.2

4. Knowledge of the definition of the word *bantu*

SS	SP	WS
Correct answers	53.4	74.5	59.5
Incorrect answers	46.6	25.5	40.4

5. Knowledge about Leopold Senghor

SS	SP	WS
Correct answers	5.2	27.6	23.8
Incorrect answers	94.8	72.4	76.2

6. Main sources of information

SS	SP	WS
Television & Radio	76.2	63.3	70.2
Newspapers & magazines	47.7	71.4	83.3
Books 14.5	26.5	23.8	
Friends & acquaintances	17.6	18.4	31.0
Direct/Interpersonal communication with Africans	16.6	17.3	13.1
Films 16.1	5.1	14.3	
Lectures	1.0	-	15.5
Other sources	1.0	1.0	6.0

7. Sources of information [periodicals]

	SS	SP
Komsomol'skaya Pravda	51.8	38.8
Izvestiya	16.6	42.9
Novoe Vremya	15.0	25.5
Pravda 7.3	17.3	
Trud 6.7	1.0	
Other sources	16.1	25.5

8. Interpersonal communication with Africans

	SS	SP	WS
I interact with Africans fairly frequently	6.8	16.7	14.3
I interact with Africans of and on	20.9	40.6	45.2
My meetings with Africans are by chance			
only and superficial	23.0	15.6	22.6
I absolutely do not interact with Africans	49.2	27.1	17.9

9. Reaction to a proposition to work in Africa

	SS	SP	WS
I would gladly agree.	13.0	13.3	8.4
I would think over such a proposition.	52.3	26.5	48.2
I don't know, it's difficult to say.	15.0	15.3	25.3
I would probably refuse.	10.4	31.6	16.9
I would refuse in all circumstances.	9.3	13.3	1.2

III. The image of the "dark-skinned" African

This item was based on questions about fifteen human traits that might be typical of a "dark-skinned" African. The items were arranged on a seven-mark scale. From the very beginning, my assistants and I faced the problem of respondents' unwillingness, either to fill in the questionnaire on the whole or to answer this particular question. (I had the same problem with the question regarding sympathies and antipathies to different ethnic groups).

93% of Soviet students, 90% of lecturers and only 82% of Western students answered the question regarding African traits. The latter often gave the average score 4" for all the traits, thereby rendering the answer meaningless. In regard to this item I found many notes in the margins of the questionnaire form. Half of the USA respondents gave most of the "complications." To sum the margin notes, one can observe:

1. It is impossible to evaluate race and ethnic differences, as the respondent treats only differences between living individuals as really existing.

2. Questions of this kind [item 1 above] are absurd and offensive.

3. It is impossible to sum up facts characterizing all Africans, because there are a vast number of cultures on the continent.

4. It is difficult to measure the results of this item of the questionnaire.

5. One's knowledge and experience is not enough.

6. The evaluation of certain traits (sexual behavior, for instance) depends on the type of culture the respondent belongs to.

It is important to understand that respondents' attitudes to existing stereotypes regarding various ethnic groups, races, and myths are rooted in the social consciousness of their respective societies. Thus while respondents from the USA went into a rage, treating the item as a provocation or arrant racism on my part[7], Soviet students remained calm and answered the question without any complaint. This can only be explained by the fact that the Soviet respondents were more prejudiced. They, therefore, took some of the disputable questions of the questionnaire as natural.

Because only a small percentage of the Soviet respondents who answered the question had enough interpersonal communication with Africans, we may deduce that most evaluated African traits through vicarious experience. They had formed their images of Africans through a combination of sources: the mass media, friends, stories, rumors, myths, sheer imagination, etc.

The reaction of the American respondents might have been influenced by their subconscious association of Africans with African Americans, with whom they frequently interact in their multicultural environment. On the other hand, the orientation of young Americans has been strongly influenced and changed by liberal and religious ideas connected with civil rights movements during the last three decades. During conversations with Russian interviewers afterwards, the American participants in this research mentioned drastic changes in the racial attitudes of young and middle-aged Americans. Yet, it cannot be denied that racial tolerance is not yet firmly rooted in young Americans either. Some see racial prejudice not as a sociological fact, but merely an issue of social ethics. Thus, many of the respondents considered the question on traits and racial differences as unethical. "It's not good manners to ask this kind of question," they charged.

For the Soviet respondents, Africans were mostly a category far removed from their daily lives. The African is a mythical, cryptic form of human being. This may be true for many other foreigners, bearing in mind the effect of Russians being fenced in for several decades by the Iron Curtain, and having been "sanitized" from foreign contacts.

Consequently, the image of Africa and Africans in the minds of the Soviet citizenry was imposed from above, above all by the ideological purveyors of the party; it was not formed through personal experience and by independent judgment or thought. This explains why the highest positive evaluation was given [or was it reproduced?] by members of the Communist Party, who had been under the influence of official propaganda that tended to portray the African as: "exploited, but kind and good-natured; a hero fighting for his independence."

Table 4.3
Respondents' estimation of traits of the "*dark-skinned*" African.

	Soviet students	Soviet professors	Western students
1. Peaceful-quarrelsome	3.88	3.78	3.69
2. Honest-dishonest	3.84	3.72	3.87
3. Hardworking (male)	3.63	3.08	3.69

4. Hardworking (female)	4.14	3.76	4.01
5. Brave-coward	3.77	3.62	3.69
6. Clean-dirty	3.32	3.48	3.42
7. Clever-stupid	3.69	3.63	3.70
8. Strong-weak (physically)	5.19	4.65	4.07
9. Modest-impudent	3.25	3.26	3.46
10. Handsome-plain (male)	2.92	3.40	3.20
11. Pretty-plain (female)	3.27	3.44	3.38
12. Friendly-unfriendly	4.49	4.12	4.10
13. Reserved-dissolute (sex)	2.87	3.07	2.98
14. Kind-wicked	4.30	3.88	4.04
15. Open-minded-suspicious	4.03	3.80	3.30

The bipartite apposition given was evaluated in the following way: scores ranged from 1 (the right apposition item, strongly expressed) up to 7 (the left apposition item, strongly expressed). Relatively, score 4 stood for either a neutral position, lack of information, or the position mentioned above (individuals, not ethnic groups as entity may have characteristic traits).

The physical appearance of Africans was defined by two traits: beauty and strength. Evidently, Africans seem strong to all three groups of respondents. Soviet respondents evaluated this trait highest of all. Soviet students gave it a special emphasis, 60% of them gave the highest scores (6 and 7). Soviet women evaluated strength higher than men; young professors rated it higher than middle-aged professors; democratically minded students and Communistic professors ranked it higher than politically indifferent respondents.

Noteworthy too is the fact that high scores came from those who had much communication with Africans. Beauty was not evaluated highly at all. Thus about 40% of Soviet students gave very low scores (1 and 2). The professors' total score is higher by half. The beauty of African women was rated higher, the score being nearly the same for all the three groups. Soviet women respondents thought less of the physical appearance of African men than their male counterparts. For Western respondents, the opposite was true; the total score by women was 0.6 higher. Western women rated African men and women equally. Democrats and Communist Party adherents were much more generous in their ratings than respondents who had no definite political positions. One score separated those who had had previous direct communication with Africans from those who had none: the scores were counter-proportional to knowing Africans, although this was less true for scores rating the beauty of African women. The friendliness of Africans was rated highest of all, especially by Soviet women. About 40% of Western students gave very high scores, with women giving higher scores than men. Communist professors gave the highest scores: 5.6, as opposed to 3.8 by politically indifferent respondents. The differences in ratings depended on how well respondents knew Africans personally. Soviet students who had interacted directly with Africans gave very high scores - 5.8.

Kindness was as highly rated as friendliness. Again, it was mostly Soviet women who gave the highest scores. About 30% of Soviet students and almost 40% of Western students gave very high scores. Professors were more reserved, especially the youngest and the oldest. Women gave higher ratings than men. Democrats and Communists in particular gave higher scores—5.0 as against 3.6 by respondents with definite political leanings. As in all the cases above, respondents who knew Africans directly rated them higher.

Diligence (Hard-working) - women. This trait was rated at the neutral level. Teachers, especially the youngest and oldest, gave low scores. Soviet female students gave a much higher rating than male students of the same age group. Gender differentiations for the other two groups vis-a-vis ratings were not significant. Communistic professors gave high ratings. Here too, respondents who had interacted with Africans gave the highest scores, although Soviet students' rating of the diligence of African women did not depend on how well they knew them.

The diligence of African men was rated half a score lower than that of African women. Professors gave the lowest scores. About 30% of lecturers gave very low scores; younger professors gave the minimum—2.8. As in the previous case, Soviet female students gave higher ratings than men. Communist Party supporters proved to be more liberal again. Ratings were dependent on the interpersonal communication factor, although this did not apply to Soviet students.

Regarding the remaining items on the table above, the ratings were below average. There are hardly any differences among the three groups in the way they rated such bipartite appositions as peaceful-quarrelsome, honest-dishonest, brave-cowardly, clever-stupid (where the scores were a little below the average), and clean-dirty, modest-impudent, sexually-reserved-dissolute. These traits ranked lowest of all.

For peacefulness, respondents from all three groups who had interacted with Africans, rated this trait equally high (4.8). Those who had not interacted with Africans rated them (Africans) twice as low as those who had. Democratically-minded students rated African peacefulness higher than those with no political leanings.

Honesty was rated considerably higher by Soviet female student respondents and considerably lower by female lecturers. Democrats gave high scores again. As in most other cases, higher scores came from respondents who had interacted considerably with Africans: 5.1 as against 3.4 by those who had practically no interaction.

For bravery, differences among the groups are insignificant. Lecturers (mostly young ones) and Western students gave higher ratings if they had interacted with Africans. Respondents with no political leanings offered lower ratings than Democrats and Communists. There was no difference regarding the ratings of intelligence (cleverness) either. Only Communists gave higher scores; Soviet male students gave higher scores in comparison with their female counterparts, and both the youngest and oldest lecturers proved more rigid. The interdependence of direct communication with Africans and ratings is very insignificant; no none at all with Western students.

The cleanliness of Africans was rated very low. Every fourth Soviet student gave very low scores (1 and 2). Women (excluding Soviet female students) gave a little higher rating; Communists still higher. Young professors gave very low ratings. The more interpersonal communication experience, the higher the ratings: scores differentials were 1-1.5.

Modesty was estimated with the least possible differences among the groups of respondents. Noteworthy were the strictest approach by the youngest and oldest Soviet professors, and a more favorable (partial) judgment by Communist professors. Here the influence of previous interaction was insignificant.

Sexual reserve was rated lowest of all. In fact, it was the only trait rated below 3. Every third Soviet student and every fourth Soviet professor circled the 1 and 2 scores. Soviet women gave higher scores than men, with the reverse being true for Western respondents. Communists offered higher scores than all other categories of respondents. Interpersonal communication experience did not lead to higher scores.

Finally, trustfulness was the trait rated with the highest rating differentiations.   Here, Western students gave the lowest scores. Women were stricter, although Soviet female students rated the trustfulness of Africans a bit higher than their male counterparts. Among professors, the oldest were stricter. Democrats gave higher scores than respondents with no political leanings, but Communists were still more liberal than Democrats. There was no relationship between respondents' direct contact with Africans and ratings of this trait.

CONCLUSIONS

1. Soviet students more frequently rated the various African traits than Western students or lecturers. Ratings by Western students deviated less than other groups, perhaps purposely, as most of them complained about the rationality of the preceding section of the questionnaire. Professors were much stricter with their ratings than all other groups.

2. Women rated Africans higher than men. This is more evident in Soviet ratings. Gender differentials vis-a-vis ratings were not very significant among Western respondents.

3. The age of professors influenced rating a great deal. Those in the 31-50 age group were much more liberal. Younger professors were very critical, and those above 50 gave the lowest scores.

4. Readers of various periodicals did not show any significant differences in any estimations, which means a common image-[formation] about Africans already exists in the minds of respondents, independent of any particular periodical.

5. Respondents holding various political views also differed significantly in their ratings. Thus, Democrats rated much higher than those who had no political preferences. Members of the Communist Party of the Soviet Union, however, gave the highest ratings.

6. The most important conclusion to be drawn from this survey is that the evaluation of all the traits is directly proportional to the level of direct interaction with Africans. Thus 70-90% of the analyzed traits received scores ranging below 4, i.e. below the average, closer to the negative grade of the bipartite apposition. On the other hand, those who knew Africans well enough through personal experience gave such low points in only 25-45% of all cases. Thus we see that most respondents had little or no direct contact with Africans. Contacts between respondents and Africans are the only means of shattering existing negative perceptions and stereotypes.

IV. ATTITUDE TOWARD AFRICANS

A traditional indicator of attitude toward the representative or member of a racial or ethnic group is how one reacts to marriage between a close relative or friend and a member of this race or ethnic group. As expected, 70% of Western students said "human traits, not skin color, matter." With Soviet respondents, only every second student (47.2%) and every fourth lecturer (25.8%) underscored this fact. About 69% of lecturers and 44% Soviet students were against this form of marriage, while only 16% of Western students thought it acceptable.

Female respondents among the Western students were more optimistic about marriage with Africans than the males in their age group. With Soviet students, it was the reverse. Women were more prejudiced: 48% of Soviet female students, as against 7.5% of their

Western counterparts, opposed marriage with an African.   Gender distinctions were insignificant for lecturers.   Attention should be paid to young [Soviet] lecturers who were prejudiced against mixed marriage involving an African and a close relative or a friend.   About 85% of the young lecturers who opposed intermarriage were below 30.   Prejudice reduced with age.   Even then, it was still very high among lecturers over 50 (58%).

The near absence of a direct relationship between respondents' interpersonal communication experience with their attitude towards wedlock involving an African was rather unexpected.   There was no evidence of this relationship among Soviet respondents at all.   Among Western students, both those optimistic and pessimistic about mixed marriage with an African, had some interaction with Africans.   Probably respondents' experience (both negative or positive) formed the corresponding attitude.   But we note that the majority (86.7%) of Western students with no personal contacts with Africans showed their anti-racist position: they said it was, "human traits, not skin color that matter" in such mixed marriages.

Among Soviet students of the same age group, the percentage was twice as low.   There are fundamental differences in respondents' attitude towards this issue between two groups of respondents.   These differences were observed on the basis of answers given to the question regarding respondents' attitudes (sympathies/likes and antipathies/dislikes) for various ethnic groups.   Let's call those respondents who looked upon ethnicity as an unimportant factor --they either declined to answer the question, or rated all ethnic groups as equal, using the same ratings—"internationalists."   And let's call those who rated ethnic groups differently based on their likes and dislikes "nationalists."

The research showed that the nationalists felt different degrees of prejudice against intermarriage more frequently than the internationalists.   This is the break down of the results: Teachers' 1.6 times as often; Soviet students: 2.4 times; Western students: more than five times.   The percentage of nationalists, grouped according to the factor given above—those who gave different scores dependent on their likes or dislikes—was 61.9% for Western respondents; 64.3% for professors, and 86.5% among Soviet students.   It is important to note that some nationalists are not necessarily racists; some of them, for instance, showed antipathy against Jews or Poles, but sympathized with Black Africans.

I met nationalists more frequently among Soviet female respondents than among men: among the students, 90.5% female respondents, as against 78.8% of men were nationalists; among professors, 79.3% and 58.0% respectively. The opposite is true for Western students: among the women 47.5%, and 76.7% of men are nationalists. Among professors, such "nationalism" decreases as professors' age increases. Thus 84.6% of the youngest professors are nationalists, and the percentage decreased to 58.3% among middle-aged professors.

Table 4.4
Respondents' attitude towards wedlock with Africans

	SS	SP	WS
I like Africans. I think it's possible to have a happy family life with them.	1.0	3.1	8.4
Human qualities, and not skin colour is the most important factor.	47.2	25.8	69.9
It is hardly probable that such a marriage will be successful.	21.2	34.0	12.0
I am against such a marriage and will discourage it.	22.3	35.1	3.6
Other answers	8.3	2.1	6.0

Table 4.5
Attitudinal ratings of various ethnic groups

	SS	SP	WS
Different ratings of all ethnic groups	10.4	30.6	11.9
Unequal ratings	86.5	64.3	61.9
No answers [no explanations]	3.1	5.1	26.2

To determine the general attitude toward Black Africans against the background of attitudes toward various ethnic groups, respondents were asked to indicate the "temperature" of their feelings. The Soviet respondents were to indicate their attitudes to 20 ethnic groups on a scale of -50 to +50 degrees Celsius, while Western respondents ranked their attitudes to 12 ethnic groups. This approach allowed me to determine the "nationalists" among the three groups of respondents.

Soviet respondents rated Black Africans at 0 degree i.e. neutral, without clearly expressed antipathy or sympathy, but lower than any other ethnic group. Soviet students rated Armenians at the same level as Black Africans, and just slightly higher than Azeris and other peoples from the former Soviet Republics of Central Asia. The rating for Arabs by the students was slightly lower than for Central Asians. Soviet lecturers showed greater empathy for Black Africans [+6 degrees Celsius] than they did for Arabs. Western students showed greater warmth [+10 degrees Celsius]. Arabs and White South Africans were rated far below. They put Black Africans closer to Poles, Chinese, Jews and Japanese.

Great differences were noted in gender. Women showed much more warmth for Africans than the opposite sex; this is, however, not true for Soviet students. Thus, female professors rated their attitude at +15 degrees Celsius, while men professors at 0 degrees C., placing Central Asians and Arabs far below. But they rated white South Africans at the same level. Western women rated Africans still higher—+20, compared with +5 by the men. Their rating for Africans was higher than for white South Africans, Arabs, Armenians, Japanese, Poles, Finns and Chinese. Africans were at par with Jews, but slightly behind Germans, Americans and Russians.

The age of professors was manifestly connected with whether they liked or disliked Africans. The younger lecturers disliked Africans more intensely (-7), but the rest gave positive scores, reaching +22 with the oldest professors. Political preferences also divided the respondents: Communists: +12; Democrats and those with no political leanings united in rating Africans, giving 0 degrees.

The most dramatic finding, which could serve as the basis for further research, is the attitudes of both Western and Soviet respondents towards white South Africans. While Western respondents rated white South Africans very low, but black Africans fairly high, the opposite was true for Soviet respondents. They rated blacks lower than whites, which reminds us that over 80% of the Soviet respondents were Russians. Although, the Soviet bureaucracy and the media actively took the side of black South Africans in the apartheid conflict, race prejudice proved stronger than the anti-racial attitude the Communist media sought to create. Thus my earlier thesis that ethnocentric "blood" is thicker than ideological "water" is justified by this finding.

One last remark. The ratings given by Western students reflect the opinion of only those who agreed to answer all the questions. Only half of them did so, the rest refusing to answer questions they considered politically incorrect or racially insulting. Thus the Western respondents' over-all ratings might have differed vastly from those of Soviet participants, had they all answered all questions. Hence, we may deduce that the comparatively stronger anti-racial attitude shown by young Western respondents is more widespread in real life than the results of our analysis show.

Table 4.6

   Attitudinal temperature toward selected ethnic groups (in Degrees Celsius)

SS	SP	WS	
Ethnic groups	+35	+35	+29
Russians	+29	+29	+31
Americans	+23	+28	+21
Germans	+23	+28	+21
Japanese	+22	+26	+16
Fins	+20	+26	+16
Jews	+11	+17	+14
Poles	+10	+16	+13
Chinese	+7	+15	+13
White South Africans	+9	+12	-4
Arabs	+2	+4	-5
"Dark-skinned Africans"	+6	+10	

Chapter Five
Eyes See What Eyes Want To See

i)   The colour-sensitive gatekeepers

Sports and war make much of the news headlines. Let me take you
back to the 1992 Summer Olympic Games in Barcelona, Spain and the
wars in Somalia and Sarajevo, which had reached their apogee at this
time. Two weeks before the games, the civil war in Sarajevo got top
billing on television. For two consecutive weeks the electronic media,
especially television, virtually went berserk with news about the 25th
Olympiad as television cameras and satellite stations with their long
and powerful reach brought memorable pictures into our homes.

Under normal circumstances, omnipotent satellite signals, should not
know boundaries and should not discriminate when picking events,
whether in sports or war; whether in Sarajevo or Somalia.   But
satellites, like TV cameras, are not colour blind. With their editing
techniques, media gatekeepers manage to sanitize the pictures that
appear on our television screens. And so for two weeks our powerful
sanitizers made sure the glory and glamour of the Barcelona games
appeared on our screens, while the thousands of Somalis who died of
hunger in refugee camps were kept out of sight. The men and women
who operate the TV cameras and satellite stations also know Sarajevo
comes first before Somalia in the alphabetical order. And so news
about the war in Sarajevo followed news from Barcelona. Somalia
would be the next in line, in some future time.[1]

But in the coverage of the Olympic games proper, the rule of
following alphabetical order was violated.   During the opening
ceremony of the Barcelona Olympiad, some countries were absent from
the alphabetical procession. So, if you saw the Great Britain contingent
march past and then Italy, and you did not see that of Ghana, don't
bother revising your primary school ABC. You haven't forgotten it yet.

The gatekeepers sanitized Ghana out. Other countries like Cote d'Ivoire and Nigeria had most members of their contingents edited out. You got the impression that Nigeria had only three athletes and Cote d'Ivoire one. But you got a surprise when the cameras began showing more than three Nigerian athletes qualifying for the quarterfinals, semi-finals and even the finals in boxing, relay, hundred metres and other track and field events.

As for a country like Ghana it remained permanently sanitized despite the fact that it won the bronze medal in one of the most glamorous events of the Olympics—soccer. You remember Spain beat Poland in the finals to win the gold? The gatekeepers decided it was not worth mentioning which country won the bronze. Yes, that is how powerful the gatekeepers can be. It is less worrying if the sanitization remains only with sports coverage. It is disquieting, indeed alarming, however, when it extends to the frontiers of war.

Before the end of the Cold War, the war in Somalia would have attracted as much attention perhaps as anywhere else. But the gatekeepers are not only colour sensitive; they are ideologically alert. They know when a country ceases to be of strategic importance. Since the collapse of communism and the end of the Cold War, Somalia and, for that matter, Africa have lost much of their strategic importance and the countries that received more liberal attention and coverage by the western media and generous handouts from Western governments for little more than being barriers to the spread of communism, have lost their appeal. The same is true for Russia. Long before the sudden collapse of communism in 1991, the Russian media had shown a striking indifference to events in its former African ideological colonies.

From experience we know that war is better copy than peace. We also know that war is war: human lives are lost. Yet the gatekeepers make some wars better copy than others. Two children were shot in Bosnia and that captured the headlines for weeks. Thousands of Somali children died each day but reports from that war-torn country drew yawns in editorial offices.

Thank God Somalia remained in the gatekeepers' alphabetical order yet; soon its turn came. In what was aptly described as a media circus TV cameras and satellite stations in the US and Russia beamed on the emaciated bodies of dying babies and their equally shrivelled mothers with such gusto and fanfare that it appeared the Somali story had never been heard of earlier, was some kind of breaking news, like the pulling down of the Berlin Wall.

Fast forward to 1999. Long before the West decided to intervene in Bosnia, the civil war in Sierra Leone had been raging fiercely claiming the lives of thousands of people, including children. But the war between the ragtag guerrilla Revolutionary United Front and poorly equipped government troops did not make "hot" copy. So for months, the Western media maintained general silence over the war in the West African country. The Monica Lewinsky-Clinton scandal captured the headlines until NATO declared war on Serbia. That was a "better" war. The Western media were there from day one to the end of the "high-tech war." Meanwhile, the war in Sierra Leone remained under reported, until a Sierra Leonean journalist shocked the world with his video documentary about the atrocities of the war. In short, the general picture was one of invisibility.

Decades ago, Ralph Ellison wrote his brilliant work *The Invisible Man,* in which he explored the conditions of the African American who was alienated, a stranger in the land of his birth, metaphorically and psychologically invisible to his fellow citizens whom he served as slave, entertainer and lowly-paid worker for centuries.

In African intellectual circles and elsewhere, the question is posed, is Africa now becoming the invisible continent? The coverage of events in Africa by the dominant [international] media gives reason to the sceptics to answer this question in the affirmative. As one critic once observed, "when, in fact do we 'see' Africa except where journalists, moved by compassion or sensationalism, show people in Europe and America the starving millions of Ethiopia and Sudan, or the blood-stained victims of violence in the townships of South Africa?"[2] The latest examples of invisibility are Liberia, Sierra Leone, and Somalia. The civil war in Liberia was largely ignored simply because it coincided with the Gulf crisis in 1990. Somalis had long been dying of civil war-induced famine and from the war itself. Yet the crisis did not merit any significant coverage until the outgoing President Bush showed "compassion", and as a way to mollify his conscience, launched "Operation Restore Hope." The media coverage that followed this declaration of "American compassion", appropriately described as "media circus", is now history.

But how long can six hundred million people remain invisible? As one African commentator observed, decades after Ralph Ellison[3] had written his seminal work, the United States discovered to its cost the problem of treating ten per cent of its population as if they did not exist.

ii)The price of prejudice

Ethnic, racial and colour prejudice-inspired hatreds have now become time bombs and active mines ominously ticking away on the landscapes of many countries and continents. Many of them have already exploded, leaving in their trail mass suffering, destruction and death. Ethnic prejudice and racially-clouded decisions and acts have brought untold harm to millions of innocent people whose only crime was in the difference of their skin colour, shape of their eyes, tribal or ethnic origin.

A sizeable percentage of the population of the decomposed Soviet Union are caught up in a fit of what appears to be inexorable inter-ethnic rebellions and massacres. In Africa, not only were whites arrayed against blacks (Apartheid South Africa), but also Indian minorities were expelled (Uganda 1975) and African ethnic and religious disputes in Sudan, Somalia, Ethiopia, Liberia, Sierra Leone, Nigeria, etc. have erupted in bloody massacres. In France, "which long thought itself immune from this kind of difficulty," ethnic and racial conflicts occur in Corsica, and also between African and Asian immigrants and the European population.[4]

In Britain, demands for ethnic self-assertion and independence by Northern Ireland resulted in several thousand deaths and destruction of property as the IRA, the Irish Republican Army, resorted to force to press home its demands. And in Canada, ethnic difficulties are leading to a threat of secession by the province of Quebec. History has recorded tragic examples. Hitler's genocide against the Jewish people, the Jewish pogroms in tsarist Russia, the near extermination of the native Indians in North America, the slave trade and colonialism in Africa.

During the Sino-Soviet split following the death of Stalin, the leadership of those two countries threatened, at one time, to annihilate their 1.3 billion peoples with nuclear weapons. The Soviets made secret suggestions to their capitalist archrivals, the United States of America, to sanitize the world of the "yellow peril." In response, the Chinese entered into a strategic alliance with the "foreign devils" in Washington to prevent the "Slavic hordes" from invading the sacred soil of the Chinese motherland. Had Marx, Engels and Lenin lived to hear the crude racism, egoism and chauvinism that were perpetrated in their names, the founders of communism would probably have wished they had never been born. Using ideological "purity" as a cover for the most base ethnocentric and selfish interests the Russians and Chinese communists behaved in a manner far more "disgraceful" than the religious sectarians that Marxism was supposed to have rendered obsolete.[5]

Canadian mass media philosopher Marshall McLuhan put us all in a global village. If we are to go by the logic of McLuhan's postulate, we are all [citizens of the global village] to speak out and be heard equally. However, that village does not give all of us equal say in the day-to-day running of the affairs of the village; the principle of democracy is subverted by village members who happen to have acquired the ability to speak louder than the rest; McLuhan's other postulate that the "medium is the message" has taken another ironic twist—power is the message [and consequently is right]. Thus the powerful wielders of "loudspeakers" and amplifiers, i.e. the dominant media in the North, have arrogated to themselves the right to shape the attitudes and feelings of other inhabitants of the village.

In a nutshell, the responsibility of the mass media in moulding the feelings and perceptions of the average person on international affairs becomes even more crucial, considering the diverse cultural norms, beliefs and practices of peoples in different parts of the world. In acting as observers, participants and catalyst[6], the news media provide the information that we need to create an image of the world. If that information is distorted, so too is the picture of reality. Observation and participation are closely linked; the media not only inform but they inform selectively[7]. Their ability to select enables them to influence our perception of the events that they report to us. By reporting some events and ignoring others and by giving prominence to some and trivializing others they place "important" and "non-important" tags on these events in our minds.

In addition, the media tend to put a nationalistic twist on international affairs and this, inevitably, influences our vision of world events. This vision is in many cases, tinged with our own prejudices, both positive and negative. The price we pay for these prejudices, especially negative ones are enormous. Over 139 million Africans died in the slave trade, while the scramble and partition of Africa by the slave masters left the continent with 34 nations and a population of less than five million.[8] Sixty million Jews perished in the holocaust, several thousands of Native Indians at the hands of European settlers, and thousands of citizens of the former Yugoslavia have also died as a result of ethnic cleansing. In all these instances, the media have been involved either by commission or omission in legitimizing these atrocities.

Some thirty years ago, African American W.E.B. Du Bois proclaimed that the problem of the 20th century is the problem of the colour bar. Had Du Bois lived today he would have broadened his perspective; he would probably have added [the] ethnic bar[9]. That said, however, the essence of Du Bois' warning is not lost. Today, at the beginning of the 21st century, humankind has not been able to prove Du Bois wrong in spite of the fact that the human race has developed powerful and far more effective means of communication through which mutual tolerance and respect, civilized and enlightened relationships between peoples of all races, cultures, countries and continents could be cultivated. Instead, the mass media appear to be only capable of recycling stereotypes, many of which tend to feed our base instincts of fear, suspicion and consequently hatred for people who do not "belong to us." Instead of becoming real tribunes for civilized interaction, mutual tolerance, and mutual respect for the cultures of others, the international media have merely succeeded in bolstering our capacity for racial and ethnic hatred, intolerance and bigotry.

It would be wrong, however, to fault the media for deliberately spreading ethnic and racial prejudice. The media are products of the societies in which they operate, and to paraphrase Lenin, they cannot exist in these societies and be free from them [societies]. The mass media in the capitalist world are prisoners of the capitalist society itself, which is rooted in a constant quest for and maximization of profit. Although, the quest for profit did not account for the culpability of the former Soviet media[10] in this shortcoming, it can be said that the ex-communist media operated by and large on similar principles as the capitalist media. In fact, as was shown earlier on in this study, the Soviet system was more state capitalism than socialism.

The objective of this book was to examine the socio-cultural and historical factors underlying news coverage of Africa by the press in the former Soviet Union. Its major focus has been on stereotype-formation — how stereotypes were employed both under communist rule and after the demise of Soviet-style communism to portray specific images of Africans in the news media. For comparison, I also analysed the differences and similarities in the news coverage of the press in the former Soviet Union. The book also attempted an evaluation of how the socio-cultural and philosophical foundations of the two former rival systems shape media gatekeepers' perception of what constitutes news emanating from the African continent.

The approach adopted by the Soviet/Russian press to the coverage of events in Africa offers a lucid lesson in how eurocentrism [ethnocentrism] and stereotyping operate and leads to a series of questions:

1)   What is it that the media of the two systems wanted to achieve with their strange suppression and juggling of news, which at times, tasted of manipulation?

2)   What mechanisms are set in motion when the so-called "free" Western and the "humanistic" Soviet/Russian place certain items in focus, while other issues are blacked out or misleadingly reported?

3)   Why do so many journalists in both Soviet/Russia and the West exhibit such an unwillingness to report positive events in Africa? Why do they react so one-sidedly when they report on Africa, paying attention most of the time to the "coup-famine-earthquake syndrome" while ignoring the battle for bread and butter and efforts at survival by the ordinary peoples of Africa?

4)   Do eyes see what eyes want to see when it comes to media coverage of African events and issues?

I do not contend that I answered these principled questions satisfactorily in this book. Suffice it to say I did try.

I tackled my research on three main hypotheses:

1)   Press or mass media systems are influenced and influence or reinforce the socio-cultural, psychological and ideological systems of any given society. All cultures are ethnocentric and the press more or less reflects this phenomenon. The more ethnocentric and racist a press system is the more it will marginalize and distort the African reality. This will in effect influence or reinforce their readers or audience's views about Africa and Africans.

2)   In press reporting, as in politics, there are no permanent friends, there are only permanent interests. Ethnocentric considerations often outweigh politico-ideological solidarity.

3) The Western media, because of their propensity to make profit, look for sensationalism in Africa in order to sell, often at the expense of balanced information. The Soviet/Russian media, on the other hand, did not hanker after profits and until 1990, did not even consider it "ethical" to carry advertisements. As an alternative to the Western capitalist system, the Soviet communist media would cover African issues and events from a more dispassionate, a broader and a more balanced angle.

However, Russian culture being a white culture, and white culture being noted for its propensity to accept unfavourable beliefs about non-white people, there will be similarities in the media representation of Africans in Russia with that in the West.

With these considerations in mind, I sought to find out how steadfastly the Soviet/Russian press held on to its proclaimed ideological solidarity with the "oppressed peoples of Africa" during the Cold War years, and how Gorbachev's "New Thinking" affected this ideological solidarity.

To test my hypothesis that "the ethnocentric blood is thicker than the ideological water," I analysed the extent of the marginalization of Africa along the twists and turns of the Kremlin's politics both domestically and internationally, as well as the interaction of politics and the press from the immediate pre-glasnost years through the six Glasnost years to the post-Glasnost years.

The following conclusions were drawn:

- The physics and the dynamics of superpower relations determined and still do determine Soviet/Russian press interest in African events. So did the dictum: "In politics there are no permanent friends, only permanent interests." The Soviet press lost interest in Africa as soon as there were no longer ideological points to score against the West. For example, had Nelson Mandela been released even two years earlier, the Soviet/Russian press would have provided an entirely different coverage. His release would have been proclaimed as yet another victory for communism.

- Africa was increasingly marginalized as the reforms advanced.

- New stereotypes about Africa and Africans replaced the old ones.

- The paternalistic nature of ex-Soviet propaganda concerning the USSR-African relationship, leading to an anti-African backlash, which seeks to wrongly scapegoat Africans as "part of the problem", now seems to dictate news coverage of the continent.

- With the Communist Party no longer setting the agenda for the press in the wake of the demise of communism, previously subdued anti-African prejudice has become more transparent. The predominantly negative tone and superficial nature of press coverage of Africa did influence ex-Soviet students and lecturers' perception of Africans making them even more prejudiced against Africans.

The comparison of the Western and Soviet/Russian systems of news coverage portrayed a struggle between the ruling classes in the respective countries for world supremacy; a struggle which manifested itself in the form of an ideological rivalry between socialism and capitalism during the entire Cold War period.

The study established that:

1) The press under both systems was ethnocentric, elitist and sensation-conscious.

2) Although the Western press was largely sensation-minded, it covered Africa slightly more propitiously and more amply, if not more judiciously, than the Soviet/Russian press.

3) Both press systems did not show any interest in changing the status quo in Africa. The preoccupation of the periodicals surveyed, particularly PRAVDA, NEWSWEEK, and THE DAILY TELEGRAPH, with negative occurrences

to the exclusion of the brighter side of life on the
continent gives cause to believe that they [the
publications] wanted to drive home the message
that Africans cannot govern themselves and that
the continent "is still stuck in its primitive,
bloodthirsty past;" that nations have wasted the
"golden opportunity" to build civilized statehood
after attaining political independence.

4)   The Soviet/Russian press proved to be more
ethnocentric and even racist. Positive stories about
Africa were paltry; more often, they were
published only when they touched on Soviet
assistance to one African country or another. Apart
from the periodicals under review, the AIDS issue
for example, was portrayed as disease of African
origin and given wide publicity in the form of a
poem in LITERATURNAYA GAZETA, in a
sports   magazine   and   countless   television
programmes.

Events emanating from what Russian journalists gleefully call the
"dark continent" were treated as second rate. Unless an African story
was linked with a Soviet/Russian leader or monumental event in
Russia, it was hardly given front-page placement.

In the rest of the cases, the news items were of so negative a nature
as to give an impression of a pervading sense of dejection, hopelessness
and haplessness in all Africa. This undoubtedly influenced and or
reinforced the formation of an overall negative image of Africans in the
minds of the Russian citizenry. As the results of our opinion survey
showed, Russian students and professors were less well disposed to
Africans than their Western counterparts.

My study also showed that the much vaunted Soviet/Russian
solidarity with Third World countries in the struggle against the one-
sided flow of news via the dominant Western media and for a more
balanced and all-sided distribution of news among peoples of our
planet was not reflected in the contents of the periodicals reviewed
during the pre-glasnost era. Apart from the anti-apartheid campaign,
other aspects of cooperation and solidarity were scantily covered in the
Soviet/Russian publications surveyed in this study.

One would have expected that as both Russia and Africa take steps
on the road to democracy, coverage of the continent by the ex-

communist press would improve. However, this was not the case; the farther Russia advanced in its democratic reforms, the more Africa got sidelined. By the end of 1992, a good number of African countries made the transition to democratic rule after decades of one-party dictatorship. Yet the post-communist press in Russia largely ignored this historic transition.

This is understandable. Like their Western counterparts, Russian correspondents operating in Africa are constrained in more than one way. Media gatekeepers and corporate business owners control what gets published, thereby shaping audience interest in African stories. Coups, millions dying, civil strife or draught and pestilence, yes. Anything else draws a yawn from newspaper editors and TV producers, as well as their readers and viewers back home. As one African publicist has rightly noted, AIDS and the killing of a drunk African baboon, for instance, are not stories that let the reader or viewer yawn. The fact that the former is a sexual story makes sense, and if it is an African sexual story, it becomes more than interesting for people, both Western and Oriental, who have been brought up on ingrained racist traditions against black people[11].

Africans, no doubt, long recognized the disparaging and insulting image the Western media presents of them. They know the monotonous old story, starting with the same one-dimensional character, set to a jaded script. The story is one of failure, chaos, inadequacy and barbarism. The character is dependent and inferior. The script requires a Western voice evoking compassion, amusement or outrage in his ever-so-superior listener.

What they hardly knew was that the Russian media were no different from the Western ones. Like in the West, news items were selected on their merit as *ideologichesko-pravil'noe,* "ideologically correct" and *khoroshie statii,* the Western equivalent of "good stories." While the former refers to stories that stressed the virtues of socialism against the vices of capitalism; Soviet/Russian humanism against Western individualism etc., the latter were basically human-interest stories. A domestic issue will normally take priority over a foreign one. The whole three-hour speech of Gorbachev would be run by PRAVDA and IZVESTIYA in full leaving little space for international news. A report on Africa would be used only if it contained elements of one of the two yardsticks mentioned above, or both, and portrayed something out of the ordinary to the Russian audience—a famine, some brutality or cultural curiosity. But the two yardsticks are screens over Russian ethnocentrism, which dismisses African sensibilities, real concerns and needs.

All this is so unfortunate and tragic. It is also dangerous, because as Gilbert Seldes notes, the mass media inculcate in people [in audiences] a weakened sense of discrimination, a heightening of stereotypical thinking patterns, and a tendency toward conformity and dependence. In the long run, Seldes contends, the mass media may discourage people from forming independent judgements. Even in their packaging of the news, let alone its persuasive components, the media are said to have the power to establish our agendas and help shape our view of the world.[12]

Thus, what Africa needs from the international news media is not a never-ending stream of disasters about to engulf the continent, but informed understanding of its seemingly intractable problems. Instead of lumping all African countries into one "hopeless" pile, the international media has a duty to distinguish between disasters such as Somalia and Liberia and successes such as Botswana and Zimbabwe (before the drought); to highlight, side by side with failures and corruptions among the African ruling elite, the many courageous and innovative responses to crisis on the part of civil associations; to consider the historical context of poverty, economic crisis, political violence, and arbitrary rule.

As professor Richard Sandbrook of the University of Toronto explains, the international media representation of Africa glosses over the historical context of Africa's current problems, which reinforces a very one-sided view. He sheds light on the root causes of Africa's myriad problems:

> Without the formation of cohesive nation-states with governments able to govern, economic development is likely to falter. Yet the process of creating such nation-states is generally long and violent. European nation-states emerged out of a couple of centuries of sporadic warfare, rebellions, and repression.[13]

Professor Sandbrook further writes:
> Most Latin American countries suffered a century or more of political violence and rule by *caudillos* before a basis of consensual government was established. In sub-Saharan Africa, owing to the arbitrary nature of colonial boundaries and administration, the process of state formation really began only with the anti-colonial movements of the early and mid-20th century.[14]

Concluding, he notes:

> It is therefore hardly surprising that bad governance and political
> disorder obstruct development in some African countries in the
> 1990s.[15]

Africa is a victim of historical tragedies, the trilogy of slavery colonialism, and neo-colonialism. All the international media can do is to give the continent its due; the problems of the continent must be understood and analysed in their historical context. One wonders if one would be asking the impossible to call on journalists of the North to remove the coating of moralism, ideology and sentimentality from these phenomena. Once this is done, to quote an African journalist, they shall see slavery as the equivalent of removing all the scientists, engineers and computer programmers from a modern industrial economy such as the USA. How many hours will the USA economy last without its scientists, computer programmers and engineers? Yet, this is the parallel of what happened to Africa when slavery robbed her labour-intensive, subsistence agricultural economy of its most productive man- and woman-power for four centuries.[16]

Without this historical parallel it is easy for ordinary people to be taken in by racist theories, which tend to dismiss Africans as genetically and intellectually inferior, incompetent, and lazy.

It is more than axiomatic that we live in an interdependent, interacting world. From the demise of communism in the former Soviet Union and the Eastern European block countries and the Gulf War through Somalia down to Bosnia, it has become abundantly clear that our planet, thanks to the scientific and technological revolution, has shrunk to a little balloon; a small ripple in one spot sends reverberations to all parts. What is more, in our new "global" world, nations are drawing closer together; an improvement discovered by one people becomes the common property of their neighbours.

We live in an era when the borrowing of achievements from each other has not only become the norm, but also an inevitable necessity. Yuri Igritsky a member of the former USSR, now Russian Academy of Sciences put it slightly differently. He said that since at a given time peoples may be passing through an essentially single process, the mechanistic idea of separate historical development does not hold water.[17]

Another Soviet scholar adds:

There are no inherently advanced and inherently backward peoples. All great civilized nations... have over their history, experienced periods of rapid progress and slow-downs and even zero movements which resulted in temporary lag.[18]

In his book *Spiritual Neo-Colonialism*, N. Yermoshkin writes:

True blossoming of national cultures presupposes mutual penetration and enrichment of cultures of various countries and peoples along with the preservation and development of their own distinctive heritage.[19]

Since wars begin in the minds of men, to borrow the famous phrase from the UNESCO constitution, it is in the minds of men that the defences of peace must be constructed.[20]   By accurately, dispassionately reporting international events, the media will be helping to construct the "defences of peace" and positively shape "the perception of national interests" by promoting the cross-fertilization of ideas, mutual exchange of knowledge and understanding, campaigning against racial and cultural prejudice and arrogance.

Of course the real situation in Africa cannot be called absolute prosperity, and it would be dishonest to assert that the continent is bereft of poverty, epidemics and disasters. However, the experience of human development has shown that: hopelessness often exists side by side with creativity, submission lives together with a passionate desire to struggle.   Side by side with poverty and misery, despair and hopelessness exists a constant struggle of Africans towards the resolution of their myriad problems. Of course, Africans themselves have contributed to the creation of many of these problems; have added to or even compounded them through the excesses of their leaders. For example, there was an incident in Nigeria where the government sent soldiers to wipe out an entire village for expressing dissent against certain government policies. African journalists have made no bones about these excesses, and poor governance. One does not expect Russian and Western journalists to become public relations officers for the continent, extolling its virtues.   But we expect from these journalists, reports of high quality, based on research journalism and careful analysis of events and issues, positing progress and retrogression; success and failure shown together, no matter whose ox is gored.

At the risk of sounding moralistic, I wish to re-emphasize a piece of advice given by American journalist James Reston to his colleagues nearly thirty years ago. In the introduction to his book *The Artillery of the Press*, Reston advocates "a less provincial, even a less nationalistic press, because our job in this age, as I see it, is not to serve as cheerleaders for our side in the present world struggle but to help the largest possible number of people to see the realities of the changing world in which American policy must operate. It also means a redefinition of what is 'news,' with more attention to the *causes* rather than merely the *effects* of international strife - at least by those American agencies, newspapers, and networks covering and influencing world affairs.[21]

Seeing, they say, is believing, and how people see themselves and others and the world around them is often how they believe themselves and the world to be. Images represent views; the press presents particular kinds of views. These views are ideological. But, to quote Nichols, "we are more than ideology makes of us."[22] There is nothing closer to the truth in Nichols' assertion than "it is the realm at the horizon of ideology that makes wisdom and change possible, and if our goal is to change the world access to the realm becomes essential."[23]

Nichols' assertion is of special significance when weighed against the background of Mikhail Gorbachev's philosophy of deideologization of inter-state relations, a philosophy, which sought to smooth the way towards ensuring the long-range survival of the global system. Wisdom means, and dictates, finding collective ways towards such a survival in the emergent New World Order. The demise of communism and the end of the Cold War has lessened, if not removed, the risk of an ideologically inspired world war. But there is a new kind of danger in the world today. It is the danger of a class war between the rich white, industrialized nations of the North and the poor non-white agricultural nations of the South. Bridging the ever-widening gap between the two sets of nations, in order to avert such a war, should be one of the major preoccupations of the international news media in our post-Cold War New World Order.

That said, however, Africans cannot hope to attract any better coverage by the international news media unless conditions on the continent improve to enable Africans to counter the pervasively negative presentation of their continent to the outside world. The charge by western journalists that there is nothing positive to report about in Africa[24] is a red herring. We know of the "Jap" bashing in the Western media in the periods before and soon after the world wars. Today, stories from Japan are overwhelmingly favourable both in the Russian and Western press, not because Japan has not got its fair share of negativity. Were Africa to be economically viable, like Japan, a different picture will be painted of the continent.

But conditions will not improve if African countries remain, in their isolated entities, ploughing their narrow furrows. What Africans need most is a political and economic union that will ensure the pooling of vast resources together, in order to improve the economic health of the continent. It is only when Africa is united politically and is economically strong that it can hope to enjoy the fruits the new world order are purported to yield.

To many, the idea of a union government of Africa is utopia. True, the enormity of the task ahead is quite great; the task of ironing out political, ideological differences, overcoming the vestiges of colonial divisions and neo-colonial machinations are enormous. All this has led to many concluding that a union government of Africa in any form is nothing but a utopian daydreaming. But this sense of utopia should not push Africans into resignation or inaction. After all, history has amply demonstrated that all great ventures of human civilization started in the womb of utopianism.   What is more, Africans should remind themselves that, "any programme, no matter how poorly conceived, if imaginatively executed, is better than complete inaction."

To conclude it is pertinent to note that the press like any social institution is not perfect, more than that, the press is a product of historical conditions.   The existing systems of information management, control and selection of its content within the framework of Russian and Western societies are the results of previous definite conditions. It is only fair to mention that mass media coverage of African and black issues in the Western media have seen some improvements over the past 20 years or so. In Britain and North America, for instance, the race or skin colour of the subject of a newspaper story is nowhere indicated unless it is very necessary. In other countries, for example, in the Netherlands and Germany, attempts are being made to improve media coverage of ethnic minorities. In 1989, an international conference on "Migrants, Media and Cultural Diversity" organized by the Netherlands in conjunction with the European Council in Noordwijkerhout discussed possible ways of providing better information on minorities and their cultures by journalists, editors and producers.[25] In Germany, the *Civis* Media Prize award has been instituted to encourage objective and dispassionate coverage of racial minority issues in the media. According to the sponsors and organizers of the award, it is an effort to help Germans and Europeans to be hospitable and to teach them to accept foreigners with their different approach to life.[26]

The improved coverage has, to some extent, forced positive change in attitudes among a growing section of the populations of some Western countries. Unfortunately, improved coverage has also led to complacency. For example, this is how some British television programme-makers reacted to criticism of poor coverage given to the Ethiopia famine in 1986: "We are improving. We might have been a bit late for the last Ethiopian famine, but we're right there, cameras at ready, on time, in 1988."[27] That is about the limit of self-criticism.

But the press and individual efforts alone cannot change national attitudes all by themselves. Governments have to create harmonious race relationships. At the same time, it is worth emphasizing that pro-African or pro-racial minority press campaigns may well be negative if they stem from paternalistic feelings and considerations of charity. Nonetheless, the main aim of a journalist's approach, in my opinion, should be to rise above his/her ethnocentrism, to be less nationalistic and more detached in handling African or ethnic issues; an approach that will show Africans and other ethnic minority groups not as "lazy hangers-on" or "alien hordes", but as part of the human race, a source of enrichment; that hostility and xenophobia will not solve the social problems for which Africans and other racial minorities are wrongly blamed; that differences between black and white people are only skin deep.

If Western journalists cover Africa more comprehensively and more positively, this may be explained by the longer contact of the West with the African continent. However, this does not in any way justify the Soviet/Russian press' sloppy, shallow and one-sided coverage of events in Africa. Now in the Russian media, words such as solidarity, anti-fascism, anti-racism and internationalism have fallen into disrepute. This "virtue" dictated by the Communist Party but never whole-heartedly accepted by the people, has now become a vice. The stereotyped over-simplified presentation of African problems distorts the African reality and hence the perception of Russians about Africans, who see the continent as an embodiment of eternal chaos, political instability, primitive cultures, civil disorder, corruption and exotic and barbarous customs; Africans as lazy hangers-on and parasites. One of the ways to temper this negative perception with a more benign image is through interpersonal interaction.

But with the new Russian leaders eager to cut all links with Africa (with several embassies closed and scholarships virtually cut)[28]

Russians are likely to continue to wallow in ignorance and remain removed from the African reality. The danger is that should another opportunity for broader interaction arise, it would be like starting from point zero. When the first opportunity presented itself for broader interaction with Africans during communist rule, Russians were largely discouraged to do so. In sharp contrast to their professed solidarity with and support for the development and preservation of African cultures and consequent criticism of Western cultural imperialism and arrogance, Russian communists rarely showed any real interest in African culture. African cultural troupes were rarely invited to perform in Russia.

For the whole 10 years that I lived in St Petersburg, the second largest city in the former Soviet Union, the only African cultural group that ever visited the city was the Ethiopian "People to People" Cultural Troupe, which was on a worldwide thanksgiving tour after the 1986 Ethiopian famine. Unlike in many Western countries where African music enjoys great popularity, to hear African music on Russian radio is like hearing exotic music from Mars. African films like African music have been gaining popularity in Western countries, with many winning prestigious awards. Yet not during the last 10 years was a film produced and directed by an African screened for the Russian public, besides those screened at film festivals.

Even African participation at film festivals in the former Soviet Union was largely marginalized or glossed over in the media. For example, in 1987 there were two separate film festivals in Moscow. The first involved Ghanaian films. The other featured Swedish movies. Nothing at all appeared on the Ghanaian film festival in the Soviet mainstream media. However, the media went agog with a series of reports about the Swedish film festival, which was held a week later.

The above example illustrates the double standard and *pokazukha* [disinformation or make-believe] tactics adopted by the Soviet/Russian media towards Africa and other Third World countries, which is also a reflection of the Kremlin's policy in this part of the world. The Soviet/Russian people were just as much the victims of this disinformation as were African governments and citizens.

Endnotes

Preface

[1]The name of the university was changed to its pre-revolutionary name in the wake of the anti-communist revolution unleashed by the Gorbachev perestroika-glasnost reforms.

Introduction

[1]Ridder Haggard was the English author of a number of fantastic novels that portrayed white "gods" and "goddesses", "heroes" and "heroines" on incredibly dangerous "civilizing" missions of the "Dark Continent" in search of the "lost land," the "lost race," the wonder that lies over the next mountain or beyond "the farthest sea."

[2]Mezler, Vaughan. (1989). Africa through racist spectacles. *African Events*, p.12.

[3]See N. Yermoshkin, *Spiritual Colonialism*, Prague, 1984.

[4]See *Literator*, December, 1990.

[5]*Perestroika* is Russian for "restructuring." It was the economic plank in Ex-Soviet leader Mikhail Gorbachev's two-pronged revolution "to give socialism a human face." The other plank was *glasnost*— "openness" in the political/ideological sphere.

[6]Russia will be used interchangeably for the Soviet Union or U.S.S.R. But the Russian Federation will be used to refer to what used to be known as the Russian Federation of Socialist Republics (RFSR) during the communist era.

[7]This hypothesis is based on Lord Pamelston's famous dictum.

[8]By "realistic cultural relativistic" approach I mean a system of news gathering and reportage in which media practitioners evaluate events in

other societies not only from the vantage point of the value systems of those other societies, but do not abdicate their responsibility to exposing practices that deviate from the basic human values of dignity, protection from death, hunger, and general survival.

[9]The years 1985, 1987, and 1990 are chosen because they make it easier to chart the dynamics of coverage of Africa in the course of the easing of East-West tension until the Soviet Union eventually collapsed eight months later.

[10]Condon, J. C. & Mitsuko (eds). (1976). *Communication Across Cultures: For What?* Tokyo: The Samuel Press.

[11]Ibid.

Chapter One

[1]Radical and nationalist leaders like Patrice Lumumba of the Congo, Kwame Nkrumah of Ghana and Salvador Allende of Chile were either assassinated or thrown out of power with the active collaboration of the Central Intelligence Agency (C.I.A.) of America. In neighbouring Afghanistan, the Soviets intervened in a purely internal power struggle to impose their stooge in power.

[2]I will use "American-West" and "Soviet-East" to refer to the West and the former Soviet Union and Eastern Europe in the same sense as "East" and "West" were used to refer to the two power blocks during the Cold War era.

[3]See Gromyko, A. A. (1985).*Aktualnie problemi otnoshenii so strannami Afriki*, Moscow: Progress Publishers.

[4]Albright, D. E. (1986).East-West Tension in Africa. In M.O. Shulman, *East-west tension in the third world*," New York: W.W. Norton and Co. p.136.

[5]Kortunov, S. (1989). Soviet foreign aid. *Moscow News*, No.49, p.6.

[6]*New Times.* (1990 July 4), p.18.

[7]*See Business MN - Moscow News* (1991, No 48); and also *Moscow News*, (1991, No.52), p.15; *Chas Pik*, (1991,December 12), p.5.

[8]See Furedi, F. (1988). *Superpower rivalries in the third world: New perspectives in the north-south dialogue.* London: Third World Communication and I.B. Tauris & Co. Ltd. Publishers.

[9]Morthengau, Hans. (1973). Politics Among Nations: The Struggle for Power and Peace. New York: Knopf, p.64.

[10]Shulman, M.O. (1986). *East-West Tension in the Third World*, New York, p.15.

[11]Furedi, F. (1988).

[12]Samir Amir is a prominent Egyptian scholar who has widely written on North-South issues. He is widely known for his leftist views.

[13]Valkiner, E. K. (1986). *Revolutionary change in third world politics.* No.38, p.422.

[14]*International Affairs.* (1989, June). p.137.

[15]Zaslavsky, V. *The Soviet World System: Origins, Evolution, Prospects for Reform*, Telos, 1986, p.14.

[16]*The Programme of the Communist Party of the Soviet Union*, Progress Publishers, Moscow, 1986.

[17]Magari, Yuri. (1986).*Countering Information Imperialism*, Novosti Press Agency Publishing House, p.36.

[18]*The New York Times*, June, 1970, p.81.

[19]Aronson, James. (1971) *Packing The News: A Critical Survey of the Press, Radio and Television*, New York: International Publishers, p.21.

[20]Kashlev, Yuri. (1983). *The Mass Media and International Relations*, Prague, p.63.

[21]Quoted in Laqueur, Walter. (1983). *The Patterns of Soviet Conduct in the Third World*. New York: Praeger Publishers, p. 200.

[22]Materials of the XXVII Congress of the Communist Party of the Soviet Union, (1986) Moscow: p.87.

[23]*Demokraticheski Zhurnalist*, (1982). Pargue, April, , p.25.

[24]The original name was given to the concept by its ardent proponents from both the Non-Aligned Movement and the former Soviet block countries, but was changed to New World Information and Communication Order, after bitter debates. "The" was changed to "a" to remove the implication that there could be only **one** new 'order'; one reflecting the imposition of a single standard. Moreover, 'international' became 'world' to remove the suggestion that any global communication 'order' would be formed, controlled or its messages censored by 'nations', thus threatening non-governmental, including commercial entities.

[25]*Demokraticheski Zhurlnalist*, p.26.

[26]*Asia and Africa Today*, No.3, 1989, p.39.

[27]*Asia and Africa Today*, (1990)."New Political Thinking and the Third World, No.4, pp.35-36.

[28]Cliff Tony. (1974). *State Capitalism in Russia.* London:, Pluto Press, pp 283-5.

[29]Russia will be used interchangeably with the former Soviet Union, while The Russian Federation (RF) will be used to refer to post-Communist Russia minus the remaining former Soviet republics.

[30]Binns, Peter. (1974) "The theory of state capitalism," in Tony Cliff *State Capitalism in Russia.* London:, Pluto Press, p.95.

[31]Ibid.

[32]Vasilyev, Alexei, Vladimir Lee, Yuri Popov and Vladimir Touradjev, (1990). "New Political Thinking and the Third World," *Asia and Africa Today*, No.4, p.35.

[33]For further details see *Soviet Social Imperialism in India*, (1976) Vancouver, BC; Marshall, Goldman. (1967). *Soviet Aid*, Praeger, New York,; Martin, Nicolaus (1975). *Restoration of Capitalism in the USSR*, Chicago: Liberator Press; Tsetung, Mao. (1977) *A Critique of Soviet Economics*, New York.

[34]Clawson, P. & Mehrotra, S. K. (1983). Soviet Economic Relations With India and Other Third World Countries. In *The Soviet Union: Socialist or Social Imperialist?* Cicago: RCP Publications, April, 1983, pp.129-130.

[35]Ibid, 131.

[36]Quoted in Herman, Richard. (1985). *Perceptions and Behavior in Soviet Foreign Policy.* Pittsburgh: Pittsburgh University Press, p.51.

[37]King, Preston.(1986) *An African Winter*, Middlesex: Penguin Books Ltd., pp.70-71. See also Richard B. Remnek, (1981)."Soviet Policy in the Horn of Africa: The Decision to Intervene" in *The Soviet Union and the Third World: Successes and Failures,* Robert H. Donaldson (ed.), London: Westview Press.

[38]Ibid, p. 71.

[39]Ibid, p.71.

[40]Ibid, p.72.

[41]Ibid.

[42]Ibid.

[43]*Izvestiya*, December 15, 1978; see also V. Sidenko, "The International Settlement Farce," *New Times*, No.20, May 1979, pp.10-11.

[44]*International Affairs*, Moscow, November, 1988, p.140.

[45]Frank Furedi, p.131.

[46]Kiva, Alexei (1991). "Africa's Second Liberation," *New Times*, No.52, p.32.

[47]Ibid.

[48]Ibid.

[49]Padmore, George. (1972). Pan-Africanism or Communism? New York: Doubleday & Company, Inc. p.269.

[50]Kiva, Alexei. (1991), p.32.

[51]Padmore, George. (1972). p.268.

[52]F. Fukuyama, "Military Aspects of US-Soviet Competition in the Third World" in Shulman op.cit. p.184.

[53]Frank Furedi, p.13.

[54]Ibid.

[55]See, for example, L.I. Brezhnev, "In the Name of Happiness of Soviet People," *Vital Speeches*, Vol. XL, No.12, April 1979, p. 371; V. Vorobyev, "Colonialist Policies in Africa," *International Affairs*, No.9, September 1978, pp.47-48. D. Volsky, "Southern Africa: Protracted Convulsion," *New Times,* No.22, May 1979, p.7; G. Roshcin, "International Monopoly Expansion in Africa," *International Affairs*, No.7, July 1979, pp.68-69; and *Izvestiya*, January 31, 1979.

[56]See, for example, Roschin, p.5; *Izvestiya,* January 12, 1979; *Pravda,* December 11, 1978; Radio Moscow, August 6, 1979, in Foreign Broadcast Information Service, Daily Report: *Soviet Union,*(hereafter FBIS: Soviet Union) August, 1979.

[57]See *Izvestiya*, October 26, 1978; *Izvestiya*, January 17, 1979.

[58]*Aziya i Afrika cegodniya*, No.3, 1989, p.5.

[59]Izyumov. A. and Andrei Kortunov. (1988). *International Affairs*, November, p.145.

[60]Ibid.

[61]*Mezhnarodnaya Zhizn*, (November 1988, p.143).

[62]Zeebroek, X (1984). "Soviet Expansionism and Expansive Anti-Sovietism", *Socialist Register*, London, p.290.

[63]See Makinda, S.M. (1987). *Superpower Diplomacy in the Horn of Africa*, London.

[64]Kozintsev, B. and P. Kashlov, (1978). "Economic Cooperations of the USSR and the Countries of Tropical Africa," *Foreign Trade*, No.2, February, p.30.

[65]See *Izvestiya*, February 6, 1990, p.5.

[66]Johnson, R. (1985-86)"Exaggerating America's stakes in Third World Conflicts," *International Security*, 10(3), Winter, p.67.

[67]Wolf, Brenda (1976). *Issues of Fundamental Relevance to Socio-Economic Progress of Developing Countries*, Part 3, Berlin: College of Solidarity Press, p.48.

[68]Ibid, p.47.

[69]Ibid.

[70]Ibid, p.48.

[71]Ibid, p.49.

[72]Gorbachev's 'New Thinking' draws on the work of Albert Einstein, the Western peace movement, Willy Brandt, Olof Palme, Gramsci and such marginal aspects of the Anglo-American International Studies as the World Order Project.

[73]Gorbachev, M. S. (1986). *Izbrannye rechi i stat'i*, vol. 2-5, Moscow: Polizdat.

[74]Ibid.

[75]Ibid.

[76]See Gorbachev, M. S. (1987). *Perestroika and New Thinking For Our Country and the Rest of the World*, Moscow: Progress Publishers.

[77]See *Pravda* (1987).September 17.

[78]Ibid.

[79]Ibid.

[80]*Pravda.*(1988). December 8.

[81]Gorbachev, M. S. (1989). *Izbrannye rechi i stat'i*, Moscow: Progress Publishers.

[82]Ibid.

[83]See Gorbachev, M. S. (1988). *Perestroika and New Thinking in Our Country and the Rest of World,* Moscow: Progress Publishers.

[84]*Information Buletin, Peace and Socialism.* (1987).International Publishers, Prague, p.7.

[85]Ibid.

[86]Ibid.

[87]*Demokraticheski Zhurnalist*, (1989, April). p.24.

[88]Ibid.

[89]Conteh-Morgan, Earl. (1992, May). "Soviet Disintegration and Conflict Transformation in the Third World," *Peace Research* Vol.24 (No.2), p.39.

[90]Ibid.

[91]*Pravda.* (1992, February 28). *Peterburskie Vedmosti.* (1992, February 28).

[92]Historic because it was the first visit by a Soviet Foreign Affairs Minister to Africa in more than 40 years, in spite of the fact that Shevernadze's predecessor, Anatoly Gromyko did not pay a single visit to Africa over 30 years long service, the longest ever in Soviet diplomatic history.

[93]*Novoe Vremya.* (1990, April 17-23). pp.15-16.

[94]Kortunov, Andrei. (1989). "Soviet Foreign Aid - Is it always Put to the Wisest Use?" *Moscow News*, No.49, 1989, p.6. See also *Asia and Africa Today* No.4, 1990, pp.35-45.

[95]See V.I. Lenin, "Once Again on Trade Unions, The Current Situation and the Mistakes of Trosky and Bukharin," *Collected Works*, Vol.32, p.83.

[96]Adamishin, Anatoly. (1990, February 9*). New Times*, p.6.

[97]Ibid.

[98]Ibid.

[99]Part of interview on prime time, (*Vremya*), evening news programme.

[100]Manchkha, P. I. (1986). *Afrika na puti k sotsialnomu progressi*, Moscow: Politizdat, pp. 181-182.

[101]*Mezhnarodnaya Zhizn,* (1988,November). p.145.

[102]Kortunov, Andrei. (1989)."Soviet Foreign Aid," *Moscow News*, No. 49, p.6.

[103]Ibid.

[104]Ibid.

[105]Manchakha, 1986.

[106]Ibid.

[107]Polyakov, G. (1990). *Asia and Africa Today*, No. 8, p.18.

[108]Ibid.

[109]Ermakov, Vladimir (1992, November 5). "Ne khodila biy Rossiya v Afriki "gulyat," *Izvestiya*, p.7.

[110]Vasilyev, Alexei. (1990, October 20). "Why Do We Need Africa?," *Izvestiya*, p.5.

[111]This was part of an interview conducted by collaborators of this author with Russians of all walks of life in St Petersburg in 1992 for a video documentary about African Russians.

[112]Tarutin, Igor.(1993, February 20). Afrikantsi khotyat rabotat s Ruskimi, *Izvestiya*, p.4.

[113]Ibid.

[114]Foreign Minister Kozyrev, for example, insisted that under 'normal conditions,' i.e. if no armed conflict is underway, Russia should develop relations with countries in the Third World only when there is a clear economic rationale for doing so. Kozyrev, "Dumat o svoikh interesakh," *Izvestiya*, October 2, 1991, p.3.

[115]*Trud*, (1992, March 6).

[116]Yusin, Maxim. (1992, March 9). "Angola ne namerena vosvrashat sovietskie dolgi," *Izvestiya*, p.6.

[117]Pilyatskin, Boris. (1992, March 4). "Mi stanovimciya c YuAR dryzhestvennimi partnerami," *Izvestiya*, p.8.

[118]About 80 per cent of the total number of former Soviet missions earmarked for closure by the Russian government as part of cost-saving exercise were in Africa.

[119]Yeltsin made the statement for the first time during his presidential election campaign in the Urals in June 1991. His speech was reported, unedited by the *Mayak* radio station. The print media and television edited out "Africa". He repeated the same statement during an interview soon after the August communist revanchist coup was foiled.

[120]Several participants in the first American-style TV talk show program, *Tema* (Theme) did not shy away from their racist sentiments. One said in reply to a question, that he would emigrate to South Africa should the future president of Russia be a black man. According to him it is easier to fight blacks in South Africa. Russians, he claims, are too soft. Taking a cue from the mainstream media are the fledgling fascist alternative media. The St.Petersburg *Otechestvo* wrote in its February. 1992 edition: "American blacks, who earn five dollars per hour wages

could come to our country and pose as millionaires and take liberties with our girls and contaminate the Russian blood."

[121]The effect of this negative propaganda on Russian public opinion has been quite considerable. A survey I conducted among Russian lecturers and students and western exchange students in St. Petersburg institutions of higher learning showed that the Russian students were more prejudiced against Africans than their western counterparts. When asked of their reaction to wedlock between a close relative and an African, 22.3 per cent of the Russian students and 35.1 per cent of the Russian professors said they were categorically against such wedlock, while only 3.6 per cent of the western students gave a similar response.

[122]See Natasha Singer. (1994). "Yeltsin and Ilya Glazunov," *Moscow Times*

[123]Ustimenko, O. (1991, December 13). A byili zloveshimi eti tri bukviy--YuAR. *Sovietskiy sport*, 6.

[124]Dubrovskiy, A. (1991, July 18). Beliy rai? *Znamya yunosti*, 3.

[125]Nalbadyan, Z. (1991, December 11) Russkie v Yuzhnoi Afrike. *Trud*, 7.

[126]Pilyatskin, B. (1991, November 23). Zakriyvayutsiya 9 posoltsv. Pochemy ne 50? *Izvestiya*, 10.

[127]Tetekin, S. (1992). Russiya I YuAR, *Izvestiya*, February 10, 1992, p.5.

[128]See *Gemini News Bulletin.* (1987, November). 8; (1991, March), 4

[129]Chaplina, N.(1992, October 19). Zebra po imeni YuAR. *Chas pik*, 12.

[130]Dubrovskiy, A. (1991, July 18). Beliy rai? *Znamya yunosti*, 3.

[131]Adade, C.Q. (1992, March 23). "Russians Queue Up To Live in South Africa," *African Concord*, p. 18.

[132]*Izvestiya.* (1991, December 9). p.3.

[133]Adade, C.Q. (1992, March 3). "Russians Queue Up To Live in South Africa," *Gemini News Service Buletin.*

[134]For further details, see Boris Pilyatskin's article : "N. Mandela ne smog k nam priekhat. On sei chas v S SH A," *Izvestiya*, December 9, 1991, p.3.

[135]See *Chas Pik*, December 15, 1991. See also *Nevskoe Vremya*, October 3, 1991, p.1.

[136]*Izvestiya.* (1992, January 24).

[137]*Izvestiya.* (1992, February 10). p.5.

[138]See *Chas Pik.* (1991, December 15). See also *Nevskoe Vremya.*(1991, October 3). p.1.

[139]The shooting to death of the General Secretary of the South African Communist Party Chris Hani by a Polish immigrant and member of a neo-Nazi group, whose aim is to wage a race war to ensure "the survival of the white race" in South Africa, makes it difficult to dismiss Black fears over the influx of citizens of the former Soviet Union and Eastern Europe.

[140]The 30th anniversary of the Soviet Union and South Africa's first "open agreement" on diamond trade relations was marked in Moscow in 1989. In attendance were Mrs. Raisa Gorbachev, wife of the former Soviet leader, and H. Oppenheimer, founder of the De Beers Diamond Marketing Company.

Chapter Two

[1]"Press will be used interchangeably for "mass media" and "media.""

[2]Davidson, A.B, Olderodge, D.A. & Solodinikov, V. G. (1986). *USSR and Africa.* Moscow: Nauka Publishing House.

[3]Blakely, Alison. (1986). *Russia and the Negro.* Washington, D. C: Howard University Press, p. 28.

[4]For a more detailed insight, read Clarence Holte's account of the "The Black Presence in Pre-Revolutionary Russia" *in African Presence in Early Europe* edited by Ivan Van Sertima, New York: Transaction, 1986.

[5]Blakely, Alison, pp. 5-6.

[6]Holte, Clarence. (1986). p.270.

[7]Blakely, Alison p. 5.

[8]Ibid. p.10.

[9]Ibid.

[10]Van Sertima, Ivan. (1986). *African Presence in Early Europe.*

[11]Ibid. p. 272.

[12]Blakely, Alison. (1986). *Russia and the Negro.* p.15.

[13]Quoted in Clarence Holte's account of the "The Black Presence in Pre-Revolutionary Russia." In *African Presence in Early Europe* edited by Ivan Van Sertima, (1986). p.270.

[14]Ibid.

[15]Ibid.

[16]For more detailed information about the life of Aldridge, read IRA ALDRIDGE: THE NEGRO TRAGEDIAN, by Herbert Marshall and Helen Stock, 1958, Rockcliff: Salisbury Square, London.

[17]Van Sertima, Ivan. (1986). *African Presence in Early Europe.*

[18]Quoted in Clarence Holte's account of the "The Black Presence in Pre-Revolutionary Russia." In *African Presence in Early Europe* edited by Ivan Van Sertima, 1986.

[19]Van Sertima, Ivan. (1986). *African Presence in Early Europe.*

[20]Ibid.

[21]Blakely, Alsion. (1986). *Russia and the Negro* , pp. 5-6.

[22]Blakely, p.26.

[23]Blakely, p.27.

[24]Wison, Edward. (1974). *Russia and Black Africa Before World War II,* New York: Holmes & Meler, p.24.

[25]See *Istoricheskii arkhiv*, 1960, No.3 p.237.

[26]Ibid.

[27]Blakely, p.128.

[28]Richard Bissel, "Union of Soviet Socialist Republics," in Thomas H. Henriksen, ed., *Communist Powers and Sub-Saharan Africa*, Stanford: Hoover Institute Press, 1981, pp.11-14.

[29]Klomegah, Kester. (1998, February). "Victims of racism in new Russia defenceless," *Sankofa News*, vol.4, 9.

[30]Ibid, p. 132.

[31]For further details, see Blakely, pp-27-38.

[32]Blakely, p.40.

[33]Dilling, Dillingworth. (1932). "What are the Soviets." *Abbot's Monthly*, pp.6-7. (Cited in Blakely, Russia and the Negro, p.81).

[34]Patterson, William L. (1971). The Man Who Cried Genocide. New York: International Publishers, p.112.

[35]McKay, Claude. (1923, December). "Soviet Russia." *The Crisis*, pp. 61-64.

[36]Adorno, T. W., *et al.* (1959). *The Authoritarian Personality.* New York: Harper.

[37]Sherkovin, Yu.A. (1985*). Social psychology and propaganda.* Moscow: Progress Publishers.

[38]Adorno, 1950.

[39]Blumer, H. 1965. "Industrialization and Race Relations." In Industrialization and Race relations: *A Symposium.* Guy Hunter (ed.). London: Oxford University Press.

[40]Augie, Fleras and Jean Leonard Elliot. (1996). Unequal Relations: An Introduction to Race, and Aboriginal Dynamics in Canada. Scarborough: Prentice Hall, Inc. 67.

[41]Ibid.

[42]McKenna,Ian. (1994) "Canada's hate propaganda laws – A Critique," *British Journal of Canadian Studies:* 15—2.

[43]Augie Fleras and Jean Leonard Elliot, (1996) *Unequal relations: An introduction to race, and aboriginal　　dynamics in Canada.* Prentice Hall, Inc. Scarborough, 67.

[44]Kon, 1967.

[45]Tuen A. Dijk, (1993) *Elite discourse and racism.* Newbury Park, CA: Sage Publications.

[46](McQuail, 1959; 1964; 1968).

[47]Klapper, J.T. (1960). *The Effects of Mass Communications.* London: Free Press.

[48]McCombs, M. Gilbert, S. (1986). "News influence on our pictures of the world." In D. Nimmo and D. Zillmann. *Perspectives of Media Effects.* Hillsdale, NJ: Lawrence Erlbaum, 1-16.

[49]Lang, K., Lang, G.E. (1966). "Functions of the mass media." In Berelson and M.Janowitz (eds) *Public Opinion and Communication.* New York: Free Press, 466.

[50]Cohen, B. C. (1963). *The Press and Foreign Policy.* London: Princeton University Press, 120.

[51]McCombs, D. & Bernard Shaw. (1981).

[52]Ankomah, Baffour. (2000, July/August). "In the name of national interest," New African, p.19.

[53]Ibid.

[54]Ibid, pp.19-20.

[55]Ibid, p.20.

[56]Adade, C.Q. (1985, August 16) "African Students in the USSR," *African Times*, London, 8-9.

[57]In interviews conducted by this author in St. Petersburg in the late 1980s and early 1990s, African students related their specific experiences in the classrooms. Many of the anecdotes reflected the general stereotypical views of the general Russian public, but some were very specific to academic life. For example, some students mentioned cases in which they had to go out of their way to praise the achievements of the Soviet socialist state, heap adulations on Lenin and other Soviet leaders and to castigate Western imperialist machinations in the Third World in attempt only to win the favor of their professors, but also to score high marks in examinations.

[58]For a detailed analysis of the Soviet media, see Mark W. Hopkins, The Mass Media in the Soviet Union, Pegasus, New York, 1970.

[59]Asoyan, B. (1987, November 7) "Afrika uzh tak daleko," *Literanturnaya gazeta*, 14.

[60]Tuen A. Dijk, (1993) *Elite discourse and racism*. Newbury Park, CA: Sage Publications.

[61]Hartman P., & Husband, C. (1970). *Racism and the mass media.* London: Davis-Poynter.

[62]Rose, E.I.B. (1969). *Colour and Citizenship.* London: Oxford University Press.

[63]Deakin, N. (1970). *Colour citizenship and British society.* London: Panther Books.

[64]Hartman & Husband, 1970.

[65]Likhachev, D. S. (1991, No.1). Russkaya kul'tura v sovremennom mire. *Novyi mir*, 3-9.

[66]Kingston-Mann, Esther (1999). *In Search of the True West. Culture, Economics, and Problems of Russian Development.* Princeton: Princeton University Press, 1999. p.195.

[67]Kingston-Mann, Esther (1999).

[68]Plehakov, K. (1992, No.9) The Russian tragedy. *New Times*, 9-11. Pleshakov, P. (1992 No.2).

[69]See Davidson, Olderogge, and Solodonikov, 1966.

[70]Blakely, p.34.

[71]Blakely, Ibid.

[72]Griboedov, A. S. (1923) Gore ot uma [Woe from Wit]. *Moscow Neva.*

[73]Works of art that portrayed blacks in subservient roles include *Countess Samoilova and Her Foster Daughter,* and *Bathesheba,* 1832 by Kar Briulov, one of the important Russian artists of the early nineteenth century.

[74]*Den'* September 9, 1862, no. 39, pp 17-18.

[75]Hartman & Husband, 1970.

[76]The largest number of Africans to have emigrated to Russia are the African Abkhazians numbering about 50 families. Other sources put their number before the First World War at 500. They are believed to be African slaves brought to the Black Sea Coast in the 16th, 17th, and 18th centuries by the Arabs. When Abkhazia became part of Russia in 1918, some of them fled to Turkey. The rest remained in Russia.

[77]*Le Nouvel Observatuer,* (1988, December 14), 15.

[78]The end of 1988 and the beginning of 1989 marked the beginning of full-blown glasnost in the mass media.

[79]Adade, C.Q., 1985

[80]See Curtis Keim, (1999). *Mistaking Africa: Curiosities and Inventions of the American Mind.* Oxford: Westview Press. See also Downing (1980). *The Media machine.* London: Pluto Press; Hartman & Husband, 1974, Wilson & Gutierrrez (1985*) Minorities and the media.* Beverly Hills, CA & London: Sage.

[81]Hall, E.T. (1959). *The silent language: The hidden dimension.* New York:Fowcet Premier Books, 166-167.

[82]This and many such anecdotes were repeated by fellow African students to the point of boredom, in the form of comic relief. Similar anecdotes are prevalent in the West. For examples, see Curtis Keim's Mistaking Africa, Westview Press, Boulder, Colorado, 1999.

[83]By virtue of the fact that they look much like other Soviet minorities in Central Asia and the Caucasus, students from North Africa received more favorable treatment than Africans from South of the Sahara. Sometimes Russians could not distinguish an Algerian from an Azeri, unless he/she is told.

[84]Asoyan, B. (1989, August 7) Sgushennoi krasok. *Komsomoslkaya pravda,* 4.

[85]This is based on the author's own personal experience and interviews granted him for his video documentary, *The Ones They Left Behind: The Life and Plight of African Russians,* 1993.

[86]For American versions of this antiquated and racist perception of Africans see Curtis Keim, 1999, p.63).

[87]Hartman P., & Husband, C. (1970).

[88]Ibid.

[89]African Russians are the children of mainly African students and Soviet[Russian] mothers who for various reasons, were left behind in the former Soviet Union by their departing fathers.

[90]Simmons, A. M. (1991, December 2). Black like Misha and Yelena. *Time*, 40.

[91]This section is based on in-depth video interviews conducted by this author among more than fifty African-Russians, their mothers, African students, African diplomats, and a cross section of residents of St. Petersburg and Moscow.

[92]The Russian word for 'black' is cherny, but Russians prefer calling Blacks *negr*, pronounced *niegr* somewhere between 'negro' and 'nigger'.

[93]"Ostavaites' dazhe esli yedite," [Do not go even if you have to leave] *Rabochaya Smena,* No.10, 1987 pp.38-39.

[94]The New African magazine (January 1997, p.35) reports that, in a recent incident in St. Petersburg, African students who were acquitted by a court when drunken detectives who had harassed them and hauled them before the court for no apparent reason, refused to file a suit against the drunken detectives for fear they would expose themselves to further harassment if they did.

[95]Sergei Minayev, "A Black Russian Fights the Odds" *Moscow Times*, Tuesday, July 28, 1998.

[96]The son of a Russian accountant and a Tanzanian medical student is the only black man currently serving in the Russian armed forces. While thousands of ordinary Russians live on the run from the police after dodging the dreaded draft, Molisa has embraced his comrades with open arms, despite the armed forces' unenviable reputation for brutality toward new recruits. "I have been dreaming of becoming an army officer all my life, because I think the army is a job for a real man," said Molisa. "I also realized that the army is the only opportunity for me, as I'm not rich, to get a higher education and enter a relatively prestigious profession. I did not have any other choice, but I like it," he said.

But while Molisa was ready for the rigors of the Russian army, the army was less than ready for him, admits Colonel Andrei Sakhno, head of a department at Moscow's Military Institute for the Federal Border Service. "A black officer in the Russian armed forces is an extremely unusual event," Sakhno said. "There has never been such a case in the Soviet or Russian army before. He is the first and probably the last," he said. "It is difficult to say at present whether it's a good thing or not, but what I am sure of is that he will experience a lot of problems because of his skin color," Sakhno said. Those troubles began even before he signed up; the 18-year-old had to battle racism at the staff college just to have the right to take the entrance exams. Officers, baffled by the Russian citizenship stamp in the passport of a black man, were reluctant to believe his story. "They had no legal foundation to refuse me for race reasons, but I felt they looked on me as a spy," he recalled. "They treated me with a great deal of suspicion, kept checking my documents again and again, trying to find even the slightest evidence of forgery. But their efforts were in vain," said Molisa, who passed the entrance exams with flying colors.

His difficulties did not stop there, as the young recruit had to win over the staff and his fellow students. "There are a lot of guys from small villages in the academy. Many of them had never seen a black man," Molisa explained. "One day our platoon went to the banya [a Russian sauna], and as we got in I noticed that one guy kept staring at me. He seemed to be studying every detail of my body. "At first I was ashamed because I thought he must be gay. Then he came up to me and said, 'It's so strange. You've got everything I have, and everything is almost the same.' It was really funny," said Molisa.

Standing out from the crowd can have its drawbacks, however, especially when it comes to the opposite sex. When the institute organized a disco, Molisa found he was given a wide berth when it came to the slow dances. "It didn't offend me at all. I was ready for it because I realized that I was very unusual for them," he said. The black-into-Russian-doesn't-go equation has caused Molisa problems on city streets too, where police patrols, convinced they have nabbed a foreigner masquerading as a soldier, are always forced to let him go once they see his military ID. For others, a more direct approach has been enough to prove his Russian roots.

During a training exercise in the country Molisa surprised one hapless villager by asking to buy some milk. Seeing a black man in Russian army fatigues, the unfortunate villager proceeded to beg him to spare her life. Only the red star in his cap and his masterful command of Russian army slang convinced her he was just a normal Russian lad, serving his country.

[97]Quist-Adade, Charles (1993) *The Ones They Left Behind, The Life and Plight of African Russians*, a video documentary.

[98]Reynods, Fagler, and Vine (Eds). (1987) *The Sociobiology of Ethnocentrism: Evolutionary Dimensions of Xenophobia, Discrimination and Nationalism*. London and Sydney: Croom Helm, p.17.

[99]Booth, Ken. (1979). *Strategy and Ethnocentrism*. New York: Holmes & Meier Publishers, Inc.

[100]Summer, W. G. (1906). *Folkways*. Boston: Ginn, p.13.

[101]Booth, Ken. p.15.

[102]Wiarda, Howard. (1984) *Ethnocentrism in Foreign Policy*. Washington: American Enterprise Institute for Public Policy Research.

[103]Keim, Curtis (1999). *Mistaking Africa,* p. 34.

[104]Keim, Curtis, p. 159.

[105]Ibid.

[106]Pieterse, Jan Nederveen. (1992). New Haven: Yale University Press, p. 37.

[107]*Stenografichicheski otchet VI Kongressa Kominterna* (The stenographic record of the VI comintern congress) Moscow: Government Publishing House. 1929, vol. 5, p.207.

[108]Department of State, Nazi-Soviet Relations, 1939-1941, Documents from the Archives of the German Foreign Office, ed. Raymond James Sontag and James Stuart Beddie Washington: Department of State, 1948, p.257.cited in Blakely, Russia and the Negro, p. 127.

[109]Nkrumah, Kwame,(1970) *Consciencism*. New York: Monthly Review.

[110]Nichols, Bill. (1981). *Ideology And The Image; Social Representation In the Cinema And Other Media*. Indiana: Indiana University Press.

[111]Nkrumah, 1970.

[112]Vladimir Shlapentokh, "Two Levels of Public Opinion: The Soviet Case," Public Opinion Quarterly, 49, No.4 (Winter 1985), pp.443-59.

[113] Ibid.

[114] *Rabochaya Smena*, p.38.

[115]Zinoviev, Alexander. (1984). *The Reality of Communism*, London: Victor Gollanncz, p.218.

[116]Asoyan, B., 1987.

[117]Thanks to glasnost, Soviet publications, including *Moscow News,* No 49) 1989, p.6; *Izvestiya.* February 6, 1990, p.5 _*Svobodnaya Mysl* (No.18), 1991 pp 85-93 have disclosed that much of the "disinterested" aid was military assistance. Recent research (see *New African* July 1992, p.35) revealed that over 89 % of the 13.9 billion roubles debt owed by various African countries to the former Soviet Union was in the form of arms deliveries "to defend socialist gains".

[118]Zevin, L. Telerman, V. (1991, No.18) Razvivayushie stranni v nashei ekonomicheskoi strategii. *Svobodnaya mysl,* 86.

[119]Asoyan, 1987.

[120]*Moscow News.*(1991, December 20).

[121]This has been the standard charge by Soviet authorities throughout the communist years against African and other Third World victims.

[122]Blakely, p. 135.

[123]Adade, 1988.

[124]Klomegah, K. (1998, February). "Victims of racism in new Russia defenceless," *Sankofa News,* vol.4, 9.

[125]Umar, M. K. (1989, September 11). "How blacks fare in the USSR." *African Concord,* 21; Klomegah, 1998.

[126]See *Moscow Guardian,* October, 1991.

[127]Adade, 1988, p.29; 1991, pp.24-25; Klomegah, 1998.

[128]Klomegah, 1998.

[129]Ibid, 1998.

[130]Ibid, p.9.

[131]The Moscow Times, an English language newspaper records over 15 cases of assaults against blacks, gypsies, and nationals from the Caucausus between 1996 and 1999 alone. Those attacked include a Camerounean rap artist and an African American US marine.

[132]Ibid.

[133]Ibid.

[134]Much of the envy and anger among the youth stemmed from the fact that African students, owing to their relatively better material living conditions, attracted Soviet women.

[135]One such conditions was that students must obtain permission from their embassies before travelling to the West, a condition which

embassies of certain countries, notably Cuba, Ethiopia under Megistu, Mozambique etc., exploited to debar their students from travelling beyond the former communist community in Eastern Europe.

[136]Klomegah, 1998.

[137]Vasilyev, A. (1990, October 20). Pochemy nam nuzhna Afrika? *Izvestiya*, 5.

[138]Taritun, I. (1991, October 12) Miy Afrikantsi v evropeeiskom dome. Pravda, 5.

[139]Ibid.

[140]Tarun, S. (1989, April, 1). Ya innostranets. *Smena,* 3.

[141]Ibid.

[142]Brezhnev, L. I. (1972). *Following Lenin's course.* Moscow: Progress Publishers.

[143]See Umar, 1989.

[144]Adade, 1985.

[145]Davidson, Olderogge, and Solodonikov, 1966, 46).

[146]Fokeev, G. (1991, No.5). Afrika v chem nash natsional'nyi interes? *Aziya i Afrika cegodniya*, 32, 34.

[147]The ongoing Russia-Chechenya war (October 1999-January 2000) and the clamp down on nationals from the former Soviet southern republics in the Caucuses and Central Asia in the aftermath of Yeltsin's recent [October 1993] bloody confrontation with his opponents in the former Russian parliament is a manifestation of the ill-blood that has existed between Russians and their former subjects.

[148]Adade, 1985, pp.8-9.

[149]See Plehakov, Konstatin, (1992). "Russian Tragedy," *New Times,* No.9,

pp. 9-11.

[150]Nassor, Ali S. (January, 1997). "African Students Suffer Racism." *New African*, p.34.

[151]Ibid.

[152]For example, in early 1992 when a third year Ghanaian mining engineering student was murdered in cold blood in his room in Moscow, none of the Russian media reported the incident. For the first time, though, the *Moscow Times*, a new English language newspaper put out by Western correspondents in Moscow carried the story on its front page.

[153]Belyaninov K. and D. Mochanov (August 14, 1992). "Cherno-belaya logika, Cushestvuyet li rasizm v Possii?," *Izvestiya*.

[154]Ibid.

[155]Klomegah, 1998.

[156]The December 12, 1993 parliamentary elections in which Vladimir Zhirinovsky's neo-fascist Liberal Democratic Party won the majority of the seats in Russia's new legislature (the Duma) is an indication of the growing influence of right-wing extremists.

[157]Travkin, N. (1990, December 1). *Literator*, p.1.

[158]Gromyko, A.A. (1985). *Aktualnie problemi otnoshenii s strannami Afriki*. Moscow: Progress.

[159]Asoyan (1990).

[160]Ibid, p.4.

[161]Ibid.

[162]Ibid.

[163]Ibid, p.5.

[164]Ibid.

[165]Ibid.

[166]Deeva, E. (1992, January 2). Krasnoe i chernoe. *Moskovskyi Komsomolets*, 5.

[167]Ibid.

[168]Hartman & Husband, 1970, p.435.

[169]Ibid.

[170]Ibid.

[171]Kossowan, Brenda. (1990, July 27). Soviet press still hard on blacks. *The Times*, 9.

[172]Davidson, A. B. (1986, August 28). The dark continent and us. *Moscow News*, p. 6.

[173]Ibid.

[174]Asoyan, B. (1987, November 7) Afrika uzh tak daleko, *Literanturnaya gazeta*, 14.

[175]Ibid.

[176]Tains, S. (1992, January 31). Negri v Rossii. *Nizavisimaya gazeta*, 8.

[177]Hartman & Husband, p.436.

[178]Adade, C.Q. (1993, October-December). Russia: After the Cold War: the ex-Soviet media and Africa. *Class and Racism.* Volume 35, London: Institute of Race Relations, 86-93.

[179]Ibid.

[180]Popov, Y. (1990, No.4). *Aziya i Afrika cegodnya,* 36.

[181]Adade, 1993.

[182]Gromyko, 1985.

[183]Taritun, I. (1991, October 12) Miy Afrikantsi v evropeeiskom dome. *Pravda,* 5.

[184]Gorbachev, M.S. (1988). *Perestroika i novoe myshlenie dlya nashei straniy i vsego mira.* Moscow: Progress Publishers.

Chapter Three

[1]Nkrumah, Kwame (1973). *Handbook of Revolutionary Warfare,* London: PANAF Books Ltd.

[2]Nkrumah, p.4.

[3]Ibid.17.

[4]Ibid.

[5]Ibid.

[6]Ibid.

[7]Tarabrin, Ev. (1986) *Afrika v. 80-e godiy: Itogi i perspektiviy, Moskva*: Akademiya nauk cccp. Viy, p.18.

[8]Tom Mboya, "Relations Between the Press and Governments in Africa," *Transition,* 2:4, June, 1962 II.

[9]Alex S. Edelstein, Youchi Ito and Hans Mathias Kepplinger, *Communication and Culture: A comparative Approach,* Longman, New York, 1989, pp. 96-97.

[10]Ibid, p.97.

[11]Ibid.

[12]Breed, W. (1955). "Social control in the newsroom: A functional analysis." *Social Forces,* 33, 326-335; Epstein , E. (1973*). News from nowhere: Television and the news.* New York: Random House; Gans, H. (1979). *Deciding what is news: A case study of* CBS Evening News, NBC Nightly News, Newsweek *and* Time. New York: Pantheon; Sigal, L. V. (19973*). Reporters and Officials: The organizational and politics*

of newsmaking. Lexington, MA: D. C. Heath; Tuchman, G. (19978*).* *Making news.* New York: The Free Press; White, D. M. (1950). The "gate keeper": A case study in the selection of news. Journalism Quarterly, 27, 383-390.

[13]Parenti, M. (1986*). Inventing reality: The politics of the mass media.* New York: St. Martin's Press.

[14]Hall, S. (1979).The rediscovery of "ideology : Return of the repressed in media studies." In M. Gurevitch, T. Bennet, J. Curran, & J. Wollacott (Eds). Culture, Society and the media. P. 72. Lodon: Methuen.

[15]Hallin, D. C. (1987). "Hegemony, the American news media from Vietnam to El Salvador, a study of ideological change and its limits." In D. L. Paletz (Ed.) *Political communication communication research* (pp. 3-25). Norwood, NJ: Ablex.

[16]Gans, H. (1977).

[17]Ibid, 182.

[18]McQuail, D. (1977). *The analysis of newspaper content,* London: Her Majesty's Stationery Office.

[19]Quoted in Weaver, D. H. & Wilhoit, G. C. (1983) "Foreign news coverage in two U. S. wire services": An update. *Journal of Communication,* p.134.

[20]Chomsky, N, & Herman, N. (1979). After the cataclysm. Boston: Southend Press.

[21]Carey, J. W. (1989). Communication as culture. Boston: Unwin Hyman.

[22]Hall, S. (1979). Culture, the media, and the ideological effect. In J. Curran, M. Gurevitch &J. Woollacott(Eds.), *Mass communication and society,* pp.315-348.

[23]Solomon, William. (1992). "News frames and media packages:" Covering El Salvador. In *Critical Studies In Mass Communication,* Volume 9 Number 1, March, p.63.

[24]Gitlin, T. (1980) *The whole world is watching: Mass media in the making and unmaking of the new left.* Berkeley:, CA: University of California Press; Gramsci, A. (1977). *Selections from prison notebook.* (Q. Hoare & G. N. Smith, Eds. &Trans.). New York: International Publishers.

[25]Gitlin, p. 253.

[26] Hallin, p. 4.

[27]Huang, Li-Ning & Mc Adams, Katherine C. (1999). "Ideological manipulation via newspaper accounts of political conflict: A cross-national news analysis of the 1991 Moscow coup." Malek, Abass & Kavoori, Anandam P. (Eds.). In *The global dynamics of news* p.60.

[28]Hallin, p. 4.

[29]Huang, Li-Ning, & McAdams, Katherine C. (1999).

[30]Huang, Li-Ning & Mc Adams, Katherine C. (1999), p.60.

[31]Ibid.

[32]PRAVDA was founded in 1912 on the initiative of V.I. Lenin. It is the chief organ of the Communist Party of the now disintegrated Soviet Union and until 1991 the most authoritative and influential newspaper in the FSU.

[33]IZVESTIYA was the organ of the Supreme Soviet of the USSR until 1991. Now it is the newspaper of the Russian parliament, although it still is by the constitution organ of peoples deputies of the Supreme Soviet, now renamed the "Duma". It was founded in 1917, the same year the Bolshevik revolution was launched.

[34]NOVOE VREMYA was founded in 1948 by the All Union Committee of USSR Friendship Societies with Foreign Countries.

[35]Eribo, Festus. (1993). "Coverage of Africa South of the Sahara by *Pravda,* IZVESTIYA, TRUD, and SELSKAYA ZHIZN, 1979-1987: A Content Analysis," *Journalism Quarterly*, Vol.70, No.1, Spring, p.52.

[36]NOVOE VREMYA is also published in six foreign languages. In the analysis to determine the extent of marginalization of Africa, the English language edition–NEW TIMES—was used.

[37]I was assisted in the survey by the St Petersburg Institute of Socio-Economic Research. In order not to prejudice the participants in the survey [I am African] and obviate the Hawthorne effect, Russian students were hired to conduct the survey.

[38]None of the articles published by *PRAVDA* during the period under review exceeded approximately 50 words.

[39]None of the *PRAVDA* stories about African countries exceeded 500 words approximately.

[40]The remaining 20.6% were "diplomatic" and party news about the arrivals and departures of Soviet and African official delegations to and from Moscow or an African capital. This type of news could not be classified under the above-stated categories, since it mainly highlighted the success and dynamism of Soviet diplomacy on the continent.

[41]*PRAVDA,* December 29, 1987, p.5.

[42]Lenin, V. I. *Chto proiskhodit v Rossii,* Poln.sobr. soch. T.9, s. 207-209.

[43]See *NOVOE VREMYA,* No.1 January 12, 1987; *Izvestiya,* November 1, 1985.

[44]Nkrumah, Kwame (1973). *Revolutionary Path,* New York: International Publishers.

[45]Ibid.

[46]Gromyko, A.A. (1985). *Aktualnie problemi otnosheniis strannami Afriki.* Moscow: Progress Publishers 23.

[47]*Development and Cooperation,* No.4, 1984, p.15.

[48]William Minter, *Portuguese Africa and the West,* New York, Monthly Review Press, 1972, p.166.

[49]See *Mineral Resources of the Industrialised Capitalist and Developing Countries,* Moscow, 1980.

[50]Nkrumah, Kwame. *Handbook of Revolutionary Warfare,* Panaf Books Ltd., London, 1973.

[51]H. S. Truman. "Address Before Joint Session of Congress", 12 March 1947.

[52]See Stockwell, John. (1997). *The C.I.A. in Search of its Enemies.* New York: Baker & Taylor.

[53]Barnett, R.J. (1968). *Intervention and Revolution,* London, p.23.

[54]See New African, July 2000.

[55]Furedi, Frank, p.141.

[56]Ibid.

[57]*Newsweek.* (1993, April 15), p.20.

[58]Volman, Daniel (1993). "Clinton and Africa," *New African,* March p.13.

[59]Ibid.

[60]Ibid.

[61]*African Concord* (1990, January 29), p.18.

[62]See *Sunday Express,* (1986, November 23).

[63]See *The Guardian,* (1987, February).

[64]Quoted in *West Africa.* (1992, January 13-19), p.71.

[65]*See New African.* (2000, July/August), p.44.

[66]This was less so for the Soviet media before 1990. In most cases, a three-hour, dull, dogmatic, platitude-filled speech, of the General Secretary of the CPSU was published in full, taking nearly half to three-quarters of the entire national and local newspapers, while news stories needing pressing national attention, like the washing out of the only bridge linking a village to the rest of the country, were ignored.

[67]The most recent incident was the brutal murder of a Ghanaian engineering student in Moscow early this year. As usual, the Russian media ignored it. The only paper to report the incident was the MOSCOW TIMES, an English language weekly, put together by western reporters in Moscow

[68]See *Osnovi Marksistsko-Leninskoi Filosofii.* Progress Publishers, Moscow, 1985.

[69]Before perestroika, Soviet television was saturated with the images of poor and homeless blacks queuing for charity food in Washington or London.

[70]Some of the ex-Soviet publications removed the communist slogan after the coup of August 1991.

[71]*IZVESTIYA.* (November 16, 1987).

[72]An article in *PRAVDA* and later *KOMSOMOL'SKAYA PRAVDA* (organ of the youth wing of the now disbanded Communist Party of the Soviet Union) said the AIDS disease originated in Africa.

[73]This period is also variously called the Brezhnev era, the neo-Stalinist period and the period of "advanced socialism".

[74].In Russian, the word "*cherny*" means black. In the context used here it also means dark.

[75]Lenin o pechati. (1972). Prague: *Mezhdurodnaya Organizatsia Zhurnlaistov.*

[76]*Asia and Africa Today*, April 20, 1984, p.1.

[77]Vasilyev, A. (1990) *Izvestiya*, October 20), p.5.

[78]Popov, Yuri (1990). "New Political Thinking and The Third World," *ASIA AND AFRICA TODAY* (No.4), p.36.

[79]The Russian pronunciation of "negro" is "*niegr*", something that sounds between "negro" and "nigger".

[80]See A. A. Gromyko. (1980). *Aktualnie problemi otnoshenii SSR s stranami Afriki*, Moscow: Progress Publishers.

[81]*Pravda*, (1991, October 12), p.5.

[82]See Cohen, B.C. (1963). *The Press and Foreign Policy*, London: Princeton University Press.

[83]NEWSWEEK covered Africa 21 times both in 1985 and 1990 (21:21) while *NOVOE VREMYA* (NEW TIMES)'S coverage dropped by more than 50 per cent (32:13).

[84]Asoyan, Boris (1987, Nov. 7)."Afrika uzh ne tak daleko..." *LITERATURNAYA GAZETA*, p.14.

[85]Zevin, Leon & Telerman, Vadim. (1991). "The Developing Countries In Our Economic Strategies", in *SVOBODNAYA MYSL*, (No.18), p.86.

[86]Ibid.

Chapter Four

[1]Mickiewicz, Propper Ellen. (1981). *Media and the Russian Public*, New York: Praeger Publishers, p.2.

[2]Ibid, p.3.

[3]Ibid, p.133.

[4]Ibid, p.56.

[5]"News and Editorial Content and Readership of the Daily Newspaper," *News Research for Better Newspapers*, vol.7, ed. Galen Rarick, ANPA Foundation, Washington, 1975, pp.14, 20.

[6]Originally I planned to include *Komsomol'skaya Pravda* in my content analysis but dropped the idea, since I could not find an analogous newspaper in the West.

[7]I hired Russians to distribute and collect the questionnaires, in order not to prejudice respondents and to circumvent the Hawthorne effect, since I am African.

Chapter Five

[1]I have in mind here the major US TV networks - ABC, NBC, and CBS.

[2]Hawk, B.G. (1992). *Africa's Media Image*, New York: Praeger.

[3]Ellison, Ralph. (1995). *The Invisible Man*. New York: Vintage Press.

[4]Heisler, Martin, O. (1977, 1-5 September). "Ethnic Conflicts in the

World Today: An Introduction." In *Annals of the American Academy of Political and Social Sciences*, p.433.

[5]Wilmot, Patrick.(1989, June 5)."Sino-Soviet Friendship," *African Concord,* p.50.

[6]Larsen, J. F. (1982)."International Affairs Coverage on U.S. Evening Network news." In *Television Coverage of International Affairs*, W.C. Adams (ed.). New Jersey: Ablex,.18.

[7]Mc Phail, Thomas L. and Nrenda M. Mc Phail, (1990). *Communication. The Canadian Perspective,* Toronto: Copp Clark Pitman Ltd., p.134.

[8]*West Africa,* (1993, March 8-14), p.391.

[9]See *An ABC of Color,* (1967). New York: International Publishers.

[10]Until 1989, the former Soviet media saw it as unethical to carry commercial advertisements. Advertisement was seen as a ploy to dupe or corrupt consumers.

[11]*Newsweek,* Narcg 23, 1987, No.12.

[12]Seldes, Gilbert. (1957). *The New Mass Media: Challenge to a Free Society.* Washington DC: American Association of University Women Press.

[13]Sandbrook, Richard. (1993, May 22). "Africa: Reforms are taking root." *Globe and Mail,* p.D7.

[14]Ibid.

[15]Ibid.

[16]*Africa Events.* (1988). Vol.4, No.2, p.54.

[17]*Social Sciences.* (1985). USSR Academy of Sciences, Moscow, No.1, p.189.

[18]Ibid.

[19]Yermoshkin, N. (1984). *Spiritual Neo-Colonialism,* Prague, p.11.

[20]Quoted in O.I.J. Sourcebook on NIICO, Prague, 1986, p.227.

[21]Reston, James. (1966). *The Artillery of the Press.* New York: Harper and Row Publishers, pp.vii-viii.

[22]Nichols, Bill. (1981). *Ideology And The Image,* p.2.

[23]Ibid.

[24]See Hawk, B.G. (1992). *Africa's Media Image,* New York: Praeger.

[25]*The Courier,* (1989, May-June), No.115, p.5.

[26]*The German Tribune* (1990 December 23*),* No.1449, p.14.

[27]*Africa Events*, (1988), Vol.4, No.2, p.54.

[28]It must be noted, however, that the Kremlin under Yeltsin made a few half-hearted attempts to forge new links with various African countries. It remains to be seen, however, if Vladimir Putin's government will show more interest in re-establishing partnerships with African governments.

References

Adade, C.Q. (1993, October-December). Russia: After the Cold War: the ex-Soviet media and Africa. *Class and Racism*. Volume 35, London: Institute of Race Relations, 86-93.

Adade, C. Q. (1993) *The Ones They Left Behind, The Life and Plight of African Russians*, a video documentary

Adade, C.Q. (1991, January) No glasnost for Africa. *New African* , Volume No.291, 24-25, 16.

Adade, C.Q. (1985, August 16) African Students in the USSR, *African Times,* London, 8-9.

Adamishin, Anatoly.(1990, February 9). *New Times.* p.6.

Adorno, T.W. (1950). *The authoritarian personality*. New York: Harper.

African Concord (!990, January 29). p.18.

Africa Events. (1988). Vol.4, No.2 p.54.

African Concord, March 23, 1992, p.18.

Asia and Africa Today (1990). No.4, pp.35-45.

Albright, D. E. (1987*). Soviet policy toward Africa revisited*. Washington D.C.: 1987.

Ali, Nassor. S. (1997, January). "African Students Suffer Racism*. " New African,*. p.34.

Aronson, James. (1971) *Packing The News: A Critical Survey of the Press, Radio and Television*, New York: International Publishers.

Asia and Africa Today, (1984, April 20). p.1.

Asoyan, B. (1987, November 7) Afrika uzh tak daleko, *Literanturnaya gazeta*, 14.

Asoyan, B. (1989, August 7) Sgushennoi krasok. *Komsomoslkaya pravda*, 4.

Augie Fleras and Jean Leonard Elliot, (1996) *Unequal relations: An introduction to race, and aboriginal dynamics in Canada*. Prentice Hall, Inc. Scarborough.

Belyaninov K. & Molchanov, D. (1992, August 14). Cherno-belaya logika, Cushestvuyet li rasism v Rossii? *Izvestiya*, p. 3.

Berker, S. L. & Roberts, C. L. (1992). *Discovering mass communication*. New York: Harper Collins Publishers Inc.

Binns, Peter. (1974) "The theory of state capitalism," in Tony Cliff *State Capitalism in Russia*. London:, Pluto Press, p.95

Bissel, Richard. (1981). "Union of Soviet Socialist Republics," in Thomas H. Henriksen, ed., *Communist Powers and Sub-Saharan Africa*, Stanford: Hoover Institute Press, pp.11-14.

Blakely, Alison. (1986). *Russia and the Negro*. Washington, D. C: Howard University Press.

Blumer, H. 1965. Industrialization and Race Relations. In Industrialization and Race relations: *A Symposium*. Guy Hunter (ed.). London: Oxford University Press

Booth, Ken. (1979). *Strategy and Ethnocentrism*. New York: Holmes & Meier Publishers, Inc.

Breed, W. (1955). "Social control in the newsroom: A functional analysis." *Social Forces*, 33, 326-335.

Blumer, H. 1965. "Industrialization and Race Relations." In Industrialization and Race relations: *A Symposium*. Guy Hunter(ed.). London: Oxford University Press.

Brezhnev, L. I. (1972). *Following Lenin's course*. Moscow: Progress Publishers.

Carey, J. W. (1989). Communication as culture. Boston: Unwin Hyman.

Chance, R.A. (1974). The dimensions of our social behaviour. In Benthal, J. *The limits of human nature*. New York: E.P Dutton and Co., Inc., 159.

Chaplina, N. (1992 , October 19). Zebra po imeni YuAR. Chas pik, 12.

Clawson, P. & Mehrotra, S. K. (1983). "Soviet Economic Relations With India and Other Third World Countries." In *The Soviet Union: Socialist or Social Imperialist?* Chicago: RCP Publications, pp.129-130.

Cliff, Tony. (1974). *State Capitalism in Russia*. London:, Pluto Press.

Chas Pik, 1991. December 15, p3. See also *Nevskoe Vremya*, October 3, 1991, p.1.

Chomsky, N, & Herman, N. (1979). After the cataclysm. Boston: Southend Press.

Cohen, B. C. (1963). The Press and Foreign Policy. London: Princeton University Press, 120.

Conteh-Morgan, Earl. "Soviet Disintegration and Conflict Transformation in the Third World," *Peace Research* Vol.24 (No.2), May 1992, p.39

Condit, C. M. (1989). The rhetorical limits of polysemy. *Critical studies in mass communications*, Volume 6, No.2, p.30.

Davidson, A. B., Olderogge, Solodinikov (1966). *USSR and Africa* Moscow: Nauka Publishing House.

Davidson, A. B. (1986, August 28). The dark continent and us. *Moscow News*, 6.

Deakin, N. (1970). *Colour citizenship and British society*. London: Panther Books.

Deeva, E. (1992, January 2). Krasnoe i chernoe. *Moskovskyi Komsomolets*, 5.

Development and Cooperation (1984). No.4, p.15.

Demokraticheski Zhurnalist,(1989, April). p.24.

Downing, J., Mohammadi, A. & Srebeny-Mohammadi (Eds.).(1990) *Questioning the media: A critical introduction*. London: Sage.

Dubrovskiy, A. (1991, July 18). Beliy rai? *Znamya yunosti*, 3.

Eribo, Festus. (1993). "Coverage of Africa South of the Sahara by *Pravda, Izvestiya, Trud*, and *Selskaya Zhizn*, 1979-1987: A Content Analysis," *Journalism Quarterly*, Vol.70, No.1, Spring, p.52.

Edelstein, A.S., Ito, Y., Kepplinger, H.M. (1989). *Communication and culture: A comparative approach*. New York: Longman.

Epstein , E. (1973*). News from nowhere: Television and the news*. New York: Random House.

Ermakov, Vladimir. "Ne khodila biy Rossiya v Afriky "gulyat," *Izvestiya*, November 5, 1992, p.7

Fokeev, G. (1991, No.5). Afrika v chem nash natsional'nyi interes? *Aziya i Afrika cegodniya*, 32, 34.

F. Fukuyama, "Military Aspects of US-Soviet Competition in the Third World." In Shulman, M.O. (1986). *East-West Tension in the Third World*, New York, p.184

Fundamentals of Marxism-Leninism. (1985). Moscow: Progress Publishers.

Furedi, Frank. (1988) Superpower Rivalries in the Third World, New Perspectives in the North-South Dialogue. In Kofi B. Hadjor, *Essays in honour of Olof Palme*. London: Third World Communication and I.B. Tauris & Co. Ltd. Publishers.

Galen, Rarick (1975). "News and Editorial Content and Readership of the Daily Newspaper." *In News Research for Better Newspapers*, vol.7, ed. Galen Rarick. Washington: ANPA Foundation, pp.14, 20.

Gans, H. (1979). *Deciding what is news: A case study of* CBS Evening News, NBC Nightly News, Newsweek *and* Time. New York: Pantheon.

Gemini News Bulletin. (1987, November). 8; (1991, March), 4.

Gerbner, G & Marsha S. (1989*). Communication & culture: A comparative approach*. London: Longman Inc.

German Tribune. (1990, December 23). No.1449, p.14.

Gitlin, T. (1980) The whole world is watching: Mass media in the making and unmaking of the new left. Berkeley:, CA: University of California Press; Gramsci, A. (1977). Selections from prison notebook. (Q. Hoare & G. N. Smith, Eds. &Trans.). New York: International Publishers.

Girboedov, A. S.(1923) *Gore ot uma* [Woe from Wit]. Moscow Neva.

Gorbachev, M.S. (1988). *Perestroika i novoe myshlenie dlya nashei straniy i vsego mira*. Moscow: Progress Publishers.

Gromyko, A.A. (1985). *Aktualnie problemi otnoshenii s strannami Afriki*. Moscow: Progress Publishers.

Hall, E.T. (1959). *The silent language: The hidden dimension*. New York:Fowcet Premier Books.

Hall, S. (1992, Vol.5. No.1). Race, culture, and communications: Looking backward and forward at cultural studies. *Rethinking Marxism*, 13.

Hall, S. (1979). Culture, the media, and the ideological effect. In J. Curran, M. Gurevitch &J. Woollacott(Eds.), *Mass communication and society*, pp.315-348.

Hall, S. (1979). The rediscovery of "ideology : Return of the repressed in media studies." In M. Gurevitch, T. Bennet, J. Curran, & J. Wollacott (Eds). Culture, Society and the media. P. 72. Lodon: Methuen.

Hallin, D. C. (1987). Hegemony, the American news media from Vietnam to El Salvador, a study of ideological change and its limits. In D. L. Paletz (Ed.) Political communication communication research (pp. 3-25). Norwood, NJ: Ablex.

Hartman P., & Husband, C. (1974). *Racism and the mass media.* London: Davis-Poynter.

Hawk, B. G. (1992*) Africa's media image.* New York: Praeger.

Heisler, Martin O. (1977, September). "Ethnic Conflicts in the World Today: An Introduction", *Annals of the American Academy of Political and Social Sciences.* p.433.

Herman, Richard. (1985). *Perceptions and Behavior in Soviet Foreign Policy.* Pittsburgh: Pittsburgh University Press.

Hopkins, MW. (1970). *Mass media in the Soviet Union.* Pegasus.

Huang, Li-Ning & Mc Adams, Katherine C. (1999). "Ideological manipulation via newspaper accounts of political conflict: A cross-national news analysis of the 1991 Moscow coup." Malek, Abass & Kavoori, Anandam P. (Eds.). In *The global dynamics of news* Stanford, CT: Ablex Publishing Corporation, p.60

Image of Africa: British ideas and action. (1964). Madison: The University of Winconsin Press.

Information Buletin, Peace and Socialism, International Publishers, Prague, 1987, p.7.

Istorichiskii arkhiv. (1960). No.3 Moscow, 237.

Izvestiya. (1992, January 24)

Izvestiya, (1992, February 10). p.5.

Izvestiya, (1991, December 9). p.3.

Jones, J.M. (1972). *Prejudice and racism.* Reading: Addison-Wesley Publishing Co.

Johnson, R. "Exaggerating America's stakes in Third World Conflicts*", International Security,* 10(3), Winter 1985-86, p.67.

Kashlev, Yuri. (1983).*The Mass Media and International Relations,* Prague.

Keim, Curtis. (1999). *Mistaking Africa: Curiosities and Inventions of the American Mind.* Oxford: Westview Press.

Khabibullin, K.N. (1989). Natsional'noe camosoznanie i internatsional'noe povidenie.

Khanga, Y. (1993). *Soul to soul: The story of a black Russian family 1865-1992.* New York: W.W. Norton.

King, Preston.(1986) *An African Winter,* Middlesex: Penguin Books Ltd., pp.70-71.

Kingston-Mann, Esther (1999). *In Search of the True West. Culture, Economics, and Problems of Russian Development.* Princeton: Princeton University Press, 1999.

Kiva, Alexei (1991) "Africa's Second Liberation", *Novoe Vremya,* No.52, p.32.

Klapper, J.T. (1960). *THE EFFECTS OF MASS COMMUNICATIONS.* London: Free Press.

Klomegah, K. (1998, February). "Victims of racism in new Russia defenceless," *Sankofa News,* vol.4, 9.

Komsomol'skaya Pravda (1987, August 1).

Kon, I.S. (1967*). Sociologia lichnosti.* Moscow: Progress Publishers.

Kossowan, Brenda. (1990, July 27). "Soviet press still hard on blacks." *The Times,* 9.

Kozintsev, B. and P. Kashlov, (1978). "Economic Co-operations of the USSR and the Countries of Tropical Africa," *Foreign Trade,* No.2, February, p.30.

Kortunov, Andrei.(1989). "Soviet foreign aid— Is it always put to wise use?" *Moscow News,* No. 49, p.6.

Larsen, J.F. (1982)."International Affairs Coverage on U.S. Evening Network news." In *Television Coverage of International Affairs.* W.C. Adams (ed.). New Jersey: Ablex, p.18.

Lang, K., Lang, G.E. (1966). "Functions of the mass media". In Berelson and M.Janowitz (eds) *Public opinion and communication.* New York: Free Press, 466.

Laqueur, Walter. (1983). *The Patterns of Soviet Conduct in the Third World.* New York: Praeger Publishers.

Lenin, V.I.(1927, Vol.IV*). Collected works.* New York: International Publishers.

Lenin, V.I. (1972). *Lenin o pechati.*   Prague: Mezhdunarodnaya
Organizatsiaya Zhurnalistov.

Lenin, V.I. *Chto proiskhodit v Rossii*, Poln.sobr. soch. T.9, s.

V.I. Lenin, "Once Again on Trade Unions, The Current Situation and
the Mistakes of Trosky and Bukharin," *Collected Works,* Moscow:
Progfress Publishers. Vol.32.

Le Nouvel Observatuer. (1988, December 14), 15.

Likhachev, D. S. (1991, No.1). Russkaya kul'tura v sovremennom mire.
Novyi mir, 3-9

McKay, Claude. (1923, December). "Soviet Russia." *The Crisis*, pp 61-
64.

Magari, Yuri. (1986).*Countering Information Imperialism*, Novosti
Press Agency Publishing House.

Manchkha, P.I. (1986). *Afrika na puti k sotsialnomu progressi.*
Moscow: Politizdat, Moscow, pp. 181-182.

Makinda, S.M. (1987). *Superpower Diplomacy in the Horn of Africa,*
London.

Mboya, Tom. (1962)."Relations Between the Press and Governments in
Africa," *Transition*, 2:4, June, 1962 II.

McCombs, M. Gilbert, S. (1986). News influence on our pictures of the
world. In D. Nimmo and D. Zillmann. *Perspectives of media effects.*
Hillsdale, NJ: Lawrence Erlbaum, 1-16.

McCombs, M., Shaw, D. L. (1981). "Function of the mass media". In
M. Janowitz and P. Hirsch (eds).

Reader in public opinion and mass communication. New York: Free
Press, 127.

McKenna, Ian. (1994) "Canada's hate propaganda laws – A Critique,"
British Journal of Canadian Studies: 15—2.

McPhail , Thomas L. and McPhail, Nrenda M.(1990). *Communication.
The Canadian Perspective.*

Toronto: Copp Clark Pitman Ltd.

McQuail, D. (1977). *The analysis of newspaper content*, London: Her
Majesty's Stationery Office.

McQuail, D. (1972). *Sociology of mass communications.* Middlessex:
Penguin Books Ltd.

Mezhnarodnaya Zhizn, (1988, November), p.145.

Mezler, Vaughan. (1989). Africa through racist spectacles. *African Events*, p.12.

Mickiewicz, E. P. (1981). *Media and the Russian Public.* New York: Praeger Publishers.

Minayev, Sergei. (1998, July 28). "A Black Russian Fights the Odds" *Moscow Times*, p.6.

Minter, William. (1972). *Portuguese Africa and the West*, New York, Monthly Review Press, p.166.

Morthengau, Hans. (1973). *Politics Among Nations: The Struggle for Power and Peace.* New York: Knopf, p.64

Moscow Guardian. October, 1991.

Moscow News. (1991, December 20). "Sekretnie dolgie Afriki bivshemy sovietskomy soyuzy." p.15.

Nalbadyan, Z. (1991, December 11) Russkie v Yuzhnoi Afrike. *Trud,* 7.

Newsweek. (1993, April 15). p.20.

Newsweek. (1987, August 23). No.12.

Nichols, Bill. (1981). Ideology And The Image; Social Representation In the Cinema And Other Media. Indiana: Indiana University Press.

Nkrumah, Kwame, (1970) *Consciencism.* New York: Monthly Review

Nkrumah, Kwame, (1973) *Handbook of Revolutionary Warfare*, London: PANAF Books Ltd.

Novoe Vremya, (1990, April 17-23). pp.15-16.

Padmore, George. (1972). Pan-Africanism or Communism? New York: Doubleday & Company, Inc. p.269

Patterson, William L. (1971*). The Man Who Cried Genocide.* New York: International Publishers.

Parenti, M. (1986*). Inventing reality: The politics of the mass media.* New York: St. Martin's Press.

Pleshakov, Konstantin (1992)."Russian Tragedy.*" New Times*, No.9, pp. 9-11

Pravda. (1987,December 29). p.5.

Pravda. (1992, February 28). "Peterburskie Vedmosti," 1992.

Pravda. (1988, December 8).

Pravda. (1987, September 17).

Pravda, (1991,October 12). p.5.

Pilyatskin, B. (1991, November 23). Zakriyvayutsiya 9 posoltsv. Pochemy ne 50? *Izvestiya*, 10.

Popov, Y. (1990, No.4). *Aziya i Afrika cegodnya*, 36.

Pleshakov, K. (1992, No.9) The Russian tragedy. *New Times*, 9-11. Pleshakov, P. (1992 No.2).

Rabochaya Smena, (1987, No. 10), pp.38-39.

Rabochaya smena. (1990, No.16), 38.

Respublika. (1990, No.3).

Reston, James. (1966). *The Artillery of the Press*. New York: Harper and Row Publishers.

Reynods, Fagler, and Vine (Eds). (1987) *The Sociobiology of Ethnocentrism: Evolutionary Dimensions of Xenophobia, Discrimination and Nationalism*. London and Sydney: Croom Helm.

Rose, E.I.B. (1969). *Colour and citizenship*. London: Oxford University Press.

Sandbrook, Richard.(1993, May 22). "Africa: Reforms are taking root." *Globe and Mail*, p.D7.

Seldes, Gilbert. (1957). The New Mass Media: Challenge to a Free Society. Washington D.C.: American Association of Women Press.

Sherkovin, Yu.A. (1985*). Social psychology and propaganda*. Moscow: Progress Publishers.

Shlapentokh, Vladimir. (1985)"Two Levels of Public Opinion: The Soviet Case," *Public Opinion Quarterly*, 49, No.4, pp.443-

Sigal, L. V. (19973*). Reporters and Officials: The organizational and politics of newsmaking*. Lexington, MA: D. C. Heath.

Simmons, A. M. (1991, December 2). Black like Misha and Yelena. *Time*, 40.

Social Sciences, (1985, No. 1), USSR Academy of Sciences, Moscow, p.189.

Solomon, William. (1992). "News frames and media packages: Covering El Salvador". *In Critical Studies In Mass Communication*, Volume 9 Number 1, March, p.63.

Stenografichicheski otchet VI Kongressa Kominterna (The stenographic record of the VI comintern congress) Moscow: Government Publishing House. 1929, vol. 5, p.207.

Stranger, Ross. (1965). The psychology of human conflicts. In Elton B. Mc Neil (ed.) *The Nature of human conflicts*. New Jersey: Englewood Cliffs, p.10.

Summer, W. G. (1906). *Folkways*. Boston: Ginn, p.13

Tains, S. (1992, January 31). Negri v Rossii. *Nizavisimaya gazeta*, 8.

Tarabrin, Ev. (1986) Afrika v. 80-e godiy: Itogi i perspektiviy, Moskva: Akademiya nauk cccp. Viy, p.18.

Tarun, S. (1989, April,1). Ya innostranets. *Smena*, p.3.

Tarutin, E. (1991, February 3). Afrikantsi khotyat s nami rabotat'. No nam ne nuzhna chernaya kontinenta. *Izvestiya*, p.4.

Taritun, I. (1991, October 12) Miy Afrikantsi v evropeeiskom dome. *Pravda,* p.5.

Tetekin, S. (1992). Russiya I YuAR, Izvestiya, February 10, 1992, p.5.

Travkin, N. (1990, December 1). *Literator*, p.1.

Trud. (1992, March 6).

Truman, H. S. (1947, March 12). "Address Before Joint Session of Congress."

Tuchman, G. (19978*). Making News.* New York: The Free Press.

Tuen A. Dijk, (1993) *Elite Discourse and Racism.* Newbury Park, CA: Sage Publications.

Yermoshkin, N. (1984). *Spiritual Colonialism.* Moscow: Progress Publishers.

Yusin, Maxim. (1992, March 9). "Angola ne namerena vosvrashat sovietskie dolgi," *Izvestiya,* p.6.

Umar, M. K. (1989, September 11). "How blacks fare in the USSR". *African Concord*, p.21.

Ustimenko, O. (1991, December 13). A byili zloveshimi eti tri bukviy--YuAR. *Sovietskiy sport,* p.6.

Van Sertima, Ivan. (1986). *African Presence in Early Europe.* New York: Transaction.

Vasilyev, A. (1990, October 20). "Pochemy nam nuzhna Afrika?" *Izvestiya*, p.5.

Volman, Daniel. "Clinton and Africa," *New African*, March, 1993, p.13.

Volman, Daniel. (1993). "Clinton and Africa," *New African*, March p.13.

West Africa. (1993, March 8-14). p.391.

Weaver, D. H. & Wilhoit, G. C. (1983). "Foreign news coverage in two U. S. wire services": An update. *Journal of Communication*, p.134.

Wiarda, Howard. (1984) *Ethnocentrism in Foreign Policy.* Washington: American Enterprise Institute for Public Policy Research.

Wilmot, Patrick. (1989, June 5). "Sino-Soviet Friendship," *African Concord*, p.50.

Wilson, C. C. & Gutierrez, F. (1985). *Minorities and the media.* Beverly Hills, CA, & London: Sage.

Wilson, Edward. (1974). *Russia and Black Africa Before World War II*, New York: Holmes & Meler.

White, D. M. (1950). The "gate keeper": A case study in the selection of news. *Journalism Quarterly*, 27, 383-390.

Wolf, Brenda.(1976*). Issues of Fundamental Relevance to Socio-Economic Progress of Developing Countries, Part 3*, Berlin: College of Solidarity Press, p.48.

Zaslavsky, V. (1986) *The Soviet World System: Origins, Evolution, Prospects for Reform*, Moscow: Telos.

Zeebroek, X (1984)."Soviet Expansionism and Expansive Anti-Sovietism", *Socialist Register*, London, p.290.

Zevin, L. Telerman, V. (1991, No.18) "Razvivayushie stranni v nashei ekonomicheskoi strategii". *Svobodnaya mysl*, 86.

Zinoviev, Alexander. (1984*). The Reality of Communism*, London: Victor Gollanncz.

Author Index

Subject Index

United States, xiv, 1, 8, 60
Uzbeks, 55

V
Visual information, 59

W
Washington, 2, 13, 49, 60
Western media, xii, xviii, 10,
    11, 19, 48, 49
Western press, vii, xiv, xvii,
    xix, xx, 15

western press coverage of
    Africa, vii
Western propaganda, 4, 5
Western thought, 54
white South Africans, 58
WWI, 36
WWII, 12

Y
yellow journalism, xi

Z
Zimbabwe, 49